Praise for Tom Chesshyre

'If you've done Paris and Prague and are wondering, "Where next?", then this may be a quiet revelation.'
Andrew Marr

'Splendid 21st-century railway adventure. At last this IS the age of the train.'
Simon Calder, *The Independent*

'Great fun, and an exhilarating read.'
Sara Wheeler, travel journalist and author

To Hull and Back

'Tom Chesshyre celebrates the UK... discovering pleasure in the unregarded wonders of the "unfashionable underbelly" of Britain. The moral, of course, is that heaven is where you find it.'
Frank Barrett, *Mail on Sunday*

'You warm to Chesshyre, whose cultural references intelligently inform his postcards from locations less travelled.'
Iain Finlayson, *The Times*

'Get it... definitely entertaining.'
The Salford Star

How Low Can You Go?

'A dozen of the world's most obscure and least fashionable spots... Highly readable... Chesshyre asks some timely questions.'
Clover Stroud, *Sunday Telegraph*

'Fasten your seatbelts, it's a wonderful ride.'
Frank Barrett, *Mail on Sunday*

'A hilarious r   rs of Europe.'
Celia Brayfie

About the Author

Tom Chesshyre was born in London in 1971. He has a degree in politics from Bristol University, where he was news editor of the university paper, *Epigram*. He completed a newspaper journalism diploma at City University, after which he had short stints at the *Cambridge Evening News*, *Sporting Life* and Sky Sports. He freelanced for *The Daily Telegraph* and *The Independent* before joining the travel desk of *The Times* in 1997, where he still works. He has helped with the research on two non-fiction books: *W. G.* by Robert Low, a biography of W. G. Grace, and *Carlos: Portrait of a Terrorist* by Colin Smith, a biography of 'Carlos the Jackal'. He is the author of three previous travel books: *How Low Can You Go? Round Europe for 1p Each-Way (Plus Tax)*, published in 2007; *To Hull and Back: On Holiday in Unsung Britain*, published in 2010; and *Tales from the Fast Trains: Europe at 186mph*, published in 2011 and shortlisted in the 2012 British Travel Press Awards. His travel writing has taken him to almost a hundred countries. He lives in southwest London.

A·TOURIST·IN·THE ARAB·SPRING

by Tom Chesshyre

Bradt

First published in the UK in March 2013 by

Bradt Travel Guides Ltd
IDC House, The Vale, Chalfont St Peter, Bucks SL9 9RZ, England
www.bradtguides.com

Print edition published in the USA by The Globe Pequot Press Inc,
PO Box 480, Guilford, Connecticut 06437-0480

Text copyright © 2013 Tom Chesshyre
Photographs copyright © 2013 Tom Chesshyre
Maps copyright © 2013 Bradt Travel Guides Ltd, drawn by David McCutcheon FBCart.S
Edited by Jennifer Barclay
Typeset from the author's files by Artinfusion
Cover design: illustration and concept by Neil Gower,
        typesetting by Creative Design and Print

ISBN: 978 1 84162 475 4 (print)
e-ISBN: 978 1 84162 753 3 (e-pub)
e-ISBN: 978 1 84162 655 0 (mobi)

British Library Cataloguing in Publication Data
A catalogue record for this book is available from the British Library

Extract from Jonathan Raban's *Arabia Through the Looking Glass* © 1979 Jonathan Raban

Production managed by Jellyfish Print Solutions; printed in India
Digital conversion by Scott Gibson

To the martyrs of the Arab Spring

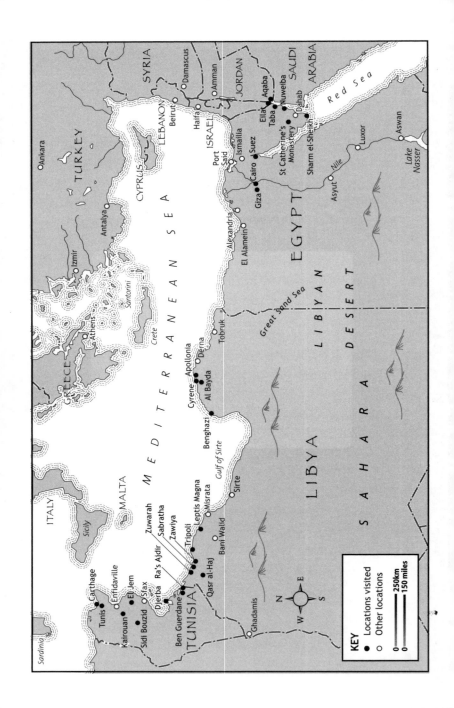

Contents

They wielded power with arrogance,
But soon it was as though their power had never been.
If they had acted justly, they would have met with justice,
But they were tyrants and Time played the tyrant in return,
Afflicting them with grievous trials.
It was as though here fate was telling them:
'This is a return for that, and Time cannot be blamed.'
'The Story of the Treacherous Vizier', *Tales from 1,001 Nights*

They didn't want to be 'dissidents', and they were waiting until the last possible minute before accepting the fact that they were moving fast into that cold paranoid world of bugging devices, imprisonment and samizdhat. I think they knew what was coming. Five weeks after my conversations with them, Sadat passed a 'measure' which brought Egyptian censorship into line with that of the most hard-headed Eastern European states; and editors and journalists who had published 'unconstructive' criticisms of the Sadat regime were jailed in a purge which aroused little interest in the West. Jonathan Raban, *Arabia Through the Looking Glass*

1

Tunis and Sidi Bouzid:

Cigarette Smugglers and Hitchhiking Heroes

IN THE long grey baggage hall at Tunis-Carthage International Airport, voices of passengers from our half-full flight echoed across the bare, dimly lit space. No other travellers were about, just a handful of officials in blue uniforms who lazily eyeballed us as we shuffled by in the early-morning February chill.

There was no sign of our baggage. With time to kill I stepped into the solitary duty-free shop, the sole customer. Followed by an assistant who sensed a sale, I perused the shelves, considering whether to splash out. Getting a drink could be tricky in some of the places I was heading, and everything in the shop was dirt cheap: bottles of rum for a handful of euros, fine French wines going for a song. I was about to embark on a voyage to Arabic lands where bars would be few and far between. This could be my last-chance saloon. But then I thought ahead to my next port of call. Alcohol was illegal in Libya during Colonel Gaddafi's rule. Whether it was still, I had no idea. What was the point in handing over a bottle to a border official? Or perhaps even being arrested later on: 'BOOZE TOURIST BEHIND BARS: SOLDIERS SEIZE SMIRNOFF'.

I didn't like the idea of that. Nobody I'd talked to seemed certain what was happening, or might happen, in Libya.

Close by, a neat row of shiny silver and green *shisha* pipes caught my eye.

Beside the pipes were colourful boxes of tobacco with curious flavours: apple, strawberry, rose, mint. Sweet smells emanated from the packaging, suggestive of another world. It was the shop's only real indication of being somewhere foreign. I closed my eyes, drew in a breath and imagined the many souks and cafés beyond the walls of Tunis-Carthage International Airport; the sense of adventure, that slightly giddy feeling of launching into unfamiliar territory, beginning to set in.

But back in the baggage hall, there was discontent; still no sign of our luggage. The inscrutable officials stared ahead blankly and indifferently. The delay was nothing to do with them, their body language said. Revolution or no revolution in Tunisia, we were going to have to wait. So we did. Eventually a distant carousel creaked into action, with a board that announced 'Paris-Orly'. An enterprising passenger ambled over to investigate, even though we'd flown from London. The bags were ours. With a growing sense of 'no-one seems to be in control here', we made our way across.

I collected my bag, and customs officers waved me through; clearly tourist material. Many of the returning locals, of whom the plane mainly consisted, were being taken to one side. With resigned looks, passengers unzipped bulging suitcases. Were great hauls of smuggled goods about to be confiscated? I didn't have time to see. A doorway led to a gloomy hall that smelt of smoke. Within moments, men in black leather jackets and jeans appeared as if from nowhere; the feeling of 'abroad' coming in a great swoop. 'Tax-eee, tax-eee, s'il vous plaît, tax-eee, monsieur tax-eee!' they urged, leaning close and gleaning that I was an English-speaker. The language of the former colonialists, who left in 1956, is widely spoken alongside Arabic, but many have English, too. They switched tack: 'You alone sir, ver-eee good pric-eees sir, where is your hot-eel, tax-eee, you wan tax-eee?' They hopped from foot to foot and gesticulated, all conspiratorial smiles and hurry-up-come-with-me. For sheer shiftiness and persistence the taxi touts and guides of Tunis-Carthage International Airport must rank among the shiftiest and most persistent of them all. They seemed desperate. They almost all smoked.

Eyes darted up and down, assessing my value and lingering on my shoes. Many wore trainers and appeared interested in mine. I muttered 'non merci' enough times for the message to sink in.

Another smoker in a black leather jacket and jeans leant against the front of the Europcar kiosk. I had booked a car for the four-hour drive south to Sidi Bouzid, the city in which the Arab Spring of revolts had begun just over a year previously. He turned out to run the hire car company. He ushered me into a dingy room with aquamarine walls. It was eye-stingingly smoky. A sign on a wall showed a glamorous woman on a beach and said: 'VIVEZ CETTE SENSATION.' We discussed the booking, and for the first time that I can remember I was not hassled to buy extra insurance. I was even told the price was less than the amount originally quoted.

'Vous êtes certain?' I asked, imagining there must have been a mistake. No rental car company, anywhere, charges less than you expect.

'Oui, c'est moins,' he replied matter-of-factly.

I paid and was led across a windy car park to a dented silver KIA. It, too, reeked of cigarettes, and was almost empty of petrol. I gazed across the car park towards a stream of traffic on a busy road. Horns blasted. Engines roared. Vehicles swept by as though tied together by an invisible rope. How could I possibly find a gap amid all of that? It looked totally chaotic; barely controlled mayhem. What was it like in a country that had just had a revolution? Would chaos be king? I was about to find out. I slipped the car into gear and headed towards the hurly-burly.

🐪 🐪 🐪

So began my journey across the countries of North Africa's Arab Spring revolutions. I was beginning to wonder what I was doing as I tentatively made my way on to the Trans-African Highway, going south on a six-lane monster full of cars honking madly, weaving and lurching. I could not speak Arabic. Some of the places I was going were potentially dangerous. I was no expert on North Africa, nor on the Middle East. I was not a veteran foreign reporter with gung-ho tales from the front line in Afghanistan or Sudan. I had no experience of the sound of bullets fired in anger, and had certainly never had to dodge any or feel them whistle past.

Not that I had any intention of finding out. I was simply someone who had watched the television news and read about the great changes that were happening, and wondered what it might be like in the new world forming as dictators disappeared and democracy seemed, at least, to be coming in. It felt like a moment equivalent to the fall of the Berlin Wall; a time of total transformation. On 17 December 2010, the street vendor Mohamed Bouazizi had set himself on fire in a remote Tunisian town in protest about ill-treatment by corrupt officials. A year on – with despots toppled in rapid succession in Tunis, Cairo and Tripoli – what would it be like to see these countries starting anew in the wake of the old regimes?

The Times, the newspaper for which I work as a travel journalist (not usually straying too far off the beaten tourist track), had just named Bouazizi 'person of the year', stating: 'He was a simple fruit seller whose demand for justice cost him his life – but his defiance sparked a revolution that changed the world. We salute him.' It was an exciting time. Seeing the reports of sweeping changes and popular revolts, I got caught up in that excitement. And on the day of Gaddafi's death on 20 October 2011, which seemed such a pivotal moment in what had been so quickly termed the Arab Spring, I made up my mind to go on a journey across North Africa.

I looked at the map and plotted a route. Tunisia, where it all began with Bouazizi's spectacular and sad act, was the sensible place to start – from a tourist's point of view. Flights from London were cheap. So were the hotels and car hire. Visitor numbers had plummeted because of concerns about going to a country so soon after a major upheaval, and it was a tourist's market. It was amazing how easily I could arrange on the internet a week or so exploring the place that sparked off the Arab Spring.

Then I'd go to Libya. It appeared possible to travel by land into Gaddafi's former hunting ground from the southeast of Tunisia. There was a border crossing at a place called Ra's Ajdir that had apparently reopened, after being closed during the revolution. I'd leave Tunisia by heading into the west of Libya, making my way to Tripoli and then eastwards to Benghazi. This would not be so simple. I wasn't exactly sure how I'd get about in Libya. Even though I had a visa, I wasn't sure whether foreigners would be allowed to cross the border at Ra's Ajdir. Had I dreamt up a mission impossible?

Next would come Egypt – to complete the trio of revolutions in North Africa. With Mubarak gone after the dramatic demonstrations in Cairo's Tahrir Square, what was it like in a country that had just had an uprising; a nation with which so many are familiar from visits to the pyramids and the ancient temples and tombs of the Nile? I would go to Tahrir Square, stay at a hotel overlooking the epicentre of the clashes, and move on through desert across land tourists rarely visit, heading towards Suez and then down into the Sinai Peninsula. That seemed to be the place where the east and the west of the Arab world met: where North Africa and the Middle East joined.

Would it feel as though the Arab Spring was alive and kicking? Or would I just find a whole lot of sand, herds of camels, heat haze and scorching temperatures?

I wasn't sure what would happen. I wasn't sure how I'd get about. But I wanted an adventure… I wanted to give it a try.

It was not to be a journey about politics alone, though I knew that politics would play a big part. I was travelling as a tourist, not as a foreign correspondent with a well-thumbed contacts book and a series of appointments. I would take the temperature of the region during a key period in its history as a casual visitor with an open mind. I would see what there was to see as a traveller with a guidebook. Yet by talking to people along the way, I'd get a sense of the bigger picture.

That was my hope, at least. Being a tourist would be my way of unlocking the countries. I would take in the Byzantine ruins of Tunisia, the Roman remains in Libya and the treasures of the pharaohs in Egypt, plus some lovely beaches in the Sinai Peninsula. What would I find out about the Arab Spring as I pottered among the ancient sights? What does an Arab Spring feel like? Was this really a Berlin Wall moment? Or had so many of us, perhaps, fallen for the hype of deposed dictators and the rise of democracy?

🐫 🐫 🐫

The Trans-African Highway was the beginning – and as I followed the busy road curving south along the misty edge of Tunis, with flint-grey sea on one side and a muddle of skyscrapers on the other, I felt as though the whole of North Africa stretched ahead.

Evidence of the country's recent upheaval quickly became apparent. Soldiers in khaki uniforms with knapsacks slung over shoulders stood by junctions thumbing lifts: revolutionaries on leave, by the looks of them. They leant against concrete walls, shivering, occasionally swigging bottles of Coke, squinting into the glare of the traffic. Was that what they had fought for, I wondered, to catch lifts on the edge of a big, cold, dusty road? The temperature was a few degrees above zero. There had been snow in the north of Tunisia two days earlier according to *La Presse de Tunisie*, the French-language national paper I'd read on the plane.

I drove on amid the manic stream of cars, passing graffiti on an underpass: 'MORT AU RCD: DEGAGE!' ('DEATH TO THE RCD: GET LOST!') The Constitutional Democratic Rally was the former political party headed by President Zine el Abidine Ben Ali in his single-party state. The unpopular leader had, quite unexpectedly, fled Tunisia precisely 28 days after protests against his dictatorship began. He was living in exile in Saudi Arabia at the time of my visit.

Strange images began to flicker ahead, almost as though I was driving through a dream. More hitchhiking heroes appeared, remarkably cheerful-looking despite the biting wind. For a moment I considered offering a lift, but not fast enough. The Trans-African Highway was not a place to dawdle. Yellow taxis darted ever more daringly, accelerating through impossibly tiny gaps between dented buses and pick-up trucks piled high with plastic containers. I kept in a steady, straight line, hoping they'd all stay out of the way.

Tunis thinned into scrubland and shanty-town dwellings. The traffic became quieter. By the side of the highway, chickens pecked amid debris. Nothing prevented them crossing the road (other than common sense). A farmer in a caramel tunic with a pointed hood stood on a hillock, looking like a figure out of the Bible. A man pushed a bike heaped with bundles of bags along the highway's verge. I stopped to buy petrol from an OiLibya station, and a friendly but wordless assistant passed over my change in a handful of coins so worn they might have been scraped from an archaeological dig. The landscape opened up, the horizon spreading ahead. Great grey clouds billowed towards the heavens, as though the end of the world was nigh. They were streaked with an ethereal sand-coloured light, unlike any I had seen before. Then there were cacti... thousands upon thousands of cacti. Their green, spiky, humanoid shapes populated the scrubland as the highway rolled towards Hammamet, the beach resort: not a single tourist coach in sight.

After Hammamet, I took the turn for Sidi Bouzid. I knew it was the right road as somebody had kindly spray-painted '190KM TO SIDI BOUZID' on a rusty sign previously covered in Arabic scrawl. The city that ignited the Arab Spring did not get any other mention, not in English at least. Pausing in a car park by a tollbooth, I heard a tap on the window. A figure wearing a blue hooded top peered downwards. He stood grinning, looking hopeful. He was in his twenties and had a stubbly face, thin nose and coal-black eyes. He clutched a white plastic bag. He did not appear to be a revolutionary soldier. I rolled down the window and he indicated in gestures that he'd like a lift. I hesitated, thinking to myself 'what the hell', and as if reading my mind, he stepped around the vehicle and opened the passenger door.

This was how I met Hasen, the cigarette smuggler. As we drove along a single-lane road through a long, symmetrical olive grove, I asked what he did for a living. He looked at me sheepishly, keeping his hoodie up, his face poking out like a sea creature half hidden in a shell. '*Les cigarettes*,' he replied, pulling a packet of 200 from his white plastic bag. 'I drive trucks.'

We spoke in a mixture of French and English. He pointed at a pick-up truck and explained that he was making his way back from Tunis after completing a run. He lived in the village of El Haouareb, about seventy kilometres north of Sidi Bouzid. He showed me the village on my map.

'*Le Marlboro, le Merit,*' Hasen said, referring to his latest delivery while peering forwards through the gap in his hoodie. '*Le Dunhill, le Carlton.*' He had picked up the cigarettes somewhere in the south.

Hasen made 300 dinars a month from smuggling – about £125. That was not enough to live on properly, he said, and nothing had changed to improve his fortunes since the revolution. He glumly shrugged his shoulders as if to indicate he was not particularly impressed by the Arab Spring – which so many had hoped would transform the economy after the widespread corruption of the Ben Ali regime. The Tunisian National Institute of Statistics had recently reported that unemployment stood at 18.9 per cent, a slight rise since the revolution, with the highest rate of around 30 per cent where I was going in the south.

'Trois cents dinars,' he repeated, holding up three fingers, sounding particularly unimpressed by the figure. 'Trois cents.' He shook his head. We continued in silence through another olive grove.

Further on, we came to a series of roadside stalls consisting of neat rows of canisters. The sun broke through and the liquid inside the canisters took on a golden glow. 'Petrol from Libya,' said Hasen, 'smugglers.' He smiled approvingly, as though he was part of some kind of unofficial smugglers' union. It seemed that people in these parts were doing whatever they could to get by, whoever might happen to be running the country.

Beyond the petrol stalls, the road narrowed and we came to a small settlement consisting almost entirely of barbecue kiosks. By each business, the carcass of a sheep was hung to advertise the day's fine dining. The effect was ghoulish, as though we'd entered the site of some kind of terrible massacre. The smell of grilled mutton wafted across the smoky street. I pulled up by a stall with a few tables and chairs, and Hasen and I went for lunch.

As Arabic music played and a (live) sheep tied to a post watched, plaintively baaing as if sensing its fate, we dined on a spicy soup and chunks of bread followed by succulent chicken served with chips – Hasen insisted on chicken, mumbling a reason that I could not make out. We discussed the Africa Cup of Nations: Tunisia was to take on Ghana in a key match in a few days' time. Hasen felt that Tunisia had a *bonne équipe* (a good team), though he did not think they would win. We drank thick, sugary coffee, and fell into silence. A man with 'SECURITY' written on his jumper stepped from behind a barbecue and began to skin a recently slaughtered sheep with a machete. We looked on as he carefully went about his task. After a while, a waiter approached with our bill. It came to the equivalent of £3 for both of us.

I paid. And as I did, a thought occurred to me: this would never have happened back home. Quite apart from all the carcasses and the machetes, what struck me, simply, was how open Hasen had been. It was perfectly normal to him to meet a stranger and to pass the time of day as though with a long-lost friend. That was just the way things were, it seemed.

The chef with the machete began hacking through bone, as I mulled over this sense of easy openness. It had a soft, almost fatalistic quality, I realised: soft, fatalistic, yet charming, too. I was in Arabic North Africa, and new rules of behaviour applied: new to a Westerner unused to the Arabic world, that is. Life, I could already sense, moved in fits and starts: manic one moment, with the utter mayhem and crazed aggression of the Trans-African Highway, and calm and contemplative the next, quietly sipping coffees in the sunshine after an impromptu barbecue. There were hitchhiking revolutionaries. There were sociable cigarette smugglers. You just had to go with the flow.

🐪 🐪 🐪

I dropped Hasen at El Haouareb. He set off down a dirt track, still hunched in his hoodie, after scribbling his mobile phone number on a piece of paper and telling me to call if I was in trouble or needed anything. It was late afternoon. The sun had turned tangerine. I drove the last few kilometres to Sidi Bouzid in a low blaze of orange light. The landscape was arid and crammed with cacti casting eerie shadows. For long stretches, mine was the only vehicle in sight. More makeshift petrol stalls materialised. I passed a police checkpoint. The officer looked surprised to see a white face at the wheel. He turned to watch me pass. I was hardly heading off to remote (and dangerous) bends of the Congo River à la H M Stanley, or investigating Bedouin tribelands with no previous contact with the outside world in the manner of the great desert explorer Wilfred Thesiger… but I could already sense I was far enough off the beaten track to stand out in these parts.

A flat-topped mountain range rose on the horizon. Shepherds in brown tunics stood sentry-still, their eyes seeming to follow the KIA. The windswept Tunisian steppes were not exactly a hive of activity. Around the shepherds, skinny sheep with ragged coats skipped between rocks, heads down to tufts of rough grass. It looked a hard way to scratch an existence. Then the shepherds disappeared. And in the final run to Sidi Bouzid, I passed a fly-tip of rusty old refrigerators and washing machines. The tip led to a filthy corridor of cacti covered in blue plastic bags. It was a total dump: as though there had been some sort of ecological disaster. Nobody had cleared up in these parts for quite some time.

Beyond, ramshackle buildings appeared: neglected concrete blocks with washing hanging from balconies. You immediately noticed the poverty on the outskirts of Sidi Bouzid, where unemployment was particularly high even by Tunisian standards. I turned down a road that seemed to lead to the town centre; all the signs were in Arabic. In fading light, I followed the traffic along a hectic street with garages surrounded by piles of enormous black tyres, an OiLibya station, tumbledown convenience stores stacked with plastic buckets and brooms, and a square with a packed café. After the wide, arid landscape, the bustle came as a shock. I eased onwards in the traffic jam wondering how on earth I'd find my hotel. I didn't have a satnav or a smartphone. I didn't have a clue. I was in a strange city with no street signs I could read, and it was getting dark. I parked the KIA and considered what to do.

Then I looked out of the side window and got a surprise. A giant picture of Mohamed Bouazizi stared down, attached to what appeared to be, or had once been, a post office. A half-smashed notice declared the building to be La Poste. Two men wrapped in heavy purple shawls sat on a broken bench by the entrance; the temperature had dropped even further and it was as good as freezing. They looked at me. I looked back at them. The haunting echo of a call to prayer played out across the dusty centre of Sidi Bouzid.

I had reached the start of it... where the Arab Spring began.

2

Sidi Bouzid and Garaat Bennour:

It Started with a Fruit Seller

DAWN BROKE in Sidi Bouzid. An Arabic voice was rising and intoning some kind of important address from the next-door room of Hotel Ksar Dhiata. It was loud enough to hear every word, although I could not understand a syllable. The speaker sounded as though he was saying something along the lines of: 'The evils of society must be kept at bay! Nothing must let them loose! But not only that. There are other evils – terrible evils! Those evils must be held at bay, too. Do not rest easy! Fight the evils!' At least, that was how I imagined his speech. I listened to the voice on the TV blaring through the paper-thin walls, then went to the empty breakfast room for a *pain au chocolat* and syrupy coffee.

I had found Hotel Ksar Dhiata after some trouble the night before. A sign had kindly pointed in the wrong direction, taking me to an industrial district that looked as though it was involved in the production of cement. I had driven on. Trial and error, including for a moment mistaking the main mosque as my hotel (its neon lights looked a bit like the ones I'd remembered from pictures on the website), eventually led to the hotel.

It was far from bustling with tourists. The breakfast room was next to a dimly lit, freezing reception with a fountain shaped like a bowling ball. By the bowling ball was a small reception desk, behind which a short, stocky elderly man had been wearing a crumpled grey jacket and a blue tie when I arrived the night before. He had almost leapt to his feet at the sight of other human life.

'Mr Thomas!' he had exclaimed. It had appeared I was the only guest yet to check in; perhaps the only guest at all. The Ksar Dhiata was the main hotel in town.

I shivered in the cold breakfast room as I ate my *pain au chocolat*, reflecting on the out-of-the-way atmosphere of Sidi Bouzid. Then I stopped by the reception to hand over my key. A woman with an aquamarine dress and black headscarf was at the desk. She was shivering too. I asked her about the days of the protests in Sidi Bouzid, but she seemed shy talking to a male Westerner. Had it been an exciting time? 'Not exciting. It was scary,' she said carefully – and that was all she wanted to say.

I headed out into Sidi Bouzid. It was a bleak, grey day. Rain was pouring down and I had no umbrella. But despite the weather, I was looking forward to exploring Sidi Bouzid. I made my way to the centre of town, driving behind a beaten-up white pick-up truck marked 'POLICE'. I parked by a pistachio-green café, causing great consternation and honking (the reactions I'd already come to expect when performing any sort of driving manoeuvre in Tunisia), and went to look at what I took to be the governor's office. It was opposite the picture of Mohamed Bouazizi that I had seen the evening before. The poster showed him beaming, arms open in the act of clapping. He wore a sporty, grey and black stripy jacket. He looked like a nice fellow. At the foot of the picture there was a message: 'REVOLUTION OF FREEDOM AND DIGNITY'.

I took a stroll about. Was this the exact spot Bouazizi had set himself on fire? It seemed to be. There was a memorial on a plinth made of rough slabs of stone. In the centre was a sculpted version of his fruit seller's cart, a simple contraption with two wheels and handles to pull along his wares. The cart was surrounded by polished stones that had been attached to the end of metal spikes that poked up out of the plinth. Perhaps these stones were meant to represent the fruit and vegetables he sold. Somebody had scrawled in red spray paint the message: 'FOR THOSE WHO YEARN TO BE FREE'. It was already clear that the people of Sidi Bouzid were proud of the town's historic place in the Arab Spring.

I crossed the street to take a picture of the Bouazizi poster, dodging the flow of vehicles. On the other side of the road from the memorial there was a grimy white building with a pale-blue metal gate with rusty bullet marks and the crescent and star of the red Tunisian flag hanging limply on a short pole. An open doorway led to a pale-blue room with a wooden table, a peaked policeman's hat on its surface. Curious, I peered inside. Was this the governor's office outside which he had set himself alight? There were no guidebooks yet to explain the new Tunisia. The officer to whom the hat belonged appeared, holding a rifle. He regarded me with half-opened eyes, as though he'd been sleeping. He seemed irritated.

'Ça va?' he asked abruptly in a tone that suggested: 'Move along now.'

'Ça va bien,' I replied, and I moved along. I didn't want trouble with the police on my first day.

A few steps away, a man was sleeping rough in a squalid heap of blankets next to a damp wall – a stark reminder of the poverty that sparked the uprising. A ruffled head and glazed eyes peered out at one end of the bundle, where a cigarette glared. No matter how hard your circumstances, it seemed, there were always enough millimes for a smoke in Tunisia.

I took my picture of Bouazizi. Then I walked down a side street by the building I assumed was the governor's office. Graffiti had been whitewashed off the walls and there were few people about. I continued along the perimeter fence on a filthy pavement covered in crumpled cigarette packets and biscuit wrappers – and suddenly stumbled upon 'life'.

But it was not very lively life. A café was packed with men wearing black, many with moustaches, and all of them either idly playing or idly watching people play cards. Every seat was taken. There was not a single woman. From inside came a steady slap of cards. Young men sat with the elderly sipping coffees and smoking. Hardly anyone spoke. They looked terribly bored; as though they were gathering at the café to pass the time of day, not to be sociable. I stepped in and immediately felt an awful sense of stagnation. On my first morning I was quickly witnessing what the revolution had been all about: unemployment and the whiling away of hours with nothing much to do (the legacy of a corrupt dictator who had ceased to care for his subjects). Over a year on, time still seemed to drift slowly in the city where the insurgency began.

Down a side street, small rundown shops sold lettuce, runner beans, beetroots and carrots. Chickens were roasted over tiny, teetering charcoal barbecues. Nike and Diesel trainers – perhaps not the real things – were for sale. A cow's head hung outside a butcher's, where not much else was on offer. Small silvery-pink fish lay in crates of ice in an otherwise empty fishmonger's. A beggar approached, holding an empty cup. He grinned, exposing stumps of yellow teeth, and I handed over a couple of coins. A smart-looking shop amid the ramshackle stalls sold Orange mobile phones. An old man wearing a brown tunic with a pointed hood shuffled past, just like the farmer I'd seen from the car yesterday.

There may have been glimmers of wealth, but the overall impression was of hardship – of people scraping a living to get by. The GDP per capita in Tunisia in 2011 was US$800, according to the US Central Intelligence Agency's World Factbook. That ranked Tunisia at 112 highest out of 226 countries, when I visited: one place below Cuba in terms of earnings, and one place above Suriname. And it showed.

I returned to Bouazizi's memorial, where folk walked past graffiti, heads down, not giving the words a second glance. 'GIVE ME FREEDOM', 'DIE FOR SOMETHING, LIVE FOR NOTHING' and 'NO MORE WAR JUST FREEDOM' were written in English (as though for international TV cameras). Then there was 'GLOIRE AUX MARTYRS', and 'RESTEZ DEBOUT LES TUNISIENS, TOUT LE MONDE EST FIER DE VOUS' – 'STAND UPRIGHT, TUNISIANS, THE WHOLE WORLD IS PROUD OF YOU'. I crossed the filthy parade in front of La Poste, and asked a jockey-sized man with a pinched face and a wool hat where exactly Bouazizi had set himself alight. 'Pas ici,' he replied. 'La maison du gouverneur, c'est là.' He pointed to a building with a grand tan-coloured entrance at the other side of a crossroads (the building I had thought was the governor's office was actually a police station).

We got chatting on the corner. 'This should be a country for celebration,' said Wassila Ghoulsi. 'We're free and I'm happy we're free. I can say what I want to you now: freedom of speech. You come from England: the mother of freedom. You know about this. But we have seen nothing about jobs. Nothing about work. What can we do about eating?'

It was not a rhetorical question. He seemed genuinely to want a reply. The realities of Tunisia's Arab Spring in Sidi Bouzid were hitting me straight away. I shrugged my shoulders and offered what I hoped was a sympathetic smile. I was just a tourist in the Arab Spring – I did not have the answers he wanted.

We were joined by a woman wearing a green headscarf. Sidi Bouzid has a population of around 40,000, yet its centre had a village atmosphere; people paused to pass the time of day. 'Listen to me, I just want to say this: I want Tunisia to be more beautiful than before,' said Hedi Gamoudi, a 22-year-old teacher. She looked at me with piercing, almost pleading, eyes. 'We want to work forever. We want security.'

I wished them both the best and we said goodbye. Then I stopped on the road at the point where Bouazizi poured two bottles of paint thinner over his body and set himself alight. I shuddered for a moment as I thought about what had happened at the spot that had led to so many revolutions across the Arab world: for it was the ousting of Tunisia's President Ben Ali that helped inspire Egypt's uprising against President Mubarak (less than 30 days later) and Libya's removal of Colonel Gaddafi (within eight months). A guard wearing an olive uniform and jackboots, with a rifle over his shoulder, watched as I approached the governor's gate, where Bouazizi had sought recourse when his produce and precious electronic scales were confiscated after an argument with a female municipal officer on 17 December 2010. It is not entirely certain what happened during the dispute, but it is said that the woman had confronted him about not having the correct permit for a stall. This was a common method of harassment with which local stall owners had become only too familiar. Bouazizi had suffered bullying for years. Only six months before he had been fined 400 dinars (about two months' wages) for a similar 'transgression'. He had had enough. Bouazizi and the officer exchanged swear words, and it is said that she slapped him and, with the help of colleagues, forced him to the ground. Furious, Bouazizi went to the governor's office to complain. When his first visit met with a blank, he returned with the paint thinner. It took an hour and a half after he set himself alight for an ambulance to arrive.

After peering through a metal gate into the gloomy courtyard of the governor's office, I walked a short distance to a market where I found men selling fruit and vegetables at the pitch Mohamed used to frequent. Bananas, apples, artichokes, runner beans and oranges were piled on wooden carts – looking a bit like one of the farmers' markets that have become so popular at weekends in Western cities. The stallholders seemed relaxed and cheerful; the days of police bullying over.

I asked the price of the apples at one stall – two dinars (about 80p) for a kilo – and fell into conversation with Cuesdi, one of the salesmen.

'Sidi Bouzid est le centre du monde Arabe!' he said, local pride shining through. 'C'est le centre de l'intellectuel! L'Egypte, la Libye: beaucoup de pays nous suivent!'

He told me that his cart cost 200 dinars and his electronic scales 500 dinars. This came to about three months' wages, so I could understand the great concern at losing them.

Cuesdi offered me a cigarette; everyone in Tunisia seemed to smoke. I declined, but stayed with him for a while, half an hour perhaps, watching the slow trickle of customers and trying to imagine what life as a fruit seller must have been like under President Ben Ali's regime. Hard toil mixed with arbitrary injustice, two hundred kilometres or so from Tunis, in a town few outsiders ever visited amid a rocky landscape filled with cacti... it could not have been easy.

After a while, Cuesdi pointed to a burnt-out building: 'C'est la Garde Nationale de Ben Ali.'

Curious, I went over to look at the wrecked HQ of the former regime's heavy men. Bullet holes marked the outer walls and the charred window shutters of the deserted building hung loose. The yard was scattered with smashed chairs, old canisters and broken glass. A battered typewriter had been flung to one side of a path, the ink running black and red across a piece of paper wound into the machine as if to write an official report. As I looked at the twisted metal, I could not help wondering how many words condemning innocent people might have been pecked out on its rusty keyboard.

Tunisia had a shocking human rights record under President Ben Ali, who was renowned for his strong-arm tactics when dealing with dissent. In 2008, an Amnesty International report entitled 'In the Name of Security: Routine Abuses in Tunisia' found 'serious human rights violations being committed in connection with the government's security and counterterrorism policies'. While in 2009, the US State Department noted in a report connected to a US$12 million aid package that 'restrictions on political freedom, the use of torture, imprisonment of dissidents, and persecution of journalists and human rights defenders are of concern and progress on these issues is necessary for the partnership between the United States and Tunisia to further strengthen'. As the man who had given me directions to the governor's office had pointed out, it was not wise to talk out loud during the days of Ben Ali.

After crunching across more broken glass through blackened hallways, I peered into rooms with charred furniture and ceiling fans melted as though part of a Salvador Dalí painting. It was Arab Spring tourism of a ghoulish sort, just as it had been at the spot where Bouazizi had set himself on fire. I looked into a section with rooms with window grills that were probably once used for interrogation: knocked-over chairs stood by charred metal desks. You would not have wanted to end up there before the revolution.

Tunisians love coffee and they make it very well: thick and sugary, served in small cups. I went to the pistachio-green café close to where I parked: Café Mon Plaisir. Sawdust had been spread on the floor, seemingly to absorb the water on peoples' shoes (it was still raining). Tables were crammed with men deep in discussion. It was desperately smoky. A waiter pointed me to a spare chair at a table with three men wearing hoodies and leather jackets. I squeezed past them and sat down. They turned to me and we got talking straight away. If you feel like exchanging opinions in Tunisia, you will not find yourself short of opportunities.

It was quickly established that I was British, and equally speedily ordained that the best English speaker should address me. This was almost formally done, and I got the impression that the waiter had placed me at the table because the best English speaker was there.

Hajbi Nizar was a 28-year-old trade unionist who worked in Sfax, a city with a port, 100 kilometres to the east of Sidi Bouzid. Although he was brought up in Sidi Bouzid, he could not find a job there. He was on a day off. He earned 10 dinars a day, of which he said he spent six on cigarettes. He kindly offered me a Merit, one of his daily six dinars of spending, which I declined. He lit up. 'Par le visage,' he said, slipping into French. 'I knew Mohamed Bouazizi par le visage [to look at].' Apparently, Bouazizi was an incredibly popular local figure, hence the uproar when he was pushed so far he set himself on fire. His local nickname was 'Basboosa' (*basboosa* is a type of sweet cake made of semolina); Bouazizi had gained the nickname for being a likeable character, and it was this personality that caused the city to react so angrily to his plight and horrific death.

I drank a thick coffee as we hatched a plan. Hajbi had nothing to do during the day, and he kindly agreed to accompany me to Bouazizi's grave, in a tiny village somewhere on the outskirts of town. I had wanted to go but had been wondering how I'd find the cemetery: the map of Tunisia I'd bought from Stanfords bookshop back in London, though good, did not cover the endless little settlements in the middle of the country's cacti-land. Hajbi said, 'No money, I go with you,' though I intended to slip him a few notes at the end, anyway.

Near the car, I took a picture of the governor's office and was surprised to find what appeared to be a row of tourists doing the same. One of the men, who had a theatrical air and wore a flowing scarf, sauntered over. It turned out that he was from the office of the Tunisian representative of the Institute for War & Peace Reporting – which also has posts in London, Washington D.C. and The Hague – and was visiting to meet local journalists unused to reporting in a country with freedom of speech. Under Ben Ali, criticism of the regime had been extremely limited, as the US State Department report had commented.

'I'm here to help journalists make sure their voice is heard,' he said, full of enthusiasm. Marwan Maalouf was from Lebanon and had a protesting past of his own, having been a student leader during the 'Cedar Revolution' of demonstrations in Lebanon in 2005 that brought an end to the Syrian occupation of the country. He also had a Georgetown University international law degree and had written articles about Tunisia's Arab Spring for *The Christian Science Monitor* and the *New York Post*.

'We're not just dealing with print journalists,' he said, waving an arm flamboyantly towards the group he was with. 'We're helping radio broadcasters and bloggers: citizen journalists. We offer mentorship and help provide a platform for voices to be heard.'

Marwan rejoined his group after we exchanged email addresses, then Hajbi and I hit the road, whereupon it quickly transpired that Hajbi did not know where the cemetery was (and did not have the greatest grasp of English either). But he figured that we'd find the graveyard somehow; he knew roughly where to go. We were about to embark on a slightly chaotic trip.

At the OiLibya station on the dilapidated outskirts of town, where I topped up with very cheap petrol, the attendant did not know where Bouazizi was buried. 'We keep going,' said Hajbi, returning to the passenger seat, keeping his leather jacket zipped up at all times, with a thick scarf wrapped round his neck. He said this with the lofty air of 'everything is going to be OK'.

We continued onwards into the hinterland down a long road surrounded by olive groves. We came to a farmer in a brown tunic herding sheep. Hajbi asked me to pull over and stepped out of the car to speak to the farmer. Then he returned. 'We keep going.' The farmer had not known where the man who sparked the Arab Spring was buried either.

I began to pull away, and glanced in the mirror. A pick-up truck was coming from behind at a rate of knots; I pulled over again to let it pass. The vehicle stopped beside us and an enormous man in a dirty white tunic and a red headscarf of the type Yasser Arafat used to wear got out. He began waving his fists and emitting an impressive stream of what could only be swear words. Hajbi, as cool as a cucumber, wound down his window and adopted his 'everything is going to be OK' response to this verbal tirade. The enormous man in the Yasser Arafat scarf mellowed. Then Hajbi, trying his luck, asked him if he knew where Mohamed Bouazizi was buried. This ignited another volley of Arabic swear words: he did not know where Bouazizi was buried and nor did he care where Bouazizi was buried! The enormous man finally returned to his pick-up, still waving his fists, and sped away.

'He was a man of contraband,' explained Hajbi, as the pick-up disappeared towards the horizon. 'He takes the contraband petrol from Libya to Algeria. He was in a hurry.'

He paused and then added: 'But he had a big heart.'

We arrived at a village that was actually on the map – Lessouda – where one policeman did not know where the cemetery was, but another did. We continued down a tiny road and then on to a dirt track with a small settlement and no-one in sight. 'Stop here,' said Hajbi.

He opened the car door and indicated that I follow him across a stony field with shrubs. Sheep were baaing somewhere close by. Wind whistled across the deserted landscape. After a few minutes we came to the tiny graveyard where Bouazizi is buried. The simple white grave was at one side of the plot, next to a thick row of prickly pear cacti, used in these parts as hedgerows 'so the sheep don't eat the olives', said Hajbi. All the graves faced the same way, he explained, because the bodies were positioned so they lie on their right-hand side facing Mecca. The dates of Bouazizi's life ('1984–3–29' to '2011–1–4') were given on a small rectangle of grey marble; it had taken nearly three weeks for Bouazizi to die from his burns. Hajbi translated the short scrawl of green Arabic script: 'Martyr Mohamed Bouazizi. Peace for his life. And in the next life, have peace as well.'

There was a low canopy of clouds and a sense of complete isolation. We were in the village of Garaat Bennour, about sixteen kilometres north of Sidi Bouzid, from where his family originated; about half the cemetery's graves were Bouazizis, and Mohamed had gone to the village school. More than five thousand people attended his burial, but today there were just a couple of olive pickers beyond the prickly pear cacti in a neighbouring field. One day, I couldn't help thinking, there might be a grand monument and a car park full of tourist buses at Garaat Bennour's cemetery. But not yet.

I looked around the empty landscape from the side of his grave. In Garaat Bennour, it felt as though I was making a pilgrimage to the Arab Spring... an important point on my trip across the revolutionary states of North Africa. Could Bouazizi possibly have known what he was setting off when he poured out the paint thinner that fateful day? Of course not. But the results had touched the world, and the man responsible lay in the corner of a rocky field by a row of cacti. It was almost as though he had been forgotten.

One of the olive pickers shuffled over; a tiny elderly woman with a nut-brown face, blue headscarf, bedroom slippers and a huge misshapen cardigan. She needed a light to start a fire to warm herself and her companion. So we walked over to the olive tree they were harvesting using a simple wooden ladder to reach the top branches. She told us that she had been working in these olive groves since she was 15; it was difficult to ascertain her current age, and I did not feel it was appropriate to ask. She lit a small heap of grass with Hajbi's lighter, and she and her companion huddled around the fire. Life was clearly far from easy on the edge of Garaat Bennour, resting place of the man who began the Arab Spring.

My edition of the *Rough Guide* to Tunisia described Sidi Bouzid as 'a notoriously drab town'. But that was before the revolution, and the sense of hope and pride that it had created. The memorial, the positive graffiti, the huge picture of their hero on the front of La Poste, and the feeling of being in a place where something very big had begun had given the town a palpable lift, even if it was still tired around the edges.

Only four people are believed to have died in Sidi Bouzid during the Arab Spring clashes, out of 338 recorded deaths in the whole of Tunisia during the 'Jasmine Revolution' (named by Western press after Tunisia's national flower). But it was the bravery of the local people in standing up to the authorities that sparked copycat protests throughout the country, with the plight of Bouazizi igniting widespread anger over unemployment, lack of democracy, and corruption, much of which sprang from the notorious extended family of President Ben Ali and his wife Leila Trabelsi. One jobless young man from the town had climbed an electricity pole in a Bouazizi-style protest and electrocuted himself after yelling his last words: 'No to misery! No to unemployment!'

As demonstrations spread across Tunisia, troops that had initially held back from using live ammunition lost their restraint. In the nearby city of Kasserine, 20 people were shot dead on 10 January 2011. These deaths led to funeral processions for martyrs, intensifying the revolt, with news of atrocities quickly spreading over the internet: more than two million people out of Tunisia's population of 11 million had Facebook accounts, a higher proportion than in countries such as Germany, Poland, Russia and Japan (the figure in Tunisia has since risen to 3.2 million). President Ben Ali, aged 74 at the time of the uprising, had been re-elected for a fifth time in 2009 with an implausible 89.6 per cent of the vote; he had originally seized power in 1987 after declaring Habib Bourguiba, the former autocratic president, unfit to rule. There had been 23 years of dictatorship. The people, just like Bouazizi, were fed up.

Ben Ali had to go, and he did. Yet unemployment and poverty, as I was discovering, had risen since his departure. And as Hajbi and I returned to the centre of Sidi Bouzid, with him directing me along impossibly tiny lanes to a side street close to the bustle of the Saturday market, I got further insight into that hardship.

After miraculously finding a parking space, we headed into the throng of people.

Along a main street makeshift stalls had been set up, leading down to a big square with a souk. If you have ever wondered where the clothes and shoes you donate to charity shops go, the market at Sidi Bouzid is one of those places. 'These come from everywhere,' said Hajbi, as we walked past stall after stall selling high-street brands familiar in the UK: crinkled Abercrombie & Fitch shirts, faded French Connection T-shirts, scuffed Adidas trainers, ragged Levi's.

It was a Third World scene; something you might expect in central Africa, not a mere matter of kilometres from the five-star hotels of Hammamet and Sousse on the coast. No care had been taken over presentation. The clothes and shoes were simply piled on top of trestle tables; part of the challenge of buying a pair of shoes appeared to require finding two that matched. The owners of the stalls were men in brown tunics with pointed hoods who stood watching customers with eagle eyes and calling out in Arabic: 'Come buy the clothes!' They looked like a strange sect of monks in charge of a bizarre car boot sale.

We walked through the jumble of clothing and crossed behind one stall to enter the Zaouia of Sidi Bouzid. A *zaouia* is an Islamic religious school, and Sidi Bouzid's attracts visitors from across Tunisia. This was as much as the town had to offer in terms of 'tourist attractions'. Entry is meant to be for Muslims only, but exceptions are sometimes made. Hajbi convinced a grouchy woman with protruding teeth and a heavy grey overcoat to let us in; I did not get the impression many tourists visited.

Inside the white-domed building, it was an oasis of tranquillity. Green and blue carpets were spread out on one side, where a teenage woman in jeans was sitting with a bag of shopping. We were asked to remove our shoes and proceeded across tiles with a geometric pattern to a room with prayer mats at the back. 'It is for the people of all religions,' said Hajbi, translating what he was told, as we entered a small chamber, and I was promptly directed to a donations box. I stuck in a note. The woman visibly cheered up.

It was a calm and restful place. Afterwards, I dropped off Hajbi outside Café Mon Plaisir, passing him some dinars. He tucked them away with a nod. Then I went in for a coffee amid the sawdust and the subdued chatter, flicking through *La Gazelle*, the Tunisair in-flight magazine (which I'd kept from the plane). Its editorial overflowed with enthusiasm. 'Tunisian youth, keen on the internet, have transformed the world around us into a village with no borders, no physical or psychological barriers, an open-minded world,' the airline's chief executive brightly wrote. He continued by saying that Tunisia had never been so open to the outside world and said that the country was proud of its newfound freedom and democracy. It had become the 'hub of democracy for the Arab world'.

I looked about the café, taking in the young men in leather jackets in the new democratic hub of Arabia. Some were not so young. They were in their forties and looked as though they had run out of hope. Unemployment made marriage financially impossible for many in Tunisia. Glum faces with glazed eyes stared into empty space.

I read on. A feature in *La Gazelle* about Habib Bourguiba, who ruled Tunisia directly after its independence from France, described his resistance against the French in the 1930s and his embrace of secularism when he gained presidential power in 1957 after combining diplomacy with the threat of stirring up further unrest to help lever the French into leaving the previous year. His nickname, earned during his early days, was the Supreme Warrior. Bourguiba's policies included the outlawing of polygamy, encouraging women's education, equal pay between the sexes, and discouraging the use of veils. The question of whether to wear the veil had once more become a hot topic since the beginning of the Arab Spring and the rise of the Islamist Ennahda Party, many of whose supporters were in favour of females covering up.

In the elections since the uprising, held in October 2011, the Ennahda Party had triumphed, using mosques to spread the word and drum up votes. Ennahda was running the country in a coalition with two liberal parties. Despite the fact that the government had paid lip-service to secularism – long entrenched in Tunisia – and refrained from basing the new constitution on Islamic law, many Tunisians remained concerned that the party could shift towards ultra-conservative Islamic ways.

I ordered another coffee and continued with the article on Bourguiba. Despite his 'good points' being listed, the feature ended with a damning verdict on President Ben Ali's predecessor: 'Unfortunately, an essential element was missed by Bourguiba: democracy. He deprived us from the freedom of opinion and political diversity. It was a fatal error which severed his popularity.' It is unlikely sentences such as those would have passed the editorial panel during Ben Ali's rule. And it was uplifting to see such outspoken words in a mainstream publication that so many international visitors would read.

🐪 🐪 🐪

Back at the hotel, I asked the receptionist in French if there were any sandwiches. I didn't want a big dinner. I was tired after my tour of Sidi Bouzid and just wanted to eat something quickly and go to sleep, ready to move on the next day.

'Cans deena,' he replied.

'Dinner is cancelled?' I asked, trying to work out his words. I could see through to an empty dining room.

'Cans deena!' he answered. 'Cans deena!'

I was mystified. He took an old envelope and wrote down the figure '15'. He had been saying 'Quinze dinars'.

I accepted, having little idea whether it was a good price for a sandwich (I hadn't quite worked out the currency yet). I had a rest in my room, a small icebox with lights that went on and off as they pleased. From the window, there was a view of the main road in town, already renamed Boulevard Mohamed Bouazizi (previously Avenue Habib Bourguiba). An empty minibar whirred below a heater that did not work.

Then I went downstairs to find my sandwich, entering the deserted dining room, where I was met by a tall, springy man dressed in black. He was the waiter. With great ceremony, he led me to a table near a flickering television.

'Je voudrais une bière, s'il vous plaît,' I said.

'Bière,' he said wistfully. 'Ah, bière.'

I asked again.

'Bière sans alcool, seulement,' he said.

I ordered a glass of water, which soon arrived – after the distinctive ping of a microwave coming from the direction of the kitchen – with a hot spicy soup. I had opted for a three-course set meal, it appeared.

The waiter and I got talking. He was interested in why anyone in their right mind would be travelling on holiday to Sidi Bouzid. I explained the purpose of my visit in a mixture of French and English and his eyes lit up. It turned out that I was being served by a Bouazizi – Ramzi Bouazizi, a distant cousin of the man who sparked the revolution across North Africa and the Middle East. I looked at him closely and suddenly realised he was almost a dead ringer: the same sticking-out ears, the same wide-set eyes, thin nose and slightly goofy grin.

He spoke excitedly in rapid French that I couldn't understand, and disappeared, returning with the stocky receptionist. The latter took my mobile phone and punched in some numbers in a manner that suggested that I absolutely had to speak to whoever he was dialling. 'Zied Bouazizi!' he then said and handed me the phone. Then they both stood back and watched, smiling big smiles, as I listened to a ringing tone. Zied Bouazizi, it transpired, was Ramzi's brother, who worked in IT in Tunis.

I introduced myself and asked him what life had been like before the revolution.

'We were living in some kind of hell,' said Zied in English. 'In Sidi Bouzid it was some kind of hell. There was nothing to do. No parks. Only coffee shops. Nothing, nothing, nothing. When I finished my studies – and I am thirty now – I was obliged to live in Tunis. There were no jobs in Sidi Bouzid.'

He explained how Ali Bouazizi, Mohamed Bouazizi's uncle, had rushed from the supermarket he owned and recorded Mohamed when he was alight, using his Samsung mobile phone to capture the horrific scene. These shocking images were then posted on Ali's Facebook page.

'We started all of this,' he said, sounding pleased to tell the story. 'I provided Ali with photos of Mohamed and with contacts in Tunis.' These photos gave Ali 'before' pictures to go along with the images of Mohamed burning on the Facebook posting; Zied, who happened to be in Sidi Bouzid when Mohamed set himself alight, said he had been surprised the authorities had not shut down the internet. His contacts had helped bring Mohamed's plight and the Facebook video to the attention of Al Jazeera and France 24, which broadcast the images that very evening. The next day, 18 December 2010, the people of Sidi Bouzid took to the streets. The revolution had begun.

I asked Zied if he was proud of what had since happened in Tunisia, Libya and Egypt.

'Yes, of course,' he replied. 'It started everything. It changed the global world. Everything comes from Sidi Bouzid and the Tunisian people.'

Just over a year since the hasty retreat of President Ben Ali, how did he feel about the future of the country? Was he worried about the creep of Islamic law? No, he replied. What he cared about was the bottom line. 'Nothing has changed at all,' he sighed. 'Every day there are just speeches and speeches and nothing happens. There is still nothing to do in places like Sidi Bouzid. No jobs. Tunisia has received money from the World Bank, the Arab Bank, the European Union, the USA – and still nothing. They talk and they talk all day.'

Just like Hasen, the cigarette smuggler, Zied seemed to have turned sour about the revolution. We switched tack, and talked about Mohamed. 'He was a very good young man, very good.'

Mohamed Bouazizi died aged 26, having been the main provider for his family from the age of 10, when he began selling fruit and vegetables in the market. Yet he had continued to study, sitting for his baccalaureate, although failing to graduate from high school (he did not attend university, despite news reports to the contrary). From the age of 19 he worked full-time at the market, having been turned down by the army. He wanted to support his five younger siblings through school. His father had died when he was three and his stepfather was too ill to work. He had lived a tough, almost Dickensian, life. When he died he was earning about 250 dinars a month (£100). To put that in perspective, my 'cans deena' meal was the equivalent of about two days' labour.

'Mohamed and I studied together and we went for coffees together,' said Zied. 'He was a good man.'

He paused, and said quietly: 'I miss my family. I like my hometown. I want the government to take care of Tunisia. I would love to have a job and come back and be with my family. I miss seeing my brother. Living in Tunisia is still…' He paused again. 'It is still like some kind of hell.'

We said goodbye. I had not expected to talk to one of the movers and shakers behind the revolution on my first full day in Tunisia. As I reflected on our conversation, Ramzi delivered another dish, presaged by another microwave ping. I asked what it was and learnt that my dinner was *salade et escalopes simples*. Ramzi beamed a big, slightly goofy smile and retreated to watch the television; he really did look like his famous relative. I ate my lukewarm *escalopes* in silence, and retired to my icebox room. I had yet to lay eyes on another guest at Hotel Ksar Dhiata.

3

El Jem and Kairouan:

Mosques, Marvels and a Near Miss

NOR DID I see another guest. And in the morning I drove on past the governor's office – epicentre of the Arab Spring – to my next port of call in Tunisia. The roads outside Sidi Bouzid were quiet, at first. I was aiming for the Roman amphitheatre at El Jem, 100 kilometres to the east and a bona fide tourist sight that's considered by some to be finer than Rome's Colosseum; the Romans had ruled in Tunisia from 146BC to the mid 5th century. I'd not heard of El Jem before planning the trip, but it was said to be one of the country's 'wonders'. It was quite close by, so why not take a look and at the same time see how visitor numbers had been hit by the Arab Spring. Tourism had accounted for seven per cent of Tunisia's GDP before the Jasmine Revolution, but takings were said to be down by a third. In a country desperate for work, this did not bode well: but would the lack of visitors really be so noticeable?

I was about to find out, before meandering 70 kilometres northwest of El Jem to stay overnight at Kairouan, the fourth most holy city in Islam after Mecca, Medina and Jerusalem. Kairouan was renowned for being a centre of anti-secularism, where people were in favour of the introduction of Islamic law. Not many outsiders visited. Who would have thought the fourth most holy Islamic city was hidden somewhere in the windswept landscape ahead? Who would have imagined a Roman amphitheatre on a par with the world's most famous lurked in a farming village? I turned up the car radio and drove for the last time by the spot Bouazizi perished. I was going to be a tourist in Tunisia.

As I passed through Sidi Bouzid's dismal suburb of fly-tips and rusting fridges – no green belts in central Tunisia – I put the foot down as the road opened into a wide horizon of olive groves and orange earth. The sun had burnt through the grey above, though fearsome ink-black clouds loomed ahead. I was in a good mood, enjoying the journey and thinking how easy it was to get about in this country I'd never visited before – and how bleakly beautiful, too.

Heading east on Route P13, I slowed to pass a small town called Fayedh, with a neat emerald mosque and barbecue stalls (the Australians have nothing on the Tunisians when it comes to charcoaling their food). Smoke filled the street. Carcasses hung from posts. People lolled about eating kebabs, having a grand old time.

The landscape took on a deeper orange as I followed the P13 onwards. I got caught behind a tractor near Ouled Haffouz, where donkeys pulled carts transporting bags of vegetables. A soldier thumbed for a lift. I hesitated but did not pull over; I was enjoying the solitude of the road. I drove on to Fatnassa, another pit stop of a town with a mosque and yet more barbecue stalls. As I moved slowly through the smoke, the heavens opened and rain rattled on the roof of the KIA. The barbecue brigade rushed for cover.

Tractors were becoming a nuisance, and Tunisians are not shy about overtaking when they are held up. Just beyond Fatnassa, feeling as though I was in sync with the local way of driving, I pulled out to overtake a slow-moving van and a tractor at the same time.

This was, as I rapidly discovered, not a good idea. In fact it was a terrible one.

The rain had reduced the grip on the road. I was in the wrong gear. The car was on an incline. The van and the tractor had seemed to speed up. The result? I found myself hurtling head-on towards a pick-up truck loaded with olives. I could not turn in; the van and the tractor were in the way. I could clearly see three men in the cab of the truck ahead. So this is what it's like before a major accident, I thought. I was close enough to look into the driver's eyes. I gesticulated madly for him to veer away; there was a verge on to which he could move. For a split second, he seemed reluctant. But he did pull to the side. I whistled past, and turned in ahead of the tractor. In two decades of driving, that was the closest I'd come to calamity. I looked in the mirror. The olive truck had stopped, as though it was about to turn and come after me: was I about to become the object of a car chase involving Tunisian olive pickers? No, but I would not have blamed them. The incident had been entirely my fault. I had been incredibly stupid, lulled into feeling I knew the roads. What had been the great hurry? Why hadn't I just bided my time and waited for the tractor to turn off?

Thinking those thoughts, I continued through the mesmerising olive groves. They seemed to go on forever. I told myself to slow down. That had been a wake-up call. I stopped at Menzel Chaker, a nowhere town with a little roundabout with a Big Ben-style clock, the hands stuck at 11. Guys wearing black leather jackets sat on the clock's pedestal, idly smoking and watching me with expressionless eyes. I was an outsider, an object of curiosity in these little-visited parts. I bought a bottle of water, a loaf of bread and some cheese from a ramshackle shop. I made a sandwich on the bonnet of the car and looked at the map, suddenly feeling an enormous sense of relief mixed with delayed shock. My trip across North Africa had almost come to an almighty halt on its second day.

But I was in one piece, as were the olive pickers, thankfully. I drove on carefully, turning left at the clock and heading down a long dirt track through farmland. This took me to the Trans-African Highway, its dual carriageway seeming suddenly enormous. At the next junction I paid the 600 millimes toll (25p) and drove past a man skinning a sheep by the roadside.

After a very near miss, I had arrived at El Jem.

🐪 🐪 🐪

The sun had come out and the sky had turned cobalt, though it was still freezing. The world above seemed to shift by the hour in Tunisia. I parked by a large mosque, and set about finding the Roman amphitheatre. I could not see any sign of the structure. It was meant to be huge: the main attraction in town. But it seemed to have disappeared.

'Où est l'amphithéâtre, s'il vous plaît?' I asked a lad lounging by a hardware store. El Jem felt sleepy; there were not many people about.

'Eh?' he replied.

I repeated the question.

'Eh?' he said again, calling for another lad, who appeared from the depths of the shop.

I repeated the question once more, beginning to feel a little like Basil Fawlty in conversation with his Spanish waiter Manuel.

The second lad scratched his head for a bit, and eventually pointed down a narrow, twisting lane.

I drove along and found *l'amphithéâtre*. At the end of the road there was a turning and ahead was the honeycomb curve of an enormous Roman edifice, rising as if by magic at the end of another lane, its hoop-shaped windows framing neat patches of sky. The afternoon light illuminated the stone, creating a warm glow. It looked absolutely marvellous: how come more people don't know about El Jem?

I parked close to 'Quick Fast Food Pizza' and a couple of cafés full of men; just as in Sidi Bouzid, it seemed they had little to do. There were shops selling tourist knick-knacks, but no tourists. I walked towards the amphitheatre and came to another café, where three Westerners were drinking glasses of freshly squeezed orange juice. They existed: there were real, live holidaymakers in Tunisia! I passed a man who was desperate for me to ride on his camel. I paid the cheap entrance fee to the amphitheatre and found myself in a walkway leading to the ring where lions and leopards were once released to take on the gladiators.

El Jem thrived in the 2nd century AD when it was called Thyrus and was an important centre for olive oil production in the Mediterranean. The oil was sold to Rome at a vast profit and the Roman plantation owners lived in giant villas. They were extremely rich, much of their money coming from taxes on the local population, which led to a revolt in AD230. The Romans were defeated, although they later took back the land. It was during this period of freedom from Rome, when an 80-year-old Imperial official was put in charge, that construction began on the amphitheatre. Since 1979 it has been a UNESCO World Heritage Site.

As I entered the main ring, two British tourists materialised from behind a pillar. They seemed as surprised to see me as I was them; the rest of the amphitheatre was deserted. They were Victoria Tidboald and her father John Tidboald. We got talking, and it transpired that Victoria was the 'Rooms Division Manager' at a hotel in Whitehall in London and lived in Tonbridge in Kent, while John was a retired arable and cattle farmer from Minehead in Somerset. They wore sensible walkers' clothes: lightweight jackets and fleeces.

Victoria proved to be an expert on El Jem. 'There are five tiers,' she said authoritatively, pointing to the rim of the amphitheatre. 'It is the second-biggest surviving amphitheatre after the Colosseum in Rome. It must have been quite a thing in its time: it could hold thirty-five thousand people.'

Who needs a guidebook when you have the Rooms Division Manager of a Whitehall hotel close at hand?

They were staying on the coast in the resort of Sousse and had come on a day trip by train. 'We've had no trouble at all,' she said, referring to the year-old revolution. Despite the Foreign and Commonwealth Office and similar departments in other countries giving Tunisia the all-clear for tourism, many people were still put off by the thought of rampaging revolutionaries. 'The only trouble we had was the hotel we booked wasn't open when we arrived.' It had been closed because there were so few visitors. 'They put us in a different one instead,' she said matter-of-factly. She didn't seem to mind.

They had recently also been on holiday to the Red Sea in Egypt, making the most of the Arab Spring prices, about a third lower than usual. 'It didn't feel any different in Egypt,' she said. 'We'd been before and after the revolution: seemed just the same.'

'We knew what to expect,' said John, taciturnly. He was a man of few words. He grinned and fell back into silence.

Their holiday in Sousse had cost £330 each for a week, with flights and hotel included. They looked pleased about this, and I wondered if there was a tribe of tourists who followed in the wake of world troubles, making the most of cut-price deals.

We looked up at the cloudless sky, with the oval shape of the amphitheatre above, taking in the impressive structure – 138 metres long and 114 metres wide. Victoria had filled me in on the dimensions. It was hard not to be blown away by El Jem's tucked-away treasure. There we were in a building that had survived more or less intact for around 1,780 years.

Victoria and John went to catch their train, and I climbed to the fifth tier. From the top I could see the Trans-African Highway and the many kilometres of olive groves that filled the countryside. Graffiti was scratched into the sandstone structure. 'J. MONTL (1914)' and 'HOFFMAN (1931)'. Tourists had been coming for some time.

I made my way down and afterwards I went to the café by the amphitheatre, where the orange juice somehow managed to be simultaneously sweet and sharp. I sat at a table listening to the crackle of charcoal on a barbecue, watched by the camel man. He seemed to be calculating the likelihood of me changing my mind and going for a ride. The waiter gave me directions to a nearby archaeology museum. It was, he said, full of wonderful mosaics from the remains of Roman villas: 'Go five hundred metres. See the mos-key. Go two hundred metres more.'

I drove to the mos-key, kept going and was soon taking in magnificent mosaics depicting Dionysus, Orpheus and Endymion, next to graphic depictions of tigers attacking horses and lions mauling wild boars. Blood dripped as claws ripped flesh. But most eye-catching of all was a scene in which a leopard had leapt on to a gladiator and was tearing at his face. Plumes of blood streaked down as the beast ate the man alive.

When I'd been in the middle of the ring with Victoria and John surrounded by the 10-feet-high walls, I'd got a sense of how menacing it must have been with nowhere to go and thousands of spectators jeering down. Prisoners of war or slaves were often tied to posts and the big cats sent in. The bloodiness and horror was captured vividly on the mosaics. The Romans were so fond of this sport that many breeds of animal including lions, elephants and bears were almost wiped out in North Africa.

After many centuries of fruitful rule, the Romans themselves were eventually wiped out in Tunisia in AD439, when the Vandals captured Carthage (Rome had already fallen to the Visigoths in AD410). Tunisia had been a key part of the Roman Empire – an important source of olive oil, grapes and wheat, as well as of ceramic pots. The clay soil around El Jem meant that the outpost was especially useful when it came to pottery; locals had also turned their hands to making statuettes and terracotta plaques for churches.

🐪 🐪 🐪

My road trip continued – onwards to Kairouan. The light was soft and hazy in the late afternoon. I followed a long straight avenue lined by eucalyptus trees. Modern villas by the roadside were built in a mock Roman style, with columns and hoop-shaped windows. They looked like pleasant places to live. I passed a roundabout with a sculpture of doves of peace near the mosque in Ouled Chamakh. A sign said that speed was *contrôlé par radar*. Across a flat desert-like scrubland, I soon arrived at the fourth most holy city in Islam.

What I found was an unholy traffic jam. It was gridlock. I looked at my map amid the honking and general mayhem. I had no idea where to go. The traffic inched forwards; I was behind a beaten-up truck loaded with runner beans. It was soon dark. Vehicles took short cuts across the pavements. Everyone jostled for position. I could not see any road signs. I was totally lost.

In desperation, I turned down a side street. The map was still no good. I got out and asked a man sitting in a white van for directions to the Kasbah Hotel. 'Oui oui! Un moment!' he said cheerfully. He pointed at a kebab shop, where he told me his son was buying supper. His son returned. I was to follow them. They'd show me the way. And a few streets later I was at the hotel. The man looked out of his van, waving goodbye with a chicken drumstick in his hand – yet another friendly Tunisian.

The Kasbah was some hotel. It consisted of a giant cream-stoned building with a huge entrance shaped like a trout's mouth. I crossed a cobbled courtyard and came to a doorman wearing a gold uniform. I was the only guest in sight but the doorman steadfastly ignored me. Was I too much of a Westerner for such an Islamic place, I wondered?

Inside, I entered a cool marble reception and was soon taking a lift to room 409. After the icebox delight of Hotel Ksar Dhiata back in Sidi Bouzid, the Kasbah was a palace. For £40 I had a wood-panelled room with a smart green and blue tiled bathroom and a balcony with diamond-patterned shutters overlooking a central courtyard and a lovely pool (pity it wasn't about 15 degrees warmer).

A muezzin started up. His voice rose rapidly, like a darts commentator announcing the score of 180, before steadying at a temporarily slower pace, as though the imaginary darts player was not doing so well. Then the tone rose once more. Other muezzins joined him, lifting and dropping their voices in a similar manner, sounds drifting across the still evening air beyond the balcony. Kairouan is so holy that seven visits is said to be the equivalent of a pilgrimage to Mecca. I closed my eyes and listened to the calls echoing above the rooftops. Then I went for a walk.

Ever since AD670 when Oqba Ibn Nafi discovered a golden cup he believed he had lost in Mecca, Kairouan had been a place of holy devotion. Just like El Jem's amphitheatre, the city was a UNESCO World Heritage Site. I was seeing two in a day; two that few people knew about. I stepped past the sullen doorman and into the heart of a holy city.

My *Rough Guide* said that Hotel Splendid was the place to go for a 'calm beer' in a 'conservative town [with] little local nightlife'. I headed in its direction along dark empty streets. It was a test of sorts: could I get a drink in such a holy, Islamic place? I was going to give it a try. Near a row of *magasins de chaussures* (shoe shops) I came to a café festooned with Tunisian flags and packed with men in leather jackets playing cards. I dallied by the café trying to make sense of my city map. A man sidled up to me. 'Let me be your guide,' he whispered in an odd voice.

'I'm looking for the medina,' I said, in English, and then repeated in French. The medina was the old walled town. 'Which way to the medina?'

'Let me be your guide,' he whispered again. 'Come, come,' he grasped my arm urgently, and attempted to lead me in a direction that I later learnt was nowhere near the medina.

I brushed him off, realising he was not one of the kindly and open Tunisians I'd met before. I said 'non merci' several times. He still would not budge. 'Do you want me to call for the police?' I asked. The p-word had the desired effect. He scuttled into the shadows of an alleyway like a crab retreating beneath a rock.

I gave up on walking to Hotel Splendid. I took a taxi instead. The hotel turned out to be on the far side of town – which wasn't a long way – down a grimy road with a building site on one side. The Splendid did not live up to its name. I climbed dark steps and entered a dull, dimly lit reception. The space was empty. To the right there was a doorway that seemed to lead to a bar. But it was locked. A rotund, bearded man who had been watching a soap opera on a television in the breakfast room approached.

'Close-ed,' he said, pointing at the doorway.

What seemed to be the only bar in town was shut.

'Close-ed,' he repeated, and then added: 'Nice!'

He was gesticulating towards the dreary breakfast room, seeming to suggest I join him to watch the soap opera. I thanked him for his kind offer, but headed back out into the Kairouan night.

The world's fourth holiest Islamic city was well stocked with cars and cats. The former ruled the roads in such a way that whenever you crossed a street a vehicle appeared from nowhere and honked at you. The latter were in charge of the cobbled alleyways of the medina, scuttling about and sleeping on steps.

At the occasional café in the medina, men with beards smoked shisha pipes, looking contentedly idle. The only shop that was open sold plates of delicately piled sweets and icing-coated pastries made of figs and sesame seeds. I could eat sesame seed sweets and smoke a shisha pipe next to a bearded Berber. Alternatively, I could return to my hotel and see what was happening there – I was hungry and thirsty and I was a tourist (who wouldn't mind a calm beer).

I walked back to the Kasbah, dodging more shady 'guides' by the café covered in flags, and entered its Golden Yasmin restaurant. I settled at a table with a pink cloth next to a large painting of galloping horses. I was the only guest. Twanging music with a clip-clop beat played in the background. Amazingly, alcoholic drinks were offered: I was delivered a beer by a wordless waiter who seemed taken aback by this rush of custom.

I collected a salad from a buffet set up as though many guests might be about to arrive, and ordered spaghetti bolognaise instead of what I already knew was the 'usual' Tunisian dish: grilled chicken and rice (I was to become only too familiar with chicken-and-rice in North Africa). It was a decent meal. The waiter kept an eye on me and brought over another beer. I settled in, listening to the twanging music and reading a novel.

Back in my room, BBC World News was reporting on the shelling of Homs in Syria, apparently by President Assad's forces. Many kilometres from Tunisia, the Arab Spring rumbled on. Hillary Clinton, the US Secretary of State, was demanding an 'end to the bloodshed' – rather optimistically in hindsight. In the face of all the evidence piled against him, President Assad was denying responsibility for any violence. An Arab League resolution condemning human rights abuses in Syria had been put to the UN Security

Council; it was blocked by Russia and China on the grounds that such a resolution could lead to international military intervention and a forced regime change. Lives were being lost as the revolutions set off by Sidi Bouzid's bold uprising continued.

There was snow in Europe, and El Jem's main competitor – Rome's Colosseum – had been closed to tourists for the first time in living memory as it was considered unsafe. The city had had its heaviest snowfall for 26 years. An item on tourism in Egypt said that authorities were hoping to 'drive tourists back to the avenue of sphinx… to make new discoveries'. I thought ahead to the country on the eastern side of North Africa. It seemed a long way away.

🐫 🐫 🐫

After breakfast, I checked out of the Kasbah and strolled up a street to the Aghlabid pools. Muezzins were calling. Cars were honking. The traffic was as bad as ever.

A handful of French holidaymakers were at the pools, which I found at the top of a short hill. The Aghlabid bathing pools date from the 9th century, when Kairouan had a population of 300,000 and was in its heyday; at the time of my visit the population was 120,000. The name came from a dynasty first headed by Ibrahim ibn al-Aghlab, which ruled from AD800 to 909, when culture thrived in the city's many palaces, schools and mosques. It was the decline of this dynasty, followed by the bloody sacking of the city in 1057 by nomadic Arab tribes, that caused Kairouan to lose its regional dominance.

Apart from the Great Mosque – which I was about to visit – the pools were among the few remains from the Aghlabid days. Originally there were 14, but only four pools had been restored. They had become the city's waterworks. I paid a ticket and climbed a staircase to a roof with a view of the impressive circles of water – great pools surrounded by stone walls in an otherwise bare plot of land. Squint your eyes and they look a little like enormous flying saucers.

On the rooftop I met Guizani Khelifa, in his late sixties. He was taking no chances with the cold, wearing a ski jacket, a scarf, a V-neck jumper and a shirt. He had a thin brush moustache and was chatty. Within seconds, without formal agreement, it was established he had become my official guide. He spoke in faltering English.

'It was sixty years ago,' he said. 'I swam here as a boy. But then two children drowned: the water is five metres deep. Swimming was banned. Very sad.'

He was a mine of information about the pools: 'In this one, the governor used to sit on that stone in the middle.' He pointed to a stone that jutted upwards with three columns grooved into the side; it was a little like a strange set of cricket stumps. 'He would go across on a boat. People would make promenades around the pool.' He pointed to the rim of the basin.

'This one is a polygon. It has forty-eight edges,' he said, gesticulating towards another pool, adding: 'The only other one like it is in Mecca.' The polygon was 60 metres across, while another was 128 metres wide. Guizani knew a great deal about the pools. He scratched his moustache, looking at them thoughtfully.

I switched subject and asked him about the revolution. Guizani's face lit up. 'For the first time in my life,' he said, 'I am very happy for democracy. Very happy!'

'I lived with the French. They left when I was ten years old. There were good French and there were bad French,' he added reflectively, seeming to lose himself in memories for a moment.

'Then came Bourguiba in 1956. He was not good for religion, but he was good for schools and for the liberty of women.' He was referring to Bourguiba's secularist policies, which included the introduction of family planning, against the wishes of many of the local Islamic hardliners.

'Maybe we were the only Islamic nation, apart from Turkey, to do this. Bourguiba was like Kemal Atatürk in many ways.' Atatürk had replaced Islamic law with Western legal institutions in Turkey in the early 20th century.

'It was a good time. Very good.'

I was getting a potted version of Tunisia's recent history, from a wise old head on a windswept rooftop. 'President Ben Ali: he was good for the first three years. Then came his wife Leila [whom he married in 1992]. She was not a very good woman. She like money.' Nobody I spoke to in Tunisia had a positive word to say about Leila Trabelsi, a former hairdresser who had adopted a lavish lifestyle after meeting Ben Ali. Her extended family, which had also enjoyed the privileges of power, was widely disliked.

'Now we have democracy! But it is very bad for tourism! The worst for forty-two years!' Guizani had been working in the tourist industry for that long. 'Maybe people will come again – Americans, Europeans – when there is better security and peace.'

We turned from the pools to take in the city. Minarets and domes stretched out under an oyster-grey sky. There were 300 mosques (and counting) in Kairouan, said Guizani, who told me that the previous night at 8 p.m., the new prime minister of Tunisia had visited to pray. Hamadi Jemali of the Islamist party Ennahda had come to the Great Mosque.

'He stayed for an hour. He only had six bodyguards with him.'

Guizani paused, scratching his beard again. 'That was unusual,' he said. 'Ben Ali would bring at least two hundred.'

We drank sugary coffees from porcelain cups at a café on the first floor of the Aghlabid pools visitors' building. Guizani seemed very much at ease with life. I could sense his great relief at being able, finally, to express opinions with strangers; not just to relate his (very) extensive knowledge of the Aghlabid pools. The French; Bourguiba; Ben Ali: he'd seen them come and go. He had a defiant sparkle in his eyes.

We finished our coffees and Guizani pulled his scarf tight. He was heading back to talk about 9th-century water features shaped like flying saucers to any tourists who had found their way to the fourth most holy city in Islam. We shook hands and I watched as he creakily re-climbed the staircase to the chilly roof.

Outside, I followed in the footsteps of the new moderate Islamic prime minister to the Great Mosque. It wasn't far. As I went I passed a women's clothes shop: 'Why Not: Prêt à Porter Pour Dames', with a pink façade and pictures of two glamorous women wearing strapless dresses and looking as though they were about to go to a ball. It seemed unexpectedly racy for the approach to Tunisia's most important mosque. Beyond, I came to a Nokia shop and a stall selling Nike trainers: further signs of 'Western' ways.

Then I turned a corner, crossed a big empty cobbled car park and came to the high tan-coloured walls of the medina. In front of the entrance, a plot of land was filled with what looked like large lumps of molten wax. I went to look closer and realised that the 'wax' was in fact wobbly stone painted white; the stones marked the tombs of an ancient graveyard. Down an alley with Tunisian-flag bunting and a heavyset man in a hooded top selling trinkets, I entered the courtyard where a sign indicated 'Grande Mosquée'.

The courtyard was enormous with a smooth limestone floor. Dozens upon dozens of archways with marble columns lined the perimeter. I went through one leading to the prayer hall, where non-Muslims were forbidden to enter. From the entrance, I could see even more columns and arches; local custom said that if you counted them all you'd go blind. A sea of red-purple carpets covered the floor of the interior. It was like a very big front room. A man wearing a woollen hat was dusting a wooden partition with a pink brush. Beyond the partition was the area where women prayed. More than four thousand people could fit in the hall. Orange water coolers stood next to piles of dog-eared books: Korans, I presumed. I was at the most important mosque in a country with a recently democratically elected Islamic leader. It somehow felt as though I had come to a symbolic centre-point of the new Tunisia.

🐫 🐫 🐫

Outside the mosque, I lost myself in a labyrinth of narrow streets lined with low-level white and pale-blue buildings. The houses had a dilapidated, broken-down look: rotten wooden doors, crumbling plaster, peeling paint. Sparrows roosted in drainpipes. Sweet wrappers and old cigarette packets had been cast about. Filthy cats stretched on doorsteps. An elderly man on a bicycle teetered past, the basket filled with baguettes. An even more elderly woman wearing slippers and red socks shuffled along.

The alleyways twisted and turned onwards, occasionally broken by little tree-lined squares around which small dented cars were parked. Most of the cars were decades old and I wondered how they'd found their way through the narrow lanes that didn't seem wide enough for vehicles. A crumpled Renault parked near a heap of rubbish was – bizarrely – filled with baguettes. It was such a striking sight I could imagine the car as an exhibit in a contemporary art gallery back home.

A man in a grey tunic with the hood pulled up glanced my way and sidled onwards. A little boy said: '*Bonjour, bonjour, un dinar, un dinar.*' He pointed to some olive-green shutters, as though he was acting as a tour guide. A moped puttered past. Sawdust spilled out from carpenters' workshops. Inside, men planed wood attached to clamps in scenes that must not have changed much for centuries (irrespective of who had been in charge of Tunisia). They kept warm thanks to buckets of charcoal that emitted thin ringlets of smoke.

Tiny carpet-weaving outfits, little bigger than the width of two doorways, gave way to tailors' workshops. Pink and orange garments were being stitched together in darkened rooms. I looked in one and could see white eyes peering out of the gloom. '*Bonjour,*' said a voice connected to one of the sets of eyeballs.

At the end of one alley, I found myself outside Bir Barouta, which was where Oqba Ibn Nafi discovered a well he believed was connected to Mecca when he visited in AD670; he had not just stumbled upon the golden cup. Up some stairs close to a shop with booming Arabic dance music, I came to the top of the well, around which a camel was turning a wooden wheel to draw the water. A sip from the well was said to bring you back to the city one day, and many pilgrims did so as part of the ritual of their visit. I took some holy water after handing over dinars to the man in charge of the camel. It tasted musty. I was the only visitor. Kairouan was a strange place, so far removed from the Tunisia of holiday brochures. I felt as though I was getting an insider's introduction to the country's strong Islamic culture… so crucial to its post-Arab Spring future.

🐪 🐪 🐪

Before heading north to Tunis, I had one further Islamic pilgrimage to make: a visit to another *zaouia* (religious school). It was built in honour of Sidi Sahab and consisted of both a school and a mausoleum built over the spot where Sidi Sahab, one of Prophet Muhammad's companions, is said to have been buried in AD685. He was believed to have always carried a few hairs from the Prophet's beard, hence the alternative name for the *zaouia*: the Barber's Mosque.

'Vous êtes français?' asked an attendant in a red fez, who manned the doorway to the tomb. He was sitting next to a bucket of burning charcoal to stay warm, and seemed very cheerful.

I explained I was British, not French.

'Musulman seulement ici,' he said jovially. Then he indicated for me to pass over my camera, which I did.

'Flash automatique?' he asked casually, as he went inside and took a couple of snaps. One was of a fine crystal chandelier; another of a tall wall covered in red, blue and gold tiles depicting star shapes and flowers. Thanks to the man in the red fez, I'd become a spy in the Barber's Mosque.

Two days, two UNESCO World Heritage Sites, one very close shave outside Sidi Bouzid: my Arab Spring tour was already taking me places I would never have otherwise gone. And I was glad to let it lead my way.

4

Tanks in the Capital

DRIVING IN Tunisia is not good for your nerves. Having seen my life flash before my eyes on the road to El Jem, I wasn't about to take any more chances. But being a cautious driver had its downsides too. It brought the tailgaters of Tunisia into play. Travelling from Kairouan back to the Trans-African Highway, I'd look in the mirror and suddenly see the grilles of giant cross-country coaches, pick-up trucks (of the petrol-smuggling variety) and jam-packed minivans right up behind the KIA. Even though I was stuck – and content to be stuck – in a queue of traffic, there they loomed in the rear-view mirror a few inches from the bumper, itching to zoom ahead. Do not expect a relaxing ride in the country that sparked the Arab Spring.

On the road heading northeast to the Trans-African Highway and Tunis, I held on tightly and left overtaking to others. The desert flatlands turned into olive groves and I joined the road I'd earlier shared with Hasen, the cigarette smuggler. I passed the café where we'd eaten grilled chicken. Then the road turned on to the highway, just south of the small nondescript town of Enfidaville.

You might easily pass Enfidaville without thinking twice. But it is a town with an intriguing history. Tunisia was the last battleground of World War II in North Africa and it was from Enfidaville that the legendary Eighth Army, led by then Lieutenant General Bernard 'Monty' Montgomery, launched what was to become an important strike in the final campaign to remove the

47

Axis forces in the northeast of the country. The dusty roads along which I was travelling played a key part in the eventual fall of Hitler.

The victory in Tunisia – Axis forces surrendered on 13 May 1943, with 275,000 prisoners of war taken – meant that all of North Africa was in Allied hands. It allowed the Allies to open up the Mediterranean Sea to the passage of ships, and concentrate on attacking Sicily, just 100 miles to the northeast of Tunisia, followed afterwards by the invasion of Italy.

Holding on to Tunisia for so long had been a strategic mistake by Hitler, as doing so used up many of his best divisions. Rommel had advised the Führer to retreat, and was put on sick leave for making the suggestion. There had been many skirmishes across central Tunisia in the lead-up to the final assault – including a heated attack known as the 'Battle of Sidi Bouzid', in which German Panzer divisions forced American troops temporarily to withdraw, inflicting heavy casualties. The town that started the Arab Spring has more than one historic claim to fame.

I pondered all of this on the Trans-African Highway, which had begun to feel like an old friend. It was three lanes each way all the way to Tunis. Sheep grazed on weeds in the breakdown lanes. The tailgaters disappeared and it was a clear drive north.

🐪 🐪 🐪

By a minor miracle, I found my abode for the next two nights without mix-up. There it was, not far from the highway, on the airport side of Tunisia's capital in the Lafayette district: the Hotel du Parc. Its name was in shiny gold letters atop a building painted garish pink. I entered through a mirrored glass door into a lobby full of supporters of the Tunisian football team drinking cans of Coca-Cola. It was 5 p.m. and the national side was playing Ghana in the Africa Cup of Nations later. The game would be shown in the hotel lounge.

I climbed steps that curled up through an atrium, dropped my bags in a very small but clean room with a highway view, and ventured outside. The streets were deserted. I strolled towards Avenue Habib Bourguiba, the most famous road in the country – where the Ministry of the Interior is based and where protesters had gathered during the Jasmine Revolution. Avenue Bourguiba was also renowned for its striking colonial-era buildings, laid-back cafés and relaxed atmosphere.

To get there I followed Avenue Mohamed V, named after a former sultan of Morocco who died in 1961. Taxis buzzed past and sometimes hovered, following to see if I wanted a ride. I soon came to a tall rose-tinted building with 'MUSEE' written on its façade. Outside the entrance was a green armoured vehicle. I crossed over expecting a military museum. It was indeed a tank, partially surrounded by coiled razor wire. The guns on top were covered by tarpaulin.

I still could not tell if it was part of the museum or for real; no soldiers were to be seen. The tank looked like a motorised version of a toad with a hunched shape and wide-set bulbous headlights. I could have stepped through a gap in the razor wire and taken a look through one of the porthole-style windows or climbed on top to examine the guns. Nobody seemed to be around.

The Musée de la Monnaie, as a sign informed me, was closed; it was not a military museum after all. But its name gave a clue to the tank's presence. Further along the road stood red sentry boxes manned by soldiers wearing camouflage in front of a pink-concrete building. I was at the Central Bank of Tunisia. Climbing on to the tank would have been a bad mistake. As I looked further down Avenue Mohamed V, I realised the street was teeming with men with guns.

It was believed that Ben Ali had spirited away as much as £11 billion of Tunisia's cash over the years, hiding his loot in Swiss bank accounts and in many other tax havens while hiring financial advisors to cover his tracks. Rumours were circulating that his wife Leila took 1.5 tonnes of gold from the Central Bank when the family fled to Saudi Arabia. They flew by private plane to Jeddah on 14 January 2011, and have since been sentenced in absentia to 35 years in prison for theft from the state, while Ben Ali faces a further 20 years for inciting 'murder and looting' during the revolt.

So the Central Bank was a sensitive spot. More soldiers were on show as I drew closer to Avenue Bourguiba. Across the way, tanks and jeeps guarded a tall tower block with mirrored glass windows. Graffiti covered the perimeter fence: 'RCD DEGAGE!' Just like the graffiti I'd seen coming from the airport on my first day, it was telling the Constitutional Democratic Rally to go away. The tower block was the former headquarters of Ben Ali's party, which had always scored so remarkably highly in the country's 'elections'. In 1994 the RCD had managed to win 97.7 per cent of the parliamentary 'vote'.

The tower attracted big crowds during the protests that forced Ben Ali's hasty retreat. The street was packed with demonstrators bravely facing up to soldiers and waving banners demanding 'FREEDOM!' and saying 'SUR LES PAVES, LE JASMIN' – announcing that the Jasmine Revolution had hit the pavements of Tunis. Many of the mirrored windows of the RCD's old base were smashed.

At the end of Avenue Mohamed V, I came to a square marked on my map as Place 7 November. This was the date when Ben Ali became president in 1987. But a new blue and yellow sign had been erected renaming the square Place 14 Janvier 2011.

The centre of the square was dominated by a rocket-shaped clock made out of metal with intricate Arabic patterns cut into the surface and a white clock face. On one side stood the Ministry of Tourism, its prominent position in the capital reflecting the importance of foreign holidaymakers to the country. There were a few fountains and an advertising board promoting yoghurts. Beyond the advert was the start of the tree-lined promenade down the middle of Avenue Bourguiba, on the far side of which was the Ministry of the Interior.

Groups of policemen stood outside the ministry, which was surrounded by two thick coils of razor wire. Behind the wire, another tank was parked next to three large police vans. Meanwhile on the opposite side of the street, a large, bright United Colors of Benetton and other fashion shops were attracting customers.

Conscious that I should perhaps not take any pictures, I quickly raised my camera for a surreptitious snap. Maybe I was naïve to be so surprised by the continued military and police presence in the heart of Tunis. About a third of one side of Avenue Bourguiba was sealed off by razor wire: Tunisia's new rulers seemed nervous.

A policeman stepped my way. 'Vous prenez une photo?' he asked.

'Non, monsieur,' I lied.

He looked searchingly at me.

I asked if these were government buildings.

'Oui,' he replied tight-lipped.

I apologised for my mistake and moved along.

At the end of the razor wire, coffee drinkers sat at a pleasant-looking brasserie. Further along was a doner kebab shop and a Zara with a sale on. I walked along the promenade heading for the medina. Life went on despite the tanks. Kids skateboarded, couples strolled arm in arm, shoppers paced towards the designer stores and elderly folk sat on benches watching the world go by.

I stopped at a fine old building: the Théâtre Municipal. Nude classical figures and horses pulling chariots were carved in stone above the three grand doorways and a balcony with balustrades. I stood in front of the theatre for a moment. I knew the building dated from 1902 – was it Art Nouveau or Neoclassical? As I was about to walk on, a middle-aged man wearing black came up to me.

'You like this building?' he asked in English. I was obviously a tourist and he must have guessed English was the best language to try.

'Yes, I do – it's great,' I said.

'This is a big street,' he continued, switching tack.

'Yes, it is,' I replied. There was no denying that.

'How about we go to a small street, where I know a small bar – I will show you the real Tunis,' he said.

'No thanks,' I replied moving along. In Tunisia there seemed to be unofficial guides wherever you turned.

Beyond the theatre, a bus crammed with police in riot gear was parked. Graffiti on a corrugated iron wall next to the bus said: 'VIVE LA TUNISIE: LIBRE ET DEMOCRATIQUE.' I kept going, coming to a tangle of razor wire surrounding armoured vehicles on Place de l'Indépendance – a square that had not needed renaming thanks to its one-size-fits-all quality. It was next to the cathedral. Soldiers in olive uniforms, red berets and jackboots stood at street corners. Above the cathedral's tall, croquet-hoop entrance, a golden picture of Christ was surrounded by angels blowing horns. The metal front gates were shut. On the filthy pavement near the steps to the entrance a homeless man lay huddled in rags next to the word 'FREEDOM' sprayed on the cathedral wall. Another piece of graffito next to the homeless man spelt out the letters 'ACAB'. It was the acronym of a maverick local group that went by the name All Cops Are Bastards.

In Place de la Victoire – a name that also survived the revolution – kids kicked a football in the early evening gloom. I crossed to enter the medina, where the stalls were closed because it was Sunday, heading up a steep alley into a mysterious world of strewn cardboard boxes, litter, cats and lurking figures. I continued into the darkness of the narrow passages with their shuttered stalls, feeling a little ill at ease. (I later read that I was right to be, as it was a notorious spot for muggers and pickpockets, while on Sundays you also needed to watch out for rubbish being heaved from windows into the alleys below.)

Hearing quickening steps behind, I walked faster. But the sound of feet ceased, and I kept on going, even further into furtive shadows and hidden alleys.

I was looking for the Great Mosque, which dated from the Aghlabid period. Eventually, I located the place of worship, with its enormous stone wall and a dome at the top of a tiered tower. I admired the impressive building. Then, having no idea where I was, I followed a couple of anxious-looking tourists back to Place de la Victoire – thankfully avoiding all muggers, pickpockets and flying bin-liners along the way.

Crossing a side street back on Avenue Bourguiba, I came to a small gap between two parked cars at the same time as another pedestrian. I gestured to him to pass and said, 'Après vous.'

The local had ruffled hair and stubble, and looked like a student. He asked: 'Etes-vous un Anglais?'

I replied that I was.

We were outside a bar called Café de Paris. The student seemed pleased to have met a foreigner, wanted to chat, and looked about the right age to have been a pro-democracy activist. I explained my journey and asked if he would like to talk about Tunisia since the revolution. I was interested to hear what he had to say. And so we entered a cavernous neon-lit room filled with men in black leather jackets. Almost all smoked and sat either sullenly or cracking jokes at circular tables cluttered with green bottles. The place felt like a cross between a waiting room at a coach station and a 1930s speakeasy.

My new friend introduced himself as Somalani Chawki, a 25-year-old tourism student from Beja, a city about a hundred kilometres west of Tunis. He looked haggard and wore a dirty fleece. He spoke in a mixture of French and English.

'My friend, après la révolution nous sommes libres, mais les problèmes sont économiques,' he said, sounding just like the people I'd met in Sidi Bouzid. 'There are 1.5 million jobless, it is very, very bad. The majority of French and British worry about coming here: it's the TV image.'

He ordered two beers, which were delivered with aplomb by a bald waiter wearing a shabby suit and a bow tie. Somalani gulped his drink.

'With Ben Ali we could not speak like this,' he said, taking a large sip. 'You would be here now and those two people there.' He pointed to two men at a table close by. 'They would be police.'

I asked if he had been involved in the protests, but Somalani skipped the question.

'This street,' he continued, 'this street was empty before. But Ben Ali is gone and for me it is much better now.'

Did he really think the police and army presence were an improvement?

He ignored this, too. And he suddenly seemed despondent; his mood seemed to teeter between bright optimism and a pessimism that bordered on depression. He abruptly asked: 'Do you have the fire?' He wanted a light for a cigarette. Smoke lay in fog-like layers in the café; consuming your own cigarettes seemed almost unnecessary.

I said I didn't smoke.

'Très bien,' he said, and disappeared hastily into the back of the bar to find some matches.

He returned, smoking, and continued his monologue, sounding glum: 'The government of Tunisia is Islamic now but people talk as though it is strong Islamic, like the Taliban. But it is not: we are like the Turks.' He put his hand up and with an alert flick of the wrist gestured to the waiter for two more beers.

The drinks arrived. He took a large draught from his second bottle. For a moment he appeared contented. But then he sighed deeply. 'I have five more months of studying and then I go out into the world. Now it is so difficult,' he said, taking a drag from his second cigarette (which he had lit with the butt of his first). 'My father is deaf and my mother is a housewife. When I work it is for my family.'

'But I thought you were a student,' I said.

He did not reply. He had become even more dejected and morose. In an effort to cheer him up, I said that tourism would almost certainly improve when things settled down.

'Where is your hotel?' he said, ignoring me and switching to a hostile tone. Somalani had a turbulent manner, for sure. He glugged his beer and stared at me.

'A long way from where we are,' I replied. I didn't like the way the conversation was going.

'Where is your hotel?' he asked again, his aggression turning plaintive.

He was glum. 'A very long way away,' I replied.

'Have you something for eating?' he asked, suddenly seeming very desperate indeed. And I looked at him again. Although he was in the uniform of any young Tunisian man in the winter – jeans, fleece and trainers – it was a very well-worn version. His ruffled hair and half-beard might not be a casual student look. It dawned on me that maybe he was sleeping rough. Perhaps he had come to Tunis from Beja in search of a job and was down on his luck. Could he be stuck in the environs of Place 14 Janvier 2011 with no money and nowhere to go?

'Please have you something for eating?' he repeated, sounding totally hopeless. Shame, sorrow and frustration showed in his eyes.

I got up and wished him luck, leaving a note worth a few more beers on the table, and stepped out of the fug of Café de Paris on to Avenue Bourguiba. I crossed the street and caught a taxi back to Hotel du Parc.

With all the soldiers, razor wire, homeless, hustlers, lost souls, police vans and tanks, the centre of Tunis did not seem like the capital of a country celebrating a glorious revolution. Despite the veneer of international brands and the few designer-clothes shoppers, the city centre felt distinctly sharp round the edges, with a strong sense of: *vive la révolution*… and now what? I found Tunis hard to work out.

🐪 🐪 🐪

The football match between Tunisia and Ghana was in full swing. The hotel lounge was connected to a bar and had been commandeered by men wearing red shirts, who were smoking, drinking beer, pontificating and cursing in Arabic at a television in a corner. Tunisia was 1–0 down. It was even smokier than Café de Paris. The hotel was next to the training pitch of Espérance Sportive de Tunis and had a big football clientele.

A garrulous waiter brought beers on trays and the fans made an elaborate show of finding the prices ridiculously steep, only reluctantly handing over cash. The waiter had a stash of green 50-dinar notes in his hand and seemed pretty pleased with the evening. The 50-dinar bill (worth about £20) was the largest note you'd usually handle and still showed a picture of Zine el Abidine Ben Ali Airport on the back; it had since changed its name to Enfidha-Hammamet International Airport.

I didn't stick around; I just wanted to rest after a long day. But as I went to my room, I heard an enormous cheer. There must have been an equaliser. I was glad: some brightness amid the trouble and gloom... though it didn't last long (they lost 2–1).

🐪 🐪 🐪

Carthage, the ancient site of important Phoenician and Roman cities, did not exactly set the pulse racing – not at first, at least.

It was not far from the hotel, about half an hour's drive just beyond Tunis's international airport in a neighbourhood of detached houses with big gardens and security signs by the sea; the old port was effectively a suburb of Tunis. I drove in the KIA and pulled up in front of one of the mansions, where I tried to work out where to start. Carthage consists of several parts including Byrsa Hill, the Archaeological Garden, the Villas Romaines and the Antonine Baths – among much else. As far as I could tell, there was no 'proper' order in which to see them.

I started at random with the Antonine Baths. I entered behind a couple of French tourists. Together we had the baths to ourselves. The sky was milky and the water of the Gulf of Tunis ashen. It was yet another nippy day. I bought a ticket and came to a wide, open plot of land with large holes covering about a quarter of the surface of a football pitch. A sign informed me that the baths (the holes) were created by the Roman Emperor Antoninus, who ruled AD138–161. Successor to Hadrian, his official, full name was 'Imperator Caesar Titus Aelius Hadrianus Antoninus Augustus Pontifex Maximus'.

Legend has it that the Phoenicians founded Carthage in the early 9th century BC when Queen Dido arrived from modern-day Lebanon. The

Phoenicians lived peacefully alone for many years before agreeing a treaty with the powerful Romans in 507BC that gave the Romans exclusive shipping rights at their excellent port. This arrangement continued until the Romans sacked and almost completely destroyed the city in 146BC. The conquerors then built up Carthage over many years, with the population growing as high as 700,000 when it was the second city of the empire after Rome. Julius Caesar had been particularly important in this development.

The attack by the Vandals in the 5th century brought an end to this period of Roman rule (although Romans returned in the 6th century). It was only with the arrival of Arab armies in the early 7th century that the Roman influence finally disappeared. After this, Carthage was again flattened, with many of the stones going to build structures in Tunis and Kairouan.

This ancient recycling of materials meant there was not a lot left to see of Emperor Antoninus's swimming pool complex. I wandered about the few remaining columns, and watched doleful fishermen casting lines into the sea. A cargo ship drifted past looking like a toy boat. Dogs barked. A ginger cat slipped along the bottom of the old Roman pool. An eerie sense of isolation hung in the air.

Heading back to the car, I met two former members of Ben Ali's presidential guard. They were leaning against a wall and looking distinctly put out. They wore olive uniforms, jackboots, blue scarves and woollen hats. They clutched rifles and appeared cold and miserable.

Their names were Salem and Walid. Salem had a long, oval face and looked as though he might play in the front row of a rugby team. Walid had rat-like eyes and was more of a scrum half in stature.

'We are here to protect the site,' said Salem gruffly. 'We control the security,' he added. I did not think he really wanted to talk.

I asked whether they liked their new jobs.

He looked at me as though that was a dumb question: 'Now we work eight to ten hours a day, in the presidential guard it was twelve hours. But it was better then.'

'Why?'

'We were in the presidential guard. There were only one and a half thousand of us in the presidential guard,' he replied.

'La liberté est très mauvaise,' said Walid.

I asked him what Ben Ali was like.

He replied enigmatically: 'Ben Ali lived in a high way, but there were things he forgot.'

Such as democracy, human rights and freedom of speech, I thought he was about to say, but he paused as the French couple walked past.

'We had no media under Ben Ali,' Salem continued; whether he considered this a good or a bad thing, I was unsure.

I asked about visitor numbers at the Antonine Baths. 'Forty per cent down, maybe,' he replied. 'C'est dommage – the unemployment.'

They looked at me with expressions that said: that's it. So I took my leave of Ben Ali's ex-bodyguards and continued with my exploration of Carthage.

The Roman villas were up a hill. The French couple were already there, and we nodded at each other as though we were comrades on an onerous mission. It was bitterly cold as I trudged up a path surrounded by old remains that did not seem to conform to any particular shape. A train rattled below, and I could see the satellite dishes on the roofs of the neighbourhood mansions – under which many ancient ruins are said still to lie. Headless sculptures were dotted between cypress trees.

That was about as much as I could say for the Roman villas. I was finding it hard to get excited about Carthage. But convinced I must be missing something, I went to Byrsa Hill, where I turned into a car park and was set upon by a man wearing Elvis Presley-style shades. He wanted to charge me for parking. But he looked so shifty I ignored him, and later discovered he had nothing whatsoever to do with the ruins of Byrsa Hill.

Shortly afterwards, I met Kalthoum Laouini, a guide who told me she was 'licensed in history'. She was inside the entrance gate and wore a plastic identification card which proved her historical qualification. Everything about Kalthoum, as I was soon to learn, had a rapid quality. She wore a thin black coat with a thick fashionable fur collar, though the body of the coat was far too flimsy for the cold. She shivered, regarded me with twitchy eyes and stated her price for a tour. I accepted without haggling, surprising her.

The tour went in fits and starts. For one thing Kalthoum's English was not so good, as she admitted when we met. She was better in Italian. 'Do you speak Italian?' she asked, looking extremely disappointed when I said no.

We proceeded to some scattered stones. 'Doric! Ionic!' Kalthoum explained, in a fit of shivers. She spoke incredibly loudly, disjointedly, and very, very fast.

'The Phoenicians came to Carthage in the 9th century BC!' she exclaimed. 'Antiquities time! From south Lebanon! It was only for trading… geopolitically important!' She paused, very briefly. 'The centre of trade with Sicily! Romans left after 1st century. Cursed place! Destroyed!'

After a machine-gun burst of this sort, delivered at a volume to attract the attention of anyone within 20 metres, she would grab my arm and lead me onwards to a new set of stones. I dared not interrupt Kalthoum's flow. Anyway, I did not want to: she was making Carthage interesting, at last.

'Hannibal!' she cried all of a sudden. 'Hannibal! Considered one of the greatest military strategists! He was abnormal! He was a genius!'

Kalthoum rattled onwards, during which she told me that Hannibal had been a military leader of the Punic Carthaginians – those who spoke Semitic – from 221 BC. He was a thorn in the side of Rome at a time when the Roman Republic was looking to expand and become an empire. During the second Punic War against the Romans he had famously taken 'war elephants – yes, war elephants!' from Spain, through the Pyrenees and into the north of Italy, which he occupied for 15 years: 'He was the public enemy number one of Rome!'

We were standing where the library once was. Kalthoum shivered violently. I asked her if she'd like to go inside the building. 'No! No!' she yelled. 'I am fine!'

She continued on to the effectiveness of aqueducts, the quality of Tunisian marble, Punic accommodation and Roman drainpipes. 'You see, we are not ashamed to learn from history!' she trumpeted proudly, in reference to Roman drainpipes.

During a moment of calm, I asked Kalthoum about the Jasmine Revolution. I was unsurprised that she had quite a bit to say about the uprising as well.

'We are so optimistic, we have suffered for so long,' she said, slowing down for once and relaxing after the Phoenician and Roman information blitz. 'We have suffered for fifty years.' She was referring to the period of Bourguiba and Ben Ali. 'We have paid a lot. There have been a lot of thieves. A lot of those thieves have gone but a lot remain.'

She paused, and said thoughtfully, looking at the stones of Byrsa Hill: 'So many years ago, so many years ago… We know we were so advanced then. But look at us now.'

She said she was a member of the Tunisian Green Party: 'I do believe that green is the future.'

A muezzin called out across Carthage. 'I don't trust the main parties,' Kalthoum said, now almost whispering. She seemed the sort of person who went from one extreme to another; a little like Somalani at the Café de Paris – perhaps it was a national trait. 'Maybe they just want to put all the money in their pockets, like Russian politicians. What we need is education and a proper health service. As human beings we need dignity first.'

She shivered a final shiver. We shook hands. And I realised I'd quite enjoyed Carthage, after all.

🐪 🐪 🐪

I dropped the KIA at Tunis-Carthage International Airport – it was due back – and went to the Europcar desk. The same man in a black leather jacket was at the kiosk, smoking a cigarette as usual.

I took a taxi to the Bardo National Museum and found myself staring at a bust of Emperor Antoninus near the entrance. So that was what the man behind the Antonine Baths looked like: flamboyant beard, flat nose, impassive stare. The Bardo has one of the world's best collections of Roman busts and mosaics. After inspecting Marcus Aurelius (prominent nose, curly locks, arrogant aspect), Hadrian (curly locks, beard, long nose, narrow eyes), I saw the beautiful mosaics. There were dozens upon dozens of them depicting gods (Dionysus, Odysseus, Apollo, Venus, Neptune), gladiators, lions, bears, hunting gods – just as in the archaeology museum in El Jem, they were fascinating and captivating. I was seeing life exactly as the Romans had... 2,000 years on. The detail in the centuries-old images of owls, ducks, herons and fish was staggering.

I spent an hour in a daze of antiquity, and waited for the taxi to go back to Hotel du Parc, sitting on a bench in a square outside the Bardo entrance. A government building of some sort was at the far side of the square. Red flags fluttered and soldiers with green berets and rifles were on patrol.

The driver finally arrived. I was irritated that he was half an hour late but he seemed unfazed. We passed a military roadblock that had been set up since I came to the Bardo.

'Un ministre est arrivé,' said the driver. By the roadblock, there were protesters with banners. It was good to see a spark of rebellion still alive and kicking in the capital of the country that began the Arab Spring – rather than the slight feeling of hopelessness in the outcome of the revolution that I had begun to expect.

On the flyover back into town, a hawker draped in Tunisian flags was attempting to sell his wares to drivers stuck in the traffic jam.

'Pour la révolution?' I asked – imagining his unusual dress was another sign of continuing pride in the uprising.

'Non, pour le football,' he replied, matter-of-factly.

I returned to the Hotel du Parc, where I got an early night. I had a 5 a.m. start the next morning for a flight on a propeller plane named *Hannibal* to the island of Djerba, close to the border with Libya. I was heading towards another country of the Arab Spring, via a place renowned for its sandy beaches, endless mosques, curious inhabitants and ancient legends.

Note: A month after my visit, the Ennahda-led government banned protests on Avenue Habib Bourguiba after violence at a demonstration involving ultra-conservative Islamic Salafists. The Salafists had attacked a group of artists performing at a separate event that happened to be taking place outside the Municipal Theatre. The Ministry of the Interior proclaimed that 'all demonstrations, marches, and any other form of collective expression' on the street were prohibited. A month after this, however, the government backed down after pro-democracy protests about the decision led to violent clashes, with police firing tear gas and using batons on demonstrators. Journalists were also attacked; some had their cameras smashed. Pro-democracy and human rights groups were furious and described the behaviour as similar to that under Ben Ali. Tunisia's fight for freedom and an open society goes on.

5

Djerba:

Lost with the Lotus-eaters

TUNIS-CARTHAGE International Airport at 5.30 a.m. was not exactly buzzing. The concourse was deserted save for a few cleaners – no sign of hustlers, check-in attendants or even airport staff manning the departure gates (which were closed). I seemed to have arrived far too early for my 7.30 a.m. flight. I sat on an aquamarine seat amid the smell of stale smoke and waited, reading *La Presse de Tunisie*. A front-page article talked about US$1.3 million being spent on improving the country's roads (a good idea, I thought). There was a piece on continuing repression in Syria; the Syrian ambassador had been asked to leave Tunisia the day before, after 200 people were killed in the city of Homs during a bombardment in Syria at the weekend. An editorial referred to 14 January 2011, saying that '*la toile de fond de toute démocratie est d'abord la sécurité*' ('the backdrop of any democracy is security first'); it went on to say that greater security would lead to confidence in tourism and economic improvement.

An hour passed and eventually the wing of the airport devoted to domestic flights opened. By then other passengers had arrived. I appeared to be the only non-Tunisian. I passed through an X-ray machine that beeped twice. The guard didn't even look up; so much for *sécurité*, I couldn't help thinking. I sat at a café where I bought an espresso and was given a free piece of cake by the owner, seemingly as a gesture of goodwill to the token holidaymaker.

Once again, a friendly Tunisian – there seemed to be so many of them.

We boarded and I was soon making yet another acquaintance on my Tunisair Express flight. After take-off my neighbour turned to me and introduced himself in a formal manner. 'Kamel Mekki, pleased to meet you,' he said.

Kamel turned out to be a trained engineer who was president of a noise-reduction company. He had a neat grey moustache and wore jeans and a brown jacket. He was flying to Djerba to 'monitor the noise between rooms' at hotels and check the noise emitted by air-conditioning units. He was one of Tunisia's foremost noise-reduction men: he had even created a 'noise map' for Tunis-Carthage International Airport, and several others in the country.

'Every time an aeroplane takes off and lands, we know the noise levels, and which areas of land are impacted,' he told me enthusiastically. 'So when someone is creating a new building – residential housing or offices – we can tell them how much insulation they need.'

Kamel had also created noise maps for airports in Senegal and Libya. He was hoping to convince Djerba of the merits of a map. He had been on a training course at the Institute of Sound and Vibration Research in Southampton in 1995, where he had learnt about acoustic walls. For a while, I was engrossed in a whole new world of noise reduction.

We turned to the Jasmine Revolution. 'It was unimaginable that we could get the president and his family out. Absolutely unimaginable,' Kamel said, beaming and clearly pleased. He was a very talkative fellow. 'It turned out to be so easy. Ben Ali was planning to send his family off and he went to the airport with them. But when he got there, his bodyguard said that the army and police had turned against him. He panicked and left.'

'If only,' I said, 'President Assad would do that in Syria.'

'Yes, yes – a very different scenario,' he replied, looking thoughtful. He scratched his chin and gazed along the line of burgundy seats. We were purring along on *Hannibal,* with a journey time of an hour to Djerba to go.

He continued his Jasmine Revolution theme. 'After Ben Ali left there were a few months of panic. Some people would go to the supermarket and take things for free. In the past year there has been so much unemployment that some have feared that it could all happen again: another revolution! But people don't realise that these things take time: like building a company. The government has been busy with elections, handling union sit-ins and sorting out the jails. It can't all happen like this.' He clicked his fingers.

'The problem is that a lot of foreigners will not invest in the country because of the insecurity,' he said. Then he turned to tourism, and complained that authorities in Tunisia had for a long time concentrated simply on selling hotels by beaches, mistakenly failing to care about cultural attractions: which was why spots such as Kairouan and El Jem were so overlooked.

Kamel had a bright and breezy – and seemingly realistic – outlook. He was in his early fifties and lived just to the south of Tunis in Hamman-Lif. He had five children ('My parents had ten, so I am feeling I am only halfway.') and a lot of opinions. He appeared to be exactly the sort of entrepreneurial person who might thrive in the new Tunisia.

'All of the top politicians have been in jails,' he said, as the plane began its descent. 'It's as if you've got to have been behind bars to hold office. The First Minister, the Minister of the Interior, the Minister of Justice and Freedom, the President: they were all behind bars at some time. It's good for their CV.'

He paused. 'In the old days it was the opposite. I know of people who talked about the president and his men on Al Jazeera when they were abroad – well, as soon as they put a foot in the airport on their return, they were arrested. And God knows what happened to them then.'

Hannibal landed to a round of applause. It was a sunny day, still cold. As Kamel and I walked towards the baggage carousel, he pointed to a man wearing an olive mackintosh: 'That is the US ambassador. I wonder what he is doing here. I met him once: he gave a talk to a group of engineers.' The ambassador, who had a furtive aspect and reminded me of a character from a Graham Greene novel, was stepping into a white stretch limo, skipping the usual queues.

My bag arrived as Kamel began to embark on another discussion about the latest advances in acoustic walls technology. Before I left, he clasped my hand and beamed. 'Welcome to Djerba! If you need anything, call!' He gave me his card, and we wished each other luck on our trips.

🐪 🐪 🐪

Djerba is about twenty-one kilometres wide and long. It is 100 kilometres to the northwest of Tunisia's border with Libya and is well known as a beach destination. Aside from a run of internationally branded hotels, the island – which is connected to the mainland by a six-kilometre causeway – has more than three hundred mosques and Islamic burial grounds. It is also home to the largest Jewish settlement in Tunisia, which consists of a thousand people living on the edge of the island's small capital, Houmt Souk. The island has 139,000 inhabitants, though the population surges (or at least it used to) when tourists arrive during the summer.

Djerba lays one of the strongest claims – along with a couple of other spots in the Mediterranean – to being the land of the legendary lotus-eaters. As told in Greek mythology by Homer, Odysseus had forcibly to collect his sailors from an island and bring them back to their ships after they tasted the sweet, narcotic flowers and fruit of the lotus plant and refused to return. When they did, they were locked in irons and Odysseus and his crew left the island (possibly Djerba) 'with all speed on their fast ships, for fear that others of them might eat the lotus and think no more of home'.

I was met by one of the locals, who did not offer me lotus leaves. Instead, he held out a sign bearing my name, spun on his heels and disappeared towards a car park as soon as he'd established I was the correct person. There wasn't even time to shake hands. I'd booked two nights at the Radisson Blu on Sidi Mahares beach with a guided tour thrown in, using an internet site. I assumed that the driver was going to be my guide for the day, or would tell me who would be after dropping me at the hotel.

We were soon moving swiftly along bright roads lined with cropped trees, their trunks painted white, which gave the island a neat and orderly look. There were donkey carts and the odd person puttered by on a moped, but little traffic. An olive grove led to the edge of Houmt Souk, where a wishful-thinking sign said *Zone Touristique*. We skirted the sleepy town, passed a Peugeot showroom and a football pitch on a beach with broken posts and clumps of weeds, and continued along the north coast of the island to Sidi Mahares.

The driver had greasy comb-over hair and was wafer thin. He introduced himself as Mr Rafik. He said little else other than confusingly asking me if I worked for the internet company through which I had booked the tour of Djerba.

I jumped out of the minivan, gathered my bags and went up the steps to the grand front entrance of the Radisson Blu Resort and Thalasso. When I turned round, realising that I had better ask Mr Rafik about the arrangements for seeing the island, I could see the minivan pulling away. Mr Rafik was going. I never laid eyes on Mr Rafik again.

Perhaps the hotel would know about the guided tour. I entered a glitzy reception with a marble floor and pillars decorated with an Arabian pattern. A bright Lacoste shop stood in a corner near a bar with a huge wagon-wheel chandelier. The receptionist smiled sweetly and said she had no idea about a tour. As she did so, a short man in a sharp suit with a badge that said 'YES I CAN' approached, clasping a packet of Dunhill cigarettes. He had overheard our conversation and was a manager of some sort. His name was Sami. He offered me a Dunhill and invited me to join him for a coffee at a metal table with a gigantic ashtray. He told me that Dunhill 'is the best, it is only tobacco, no chemicals', as though that might tempt me. We sat beneath the giant chandelier, where I could see through a window to a large pool and the beach.

I soon understood the reason why he was keen to talk. 'You have to promote our country now!' Sami said, fixing me with a penetrating gaze. 'Occupancy at the hotel is at twenty per cent!'

He blew out a great plume of smoke in exasperation at so few rooms being full. 'People say it is very dangerous to come to Tunisia, that there is a lot of risk,' he continued. 'But Djerba is an island of peace. We didn't even realise there was a revolution: no fighting, no incidents, no nothing! Our revolution was without blood.'

Sami began to rattle off some facts: 'Three hundred and thirty days of sun a year! The quality of the beaches!' He raised his eyebrows and made an expression that suggested that everybody knows about the excellent quality of Djerba's beaches. 'Very, very good quality! Twenty-seven-hole golf course! Thalassotherapy!'

He lit another Dunhill cigarette. 'Bourguiba stayed at the hotel. Dominique de Villepin [the former French prime minister]. Angelina Jolie!' He told me that the American actress had spent one night in February 2011 when thousands of refugees crossed the border from Libya. Jolie had been acting as a 'goodwill ambassador' for the UN High Commissioner for Refugees. She had visited a refugee camp seven kilometres from R'as Ajdir, the border crossing into Libya – the crossing I was heading to in three days.

Tourism in Djerba was 50 per cent down and Sami wondered if it would ever pick up again. He blamed the proximity of Gaddafi's former state for the worst of the woes: 'It is because of Libya that guest numbers are terrible.'

I mentioned the mystery tour, wondering how I was going to move about the island. Sami got on his phone, and rattled off a few words, his voice rising slightly for a moment as though in a minor dispute, before settling into what sounded like agreement and hanging up. This was how I met Tarak, who turned up 10 minutes later. But while we waited, Sami told me that Tunisia 'had a chance under Bourguiba, we were theoretically democratic, he was an intellectual, polygamy was outlawed, and he promoted health care and education'. Sami then went into some detail about his own academic qualifications achieved under the former president – there were quite a few of them.

Tarak was a Tunisian Del Boy. He wore large beetle-like shades propped on his head, with slicked-back hair in the style of a 1960s rocker. He was short and compact, and he was to be my guide for half a day. He wasted no time in cadging a Dunhill from Sami and settled into an armchair after briskly waving for a coffee.

He was keen to join our discussion. There really is very little Tunisians love more than talking about politics. 'It started with the intellectuals,' he said referring to the Jasmine Revolution. 'The size of the middle class was shrinking as education was getting worse. There were a lot of ambitious people who were from middle-class families who were slipping into the category of the poor. They were frustrated. Pressure was building. We were just waiting for an event that would be the reason [for the uprising].'

Tarak was dismissive of comparisons of Tunisia with Libya and Syria. 'We are very, very far advanced in terms of openness,' he said. 'We are close to the European thinking on this. Libya is just tribes: tribes!' He said 'tribe' as though it were a dirty word.

'We were tribes in 1956. Before independence from the French, when there was a problem between tribes, it did not go to court. It could lead into something very big and violent. Now all are equal before the law. In Libya Gaddafi encouraged tribes: Libya is just tribes! Divide and conquer, that's what Gaddafi did. Luckily they have money and petrol, so they can rebuild. In Tunisia, it will take two or three years: we are learning democracy. Two or three years: no problem!'

Tarak and I were soon hurrying through the lobby to his black Renault Megane, for which he had had to pay 'double cost taxes: Ben Ali and his government they take the money – now it's in Switzerland, French and English banks'. Tarak flicked his sunglasses down and wore them normally. They were of the type favoured by female fashion models and celebrities such as Victoria Beckham, though I did not say so to Tarak.

We charged along the road heading back to the airport as I learnt of all the places Tarak had worked in the past including Sharm el-Sheikh in Egypt, where he had once been manager of the Pacha nightclub and met 'Russians, Ukrainians and Montenegrins'. He had an involvement in a hotel on Djerba and we were soon pulling to the side of the road to pick up his assistant,

Hasna. She was sassy, in her twenties and had a shock of curly auburn hair. She was dressed as though ready to go out on the town.

But instead of hitting a nightclub, we went to Fort Ghazi Mustapha. The fort overlooked the Mediterranean Sea and there had been a structure on the site since Roman times, though the Aghlabids were responsible for developing the solid, cream-stone fort as it now stands. There were ramparts and a rooftop viewing platform. Tarak reckoned there should be a café on the rooftop: 'I proposed this, but they say "no".' He looked disgruntled and bemused, with an expression that suggested: 'I try so hard to drag this country forwards: what is the point when they cannot see the logic of my great ideas?' He shrugged his shoulders.

His phone rang (as it did regularly). While he was on his mobile, I briefly chatted to Hasna. She was from Le Kef in the northwest of Tunisia, near its border with Algeria. She worked as a receptionist at the Star Beach Hotel on Djerba, where Tarak was manager. There were very few guests at the moment, which was why Tarak had come to show me round – plus he had an arrangement with Sami, which I'd half overheard earlier. Whilst I was in mid-sentence talking to Hasna, Tarak came over and hurried us along... we were going to the capital.

At Houmt Souk, Hasna had to leave, which was disappointing as it was just about the first chance I'd had to talk to a Tunisian woman about the revolution, apart from Kalthoum in Carthage. You cannot help but notice how sharply divided Tunisia is between the sexes; how predominant men are in almost all walks of life. Women do not hang out playing cards in cafés. Nor do they drink beer in hotel lounges watching the national football team. Not a single one – in either instance. Nor do they hold positions at the top of government. Instead, the women I'd seen in public places tended to be hastily moving along while carrying bags of shopping; often wearing headscarves, which had apparently become far more common since the Islamists won power after the revolution. At a glance, Hasna appeared 'Western' in her outlook, and quite different. I hoped to catch up with her later.

Houmt Souk was by turns bustling and half asleep. There were countless souvenir shops selling colourful ceramic pots and porcelain camels – but no tourists. More men sat at cafés. A 'Turkish mosque', described as such by Tarak, had a golf ball-shaped roof and long thin minaret, just like most of the other mosques I'd seen. Pistachio- and burgundy-coloured carpets with triangular patterns and stripes covered the walls. Through doorways you could see the looms at which the carpets were made, carpets that cost up to 500 euros each. Tarak seemed keen that I buy one and began a sales patter about the greatness of Djerban rugs. But I did not want to lug a Tunisian carpet across post-Gaddafi Libya, and in any case did not have 500 euros to spare. Down twisting alleyways I could see people busy shopping at markets that sold fruits and fish, yet the main streets were quiet. We settled at a café offering *le roi de jus d'orange frais* in a pleasant square. A tall man Tarak knew walked by. He ran a small local hotel. He came over, joined us for a juice and said: 'The people here are very cool and quiet: very Zen. I am one hundred per cent Djerban. I am very Zen. During the revolution, nothing happened in Djerba. We are pacifists: Zen.'

He paused. 'The trouble is the Libyan people. They come here for drinking, drinking, drinking and looking for women. It is a big problem. They are not Zen.' There was definitely Tunisian-Libyan tension on the peaceful island of Djerba. 'But here in Djerba we are Zen. Very Zen.'

He eyeballed me, making sure I had got the message. I nodded in a Zen-like manner to indicate I had.

Afterwards, we drove around the countryside for a while, seeing olive groves and lots of small, bulbous white mosques, which Tarak, still wearing his Victoria Beckham shades, would point out. 'Mosque!' he'd pronounce, and we'd drive on. From a distance the mosques looked like strange overgrown marshmallows, breaking up the arid, cacti-filled landscape. But we did not stop; we were going a scenic way back to the hotel, moving onwards through little villages where men sold fresh fish to locals from the back of mopeds.

We arrived at the Radisson Blu and Tarak informed me that he and his wife would like to join me for dinner at the hotel restaurant. This was swiftly agreed, and off he disappeared.

🐪 🐪 🐪

The Radisson Blu was on a long stretch of sand, where fishermen were casting lines and a handful of tourists were taking perambulations. I joined them. The grey sea had a hint of blue and waves broke with a gentle hiss. I came across other holidaymakers (German by the looks of them) about once every 20 minutes on a two-hour walk heading east, passing endless concrete-block hotels flying the Tunisian flag. The hotels were so similar that I slightly worried about missing mine on the walk back.

It was a calm place. The fishermen wore baggy tracksuit bottoms and looked as though they were fishing for their suppers, not for recreation. They stood by buckets and smoked cigarettes, gazing out across the shimmering water that led to Malta and Sicily.

It was a good spot to clear my head – and also try to think straight about the journey ahead. I had reservations about visiting Libya, and I was so close now, just a couple of days away. The Foreign and Commonwealth Office advised against 'non-essential' travel to all parts of Gaddafi's former state. Well, pottering about the tourist sites while attempting to gauge the atmosphere of its Arab Spring was pretty non-essential. I was about to visit a country that the usual travel insurance firms would not touch with a bargepole. As far as they were concerned, it was no go. I had asked a veteran traveller who ran an adventure tour operator in the UK, and had had plenty of close scrapes in faraway places, about the wisdom of visiting Libya. He had simply commented, 'Go, but be careful and *bon courage.*'

After a period of quiet, there had been reports about a gun battle in Tripoli a few days before I set off for Tunisia. Militias had fought over control of a plush property said to have belonged to Gaddafi's playboy son Saadi. The dispute had apparently been settled and the country's National Transitional Government said that peace had returned. But the flare-up did not exactly put my nerves at ease – and Reuters was now reporting that 'violent crime and clashes between armed militants are running rife as the jubilation of last year's liberation fades, to be replaced by the harsh and unromantic reality of building a new state'.

I was worried. I had already paid (at some cost and via an international bank transfer to an account in Frankfurt) for a driver-guide based in Tripoli to accompany me during my time in Libya – and I had been assured by several sources that the trip would be safe as long as I was cautious. But even so *clashes between armed militants are running rife* had me worried to the point of perhaps calling it all off.

What if something bigger happened in the next few days? It was not out of the realms of possibility. Just three months previously, the border crossing at R'as Ajdir had been closed to travel due to tensions between Tunisia and Libya. Quite apart from whether it was a good idea to go, I was not entirely sure whether I would be allowed into the former pariah state, so well known for its support of international terrorism and now full of rebels with guns.

I tried to think of something else. And as I daydreamed, I heard the sound of thunder, as though a storm was coming driven by a gale. But there was no wind. I kept on walking along the undulating beach, thoughts adrift. The thunder rose. I switched into the present and turned around to see two chestnut horses galloping along the biscuit-coloured sand. They clattered past – hooves drumming a rhythmic beat. Two teenage lads were having a race. They were grinning at the sheer joy of the experience, having a wonderful time. I watched them disappear in the direction of Houmt Souk. They lifted my mood. I decided there and then to hold firm and let this Arab Spring adventure take me whichever way it went – just be watchful, use my common sense: let instincts lead the way.

Back in my room, I picked up a letter about breakfast times and activities addressed to 'Dear Sir Chesshyre'. I had been knighted by the Radisson Blu (surely a providential sign). I stepped out on to the balcony as the sun slipped away slowly in a blaze of tangerine. Sparrows tweeted in the treetops, enjoying a dusk gathering. A black and white cat had settled on a rock and was catching the last of the day's warmth. Streaks of orange and red illuminated the sky.

After the sunset, I checked the BBC News website to see if there was any further trouble in Libya: fortunately nothing. But in Egypt, Islamists had widened their poll lead in the parliamentary elections while 'secular liberals trail[ed] behind'. There was a card on my pillow with a saying-of-the-day: 'There is more to learn from defeat than with success.' It was a *proverbe japonais*. I wasn't sure whether the message boded well or ill.

In the short term, it was a bit of each. I drank a beer in the lobby bar with Tarak and his wife (who ordered a gin and tonic) while listening to a pianist tinkle out 'Blue Moon'. I picked up the tab. Then we made our way to what turned out to be the hotel's signature restaurant. The food was Arabic and Tarak made a great show of saying hello to the maître d'. Dozens of small dishes of hummus, aubergine dip, olives, octopus and sausages began to appear accompanied by baskets piled high with unleavened bread. Tarak promptly ordered a bottle of white wine, though his wife, in an elegant black dress, had opted for a glass of champagne.

We were sitting on low-level sofas with pink cushions. Twanging guitar music and drums came from a band in the corner. I could hardly hear a word that Tarak or his wife said. A belly dancer arrived to an increased beat. The belly dancer had a butterfly tattooed on her navel and wore gold high-heel shoes, bangles, a skimpy emerald top and a shawl. Tarak insisted – as though the honour of both Tunisia and Great Britain were at stake – that I dance with her, which I duly did.

'You must step, step, step!' she said, indicating how I should adjust my feet. 'Move your hips!' Tarak and his wife appeared delighted. I asked the belly dancer her name and she replied that she was Ramona and came from Lithuania. 'I have make training in Egypt and Lebanon,' she added.

I returned to the table, whereupon Tarak began telling me about a

Brazilian belly dancer he had got to know in Tunis. 'She had a body like...' and he made various curve-shaped gesticulations, his eyes swivelling.

Amid the cacophony and the continuing cascade of little dishes delivered by a team of waiters, I learnt that Tarak's wife's first name was Leila and her maiden name Trabelsi.

'The same name as Ben Ali's wife!' said Tarak. 'I chose her to be like the president!' He beamed and she smiled. She did not speak English, but enjoyed a smoke. She had got through the best part of a packet of Virginia Slims while Tarak was seeing to his supply of Merits.

I watched through a haze as Tarak went for a snake-like wiggle with the Lithuanian, left alone with Leila Trabelsi for a while. I had not imagined I'd meet Ben Ali's wife or someone of the same name in Tunisia. Tarak returned. Leila Trabelsi went to the foyer, while Tarak and I waited for the bill, which was delivered and placed on the table. Tarak regarded the piece of paper as though it were an offensive object. I fished out my stash of Tunisian dinars (which were to be no more). Then Tarak and Leila Trabelsi said goodbye and disappeared into the Djerban night.

🐪 🐪 🐪

I slept well, but in the morning I was not finished with Tarak. He had insisted on coming the next day to continue our tour – he seemed to regard himself as some sort of local tourism ambassador. He also appeared to be at a loose end. Back in the black Renault Megane we went, checking out a local golf course and then a strange crocodile farm. At the latter, Tarak was soon talking expansively to the attractive middle-aged woman who ran a gift shop, declaring that 'I am the baron of Djerba! I am the mafia in the right way! The good way! The mafia positive!' The woman seemed to find all of this amusing but was soon almost shooing us on our way.

Not long afterwards we arrived at the Star Beach Hotel, where Tarak suddenly had business. I was introduced to his boss, a tall man who said: 'I don't know why they call it the Arab Spring... it all began in December and January.' He had a point, though the Prague Spring that began all revolutionary 'springs' in fact started in January (1968). I also bumped into Hasna, who clearly wanted to talk but couldn't at the hotel. She gave me her mobile number and asked me to call her later.

Tarak was tied up with important negotiations, so I caught a cab for a tour of the island. In a whirlwind trip we stopped at Phoenician and Roman ruins at Meninx, close to the causeway to mainland Africa. Karim, the taxi driver, and I walked about the ancient half-buried, unexcavated stones, with no-one else around and no staff or ticket required for entry.

We drove on and checked out a pottery at Guellala run by Mohamed, a Berber wearing a dusty brown tunic. He tried half-heartedly to sell me an urn. A camel was tethered to a post, forlornly turning in circles. 'Pour les touristes,' said Mohamed, though there weren't any. We paused at a *huilerie*, where great sacks of olives lay all about and men dressed in plastic bags and covered head to foot in black slime were making olive oil using old-fashioned presses. Sweet aromas filled the air.

We passed a huge jar at the side of the road that Karim claimed was 'la plus grande jarre du monde'. I took his word for it; the jar was impressively *grande*. Then we went to Sidi Jemour, an ancient burial tomb of an Islamic holy man. It was at an isolated spot on the coast and was one of the settings used by the director George Lucas when he filmed *Star Wars* on the island in the mid 1970s. This was where Luke Skywalker once flashed past on a 'landspeeder' and where he climbed on to the unusual domed building to learn about the Alliance's plans to defeat Darth Vader. It did look vaguely familiar.

On the southern edge of Houmt Souk, we visited Hara Sghira, the Jewish settlement. Tourists can visit the synagogue, which dates from the 1920s, although Jews are believed to have been on Djerba since as early as 566BC. There was a security gate with a metal detector and a row of guards with guns. Ever since a terrorist attack that killed 21 people in 2002, security had been tight. There were no Jewish victims in the attack; the dead numbered German and French tourists and two Muslims.

I walked past the men with machine guns, under an archway festooned with Tunisian flags and down a lane flanked with white buildings with blue shutters. A gargantuan man who appeared to be in charge of visitors stepped out of a doorway and ushered me into an inner sanctuary, made me take off my shoes and handed me a skullcap. I put this on and was led to a small room decorated with blue tiles and candles. The enormous guide, almost bursting out of his grey jacket, pointed to three much smaller men wearing red caps. 'Ce sont les rabbins,' he commented matter-of-factly. I was asked to provide a donation, and did so. Then he showed me round the echoing empty complex, during which I learnt there are around seven hundred Jews in the rest of Tunisia while about a thousand live in or about Hara Sghira. At the end of his tour, I passed back the skullcap and the guide stretched out a hand with a euro in it. The euro was not for me; he was after a tip. I handed over a few dinars. The gargantuan man exposed a row of stubbly yellow teeth in appreciation. I had not imagined I'd visit one of the largest Jewish settlements in Africa... What would the Arab Spring eventually mean for the Jews of Djerba? It was hard to tell.

Afterwards, we stopped at Houmt Souk, where I parted company with Karim, and where the *maison des poissons* was in full swing. Barracuda, tuna and octopus were piled on ice in stalls and on two great tables in a shed at the back. On top of each of these two tables a severe-looking elderly man sat, looking regal on an elevated chair amid all the ice and fish, occasionally yelling 'Eh! Eh! Eh!' These cries were seemingly either to bring to the attention of the fish-buying crowd the great fish deals available on his table – not the other table – or else to reprimand a customer asking to pay a price considered too low. They made a comic couple.

Then I ate a delicious plate of *calamar sauté à la Djerbienne* at a restaurant where I was the sole diner. The squid was served with a spicy sauce and a sharp salad consisting of chopped tomatoes, onion, capers, cabbage and basil. After the meal, I called Hasna, and she said she would meet me at the hotel reception for a drink in about an hour.

I found her sitting in an alcove away from the main lobby. I got the impression she did not want to draw attention to herself in a prominent place. We moved to a sofa by the bar and ordered drinks: she had a Coke, I had a beer. She was wearing another tight-fitting outfit as though ready to go to a nightclub (seemingly her regular style), and her curly auburn hair hung partially over her eyes on the right side of her face. She had on thick-framed glasses and looked a little tired after a day's work, but was keen to tell me about life under Ben Ali… and particularly the role of the Trabelsi clan.

She did not pull her punches about the latter. 'It was the Trabelsi family that was the problem, not Ben Ali. They were like mafia. Like Hitler,' she said, launching straight into her attack, perched on the edge of the sofa. 'Ben Ali was a good man, but it was his family: drugs and gangs. And his wife – oh my God – she was like a dragon. The family had,' she gestured as though shooting a revolver, 'they had the pistol. Is that the right word?'

I said that it was.

'Tunis, Sousse and Hammamet: it was bad, though it did not stretch to Djerba. If someone wanted to start a business that looked as though it would make money.' She pointed her fingers like a gun again. 'You understand?' I said I did. 'My friend began a jet ski company in Sousse. He couldn't do it, as a Trabelsi, the brother of the wife of Ben Ali, he wanted a community.'

I asked what she meant by community.

'A community, a share.'

'What did they ask for: fifty/fifty?'

'No way. Eighty per cent to them, twenty per cent to my friend,' she replied, sounding animated. 'I swear, Mr Tom, I swear.'

Hasna began to tell a terrible story. 'A friend of mine was a girlfriend to one of the Trabelsis.'

She mentioned a prominent member of the family – but as I have since been unable to corroborate the details of what she went on to describe I have not used his name.

'She had trouble with the relationship, and they had had an argument.

She had said: "**** you and your family." And she stormed out,' Hasna continued, as her eyes began to well. 'But you could not say that. Not to a Trabelsi. He came back and poured gas on her and set her alight. I swear. She died. Many people know this story. I swear, Mr Tom, I swear it's true. She was about twenty-six or twenty-seven. It happened five years ago.' She paused and then whispered: 'He was a devil. He was a monster.' She sounded for a moment as if she was going to cry, but she held back.

We were silent for a while. I asked her about her plans for the future. It turned out she had a job lined up at a children's club at a hotel in Antalya in Turkey; she could no longer stay in Djerba as wages were too low with so few tourists.

A band from Mauritius was striking up in another bar by the front entrance. We went over to listen for a while. Hasna told me above the sound of the music, 'I don't like living in a warm country – I like the cold.' She seemed a little fatalistic. As we said goodbye at the revolving doors of the Radisson, she blew me a kiss and strode towards the taxi rank. I hoped things worked out for her in Turkey.

So many Tunisian lives, so many different outcomes: under the dictatorship that had touched everyone and with an unknown future lying ahead. I had enjoyed my time in Tunisia, and sensed the strong underlying will to make democracy and secularism alongside Islamism work. But tomorrow I was heading into another country and another revolution. I could not pretend I wasn't nervous: I was as anxious as I have ever been on the eve of a 'holiday'.

6

R'as Ajdir and Tripoli:

Tap, Tap, Tap
into the Night

A T THE Houmt Souk taxi rank all was confusion. Several pot-bellied men wearing jeans appeared to be in charge of proceedings – a team of Fat Controllers, each with the air of 'This is my patch, I regard with disdain anyone who says or thinks otherwise'.

I went up to one of the rank's 'commanders-in-chief', naturally upsetting all the others, who crowded round to listen and have their say. Through a fraught process of questions, charged with a sense of general indignation and competitive bitterness (the bottom line seemed to be that they all wanted to have me go in *their* vehicle even if it was not heading in the right direction), I discovered that I should take one of the *louage* (rental) minibuses to the Libyan border.

These minibuses were coloured white, while regular taxis were yellow. The latter were not licensed to go all the way to the border, though one driver had offered a 'special rate' – just for me – of about US$100.

In the end I bought a ticket from a kiosk for about US$3 and went to the appropriate white minibus. The passengers – we numbered four – had to wait until the tally reached seven. This was the profitability tipping point at which the driver would have enough cash to make the journey worthwhile. Without three more, we would be staying in Houmt Souk for the foreseeable future.

A youth strides by the fruit cart monument to Mohamed Bouazizi in Sidi Bouzid; unemployment in the south of Tunisia is as high as 30 per cent

Pro-revolution graffiti in Sidi Bouzid, written in English as though for the international media

The governor's office in Sidi Bouzid, in front of which Bouazizi, frustrated by harassment from officials, set himself alight

Author by Mohamed Bouazizi's grave – the only visitor at the isolated graveyard in the village of Garaat Bennour

El Jem, Tunisia; considered by some to be finer than Rome's Colosseum

Anti-Gaddafi cartoon in Tripoli; Libya's capital was full of street art against the former dictator

Leptis Magna, Libya; the guide had not seen a tourist since the revolution

Author by new Libyan flags near the Roman ruins in Sabratha; a reversion to pre-Gaddafi colours

Tunnel hatch at Gaddafi compound, Tripoli; it was incredibly eerie in the Brother Leader's old HQ

Scrap-metal scavengers in Gaddafi's old bunker; some gun parts could be recycled, while bullet shells would be melted down

Camel head for sale, Tripoli market

Revolutionaries from Derna in the east of Libya, posing in Tripoli with guns including a shiny AK-47

Commonwealth war graves in Benghazi; three weeks later the headstones were smashed by anti-Western Islamic fundamentalists

Berber castle in Qasr al-Haj from the 12th century, made from mud and stones

Effigy representing the 'enemy' hung by Salafists, ultra-conservative Islamists

Orange-juice salesman, Tahrir Square; he confessed that only 10 per cent of his juice was made of oranges, the rest was water

…fiti in Cairo mocking former President Mubarak,
for almost 30 years

Salafists marching towards Tahrir Square beneath the City View Hotel,
protesting about a disqualified presidential candidate

Inside the Yacoubian Building, Cairo, the inspiration for Alaa Al Aswany's anti-Mubarak novel

Man having groceries pulled up to his apartment in Suez the city was in a sorry state after many years of neglect

Suez Canal; at the Red Sea Hotel in Port Tewfik, cargo ship and oil tanker spotting is de rigueur

Mubarak's plush villa in Sharm el-Sheikh, to which he fled after the revolution

On the road northwards into the Sinai desert; for long stretches the highway was empty

Bureau de change at Jordan border; the attendant was napping on the sofa, under the poster of the omnipresent King Abdullah II

Pilgrims on top of Mount Sinai at sunrise, where Moses received the Commandments

And so I found myself on a plastic grey seat with a cigarette burn in a freezing *louage*, sitting behind a man wearing a grey tunic with a pointed hood. He had kept the hood up to stay warm. A voice on a radio rattled on importantly, before the station switched to a mournful Arabic tune. Next to the man in the tunic a younger fellow in camouflage trousers was restlessly pecking on a mobile phone. Thanks to him, I had discovered that the bus went as far as the town of Ben Guerdane – not right up to the R'as Ajdir border, as I had imagined. Another taxi was required from Ben Guerdane. But I was too bamboozled by the ticket negotiations for this taxi to worry about the next part of the journey. I settled down awaiting further travellers, while reading a piece in *La Presse Tunisie* about how Tunisia was experiencing the coldest winter for five years and that '*il continue à neiger sur le nord-ouest*'. The temperature was so low it was snowing not so far away.

Passenger Number Seven eventually arrived, and we departed. We crossed sandy scrubland leading to the causeway, where we were waved through with a nonchalant flip of a hand by a soldier wearing shades, and set out across the sun-dazzled, muddy-green water. Flocks of seagulls swept across the seascape, looking like handfuls of confetti. There was a solid stone fort on the horizon – not the one I'd visited with Tarak and Hasna.

We reached the mainland and set off through olive groves, the soul-searching Arabic music continuing on the radio. At a little town with houses hidden behind walls topped with jagged pieces of glass, we turned at a junction boasting Pizzeria Hannibal, and then hurtled onwards. We crossed another causeway with a *garde nationale* checkpoint, and I wondered if the hazy grey land I could see ahead might be the start of Libya. The landscape was flat and sandy and inhospitable – it felt as though we had come to the end of the earth.

The Ben Guerdane bus station was an unprepossessing, windswept spot. We alighted into a litter-strewn yard, where I found myself in step with the man wearing camouflage trousers. The two of us were ushered to a yellow taxi by various locals, and we were soon sharing a vehicle, heading to the border (at least I hoped so).

I asked my new companion what he had been doing in Djerba. 'Holiday, my friend,' he replied; he was a Libyan taking a break. 'Holiday. Four or five days. Rest and relaxation.' He was in his late twenties, or so I thought, and had a slightly world-weary air. He spoke as though he was dragging the words from his chest – but was perfectly pleasant.

He asked me where I was going.

I explained that I was about to set off on a trip across Libya. Upon hearing this, he turned round sharply from the front passenger seat and looked me squarely in the eyes, peering through thin-framed circular glasses. 'Just be careful, my friend,' he said alertly. 'Very careful. There are weapons everywhere in Libya: guns, guns, guns.'

He fixed his gaze long enough to be certain I had got this message, before repeating: 'Guns, my friend.' He wore black leather gloves and was smoking a Marlboro Red cigarette. His hair was long and fashioned in a style that reminded me of Michael Jackson. Yet he seemed to be old beyond his years, speaking like an elderly man reflecting on a long hard life.

He returned to examining his mobile phone, as we passed along a corridor of stalls selling tyres, ceramics, wicker baskets, cuddly camels and 42-inch televisions – I could tell the exact size as they were in cardboard boxes that displayed all the details. Ben Guerdane seemed to be a centre of cross-border commerce... and tourism, too, if the stuffed camels and other tourist knick-knacks were anything to go by.

As we made our way along a road partially covered with sand drifts and busy with lopsided trucks transporting crates, I asked my companion about Libya since the revolution: he was, after all, the first Libyan I had met and I was curious to get an early report. What was life like since Gaddafi's demise? He turned slowly again.

'Just two things have changed,' he said calmly and softly. 'The flag and the leader.'

He seemed a little suspicious of me – cautious, sussing me out. He asked where I was from.

'Ah, the British!' he said, his wary attitude disappearing in an instant and his face coming to life. 'The British! We love the British! And the French! You helped us kill Gaddafi!'

He was suddenly full of warmth. He explained that he had thought I was Dutch, German or American. 'I have met Americans: but never a British!' he exclaimed. He swivelled round completely from the front seat and was animated. 'I have longed to meet a British!'

The road had turned into a sand tunnel; the wind had whipped up and there was a haze ahead – you could hardly see more than 20 metres. My companion told me his name was Sotyn Al-Tekr and that he had fought for the rebels against Gaddafi in Zawiya. He was not in his late twenties. He was just 23 and now serving as a sergeant in the army maintaining order while the National Transition Council ran the country in the lead-up to elections due to be held later in the year.

Sotyn brought out his mobile phone and began flicking through images on the monitor. He turned the phone so I could see a picture. It was of him lying on a narrow bed. He had a huge bandage wrapped around his midriff, as though he was halfway through the process of mummification. He was grinning and making a Winston Churchill V-sign.

'For three days I was without doctor,' Sotyn explained. 'It was shrapnel. We were just pistols at the start, sometimes no pistols. Gaddafi had machine guns and tanks.'

The battle for Zawiya, a major oil port 50 kilometres to the west of Tripoli, had been an important part of the struggle that brought about the regime's demise. After Zawiya, Tripoli had fallen. The capture of the capital had marked the practical end for Gaddafi, who hung on in hiding until he was tracked down to the coastal city of Sirte – close to his hometown – and dragged out of a drainage pipe, beaten, attacked with a bayonet and killed on 20 October 2011. Nobody is sure exactly what happened – whether

Gaddafi was shot dead or not, for example – though it has since come to light in a Human Rights Watch report that 66 of his supporters were summarily executed after his capture, almost certainly including his son Mutassim. It was on that day, with the trio of North African revolutions complete, that I had first formulated the idea of my trip from Tunisia to Libya and on to Egypt.

I said to Sotyn that I thought he was very brave.

'I'm brave because I help my people,' he answered plainly, in a manner that suggested that bravery was nothing: the impulse to help in the struggle overrode any decision-making in the matter.

The sandstorm was swirling viciously, the taxi was being buffeted by wind, and we were passing along a section of road surrounded by razor wire. It had become a desolate, bitter day.

'I was a sniper,' said Sotyn. He showed me another picture from his phone, which captured him wearing a balaclava and holding a rifle. He looked terrifying: a killer, an assassin. The picture was the screen saver on his phone. With his camouflage trousers, T-shirt, fleece and Michael Jackson hair, Sotyn could pass for a member of a 1980s funk band, but in the picture he looked deadly.

'I shot at a machine gun used by Gaddafi's men,' he said. 'I got the people. I got them.'

How many did he kill, I asked.

He paused, thinking about this. We were pulling into a yard with a road leading off across the madly sandy world outside. Then Sotyn said quietly: 'Really, I don't count.'

He was subdued, and I realised that somehow that was not the right question to have asked. Perhaps his break in Djerba – which had been a centre for the rebels plotting the downfall of Tripoli – had been to take his mind off what happened in the bloody uprising. As many as thirty thousand died and fifty thousand were wounded in the struggle; no-one knows the figures for certain as there was a media clampdown during the revolution.

🐪 🐪 🐪

The border at R'as Ajdir during a sandstorm is hellish. Sotyn parted after we exchanged mobile phone numbers. He said that he could show me around Misrata, a city that was also the scene of some of the bloodiest battles during the revolution, if I liked. He took another taxi across the border. But as a foreigner I walked up to a booth at the edge of a hangar with a green roof, where a dozen people were waiting.

The winds had intensified into a full-blown gale. It was bitterly cold and horns from vehicles either impatient to leave or to enter Libya were honking almost continuously. I was the only white face. I joined the queue clutching my passport and my 'letter of invitation', which explained that I was coming on business to visit an oil company. Libya required such a document. There were no tourist visas; instead I had to collect a business visa-on-arrival. The tour company I had contacted in Tripoli had suggested that this subterfuge was the best way of getting into the country. I was their first tourist since the revolution.

A Tunisian in a blue uniform barked 'Passport!' from behind a filthy window. I handed over my passport and the letter. The official perused the documents, and slapped them to one side. He said a word that sounded very much like: 'Baloney!'

Another official appeared and took me to one side. He was short, rotund and had black curly hair that was so oily it appeared glued to his skull. 'What is this?' he said. 'We do not recognise this stamp.' He was pointing to a stamp on the letter of invitation.

I explained that it came from the embassy. He disappeared with my passport and letter.

I waited for an hour. There was no cover and I was quickly coated in sand. At one point Sotyn appeared. His taxi had made it to the front of the long, horn-blasting queue. He argued my case with the oily official, who once again shook his head. On the request of another immigration officer, I called my guide on the other side of the border to try to prove I had a Libyan contact, but his phone was not working (I later learnt the number I'd been given was typed with a digit out of place). I said there was trouble with the phones. 'That is your problem,' he replied, taking my passport away again.

I waited for another hour, at the end of which a tall man with a moustache wearing a trilby and a long black coat approached. He did not seem to be a regular official. He looked like an archetypal foreign spy out of a James Bond film. He sidled up to me. He had a suggestion. 'Perhaps,' he said, clearing his throat slightly. 'Perhaps, they would like something.'

The penny dropped. 'You mean some money?' I asked.

'Perhaps, perhaps,' he said enigmatically.

'How much should I give?' I inquired.

'How much have you got?' he replied sharply.

I showed him 60 Tunisian dinars (about £24). 'I could give them this, it's all I have,' I said, referring to what I had left of Tunisian cash.

He found this amusing. 'And so go into Libya with no money?' he asked rhetorically. He chuckled to himself. He looked at me in a way that seemed to assess my worth.

'Could you make the suggestion on my behalf?'

'I could do that for you,' he answered discreetly, his eyes twinkling under his trilby.

He disappeared and 10 minutes later a man wearing a grubby grey hooded tunic arrived. 'Are you a journalist?' he asked abruptly.

'Yes,' I replied, deciding that honesty was probably the best course of action by that stage – even though I was strictly speaking not travelling as a *journalist*, but as a *tourist*… a rather unusual tourist.

'It says here that you are an office manager,' he commented.

'I help to manage an office in which journalists work,' I said carefully, trying to twist my way out of my slight 'lie'.

He made me follow him to another grimy kiosk. I heard a reassuring thud of a stamp. He whispered the word *baksheesh*, and I gave him my dinars. He handed back my passport and letter, and I walked through the whistling wind past a sign that said 'LA TUNISIE VOUS SOUHAITE BON VOYAGE' (Tunisia wishes you a good journey), across a no-man's-land to another sign that needed no translation: 'LIBYA FREE!' Soldiers in khaki were standing by a wall. 'Nationality?' they asked, and seemed delighted by my response. 'Very good!' they said, as though I had personally flown the NATO planes that helped drive back Gaddafi's troops. I kept going along an empty pavement in the direction of yet more immigration kiosks, the ones I needed to pass to get into Libya, but before I reached them a voice called over to me.

It was – by some minor miracle – Othman al-Ghareeb, my fixer for the trip from the west to the east of Libya. 'I wasn't sure you were going to make it,' he said. He was bald, over six feet, wore aviator shades and a shiny black bomber jacket. He had a solid build and was in his thirties. He looked like the right sort of person to sort things out in post-revolutionary Libya. He took me across a sandy yard where lorries stood piled with terracotta tiles. We traversed a wasteland of weeds, went through what seemed to be a gap in a fence and arrived at a single-storey building with broken windows and a door clanging violently against its frame in the fierce wind. He gave my passport to an official; we appeared to have bypassed the regular kiosks, which might have explained the extra 'passport fee' I'd paid in advance in London. We sat on a crumbling wall under a rattling carob tree and next to a pile of old cans, waiting for the official. The passport was returned, fully stamped. We walked out of the border compound to Othman's car.

Through a hole in a fence via a fistful of dinars, I had made it into post-revolutionary Libya – I was a tourist in a land run by rebels with *guns, guns, guns*.

🐪 🐪 🐪

The 175-kilometre drive from R'as Ajdir to Tripoli takes about three hours, depending on how long you are held up at security checkpoints. You travel along the *strada litoranea* (coastal highway) laid by the Italians and officially opened by Mussolini in 1937. This road runs from R'as Ajdir right across Libya to its border with Egypt; a distance of over 800 kilometres.

The Italians, dreaming of a modern empire and picking on a next-door neighbour across the Mediterranean Sea, just like the Romans, had entered Libya and ended Ottoman occupation in late 1911. Thus began a period of extremely unpopular rule in which resistance, mainly in the east of Libya, led to the deaths of as many as seventy thousand people from ill-treatment in concentration camps and more from mass executions. Some regard these camps as being the precursor to those of World War II: deaths that foreshadowed the horrors of fascism that lay ahead. Italian control was finally brought to an end in February 1943 after the British Eighth Army occupied Tripoli on their way west to Tunisia, where their defeat of Axis forces in Tunis was such an important turning point in the war. Travelling across North Africa's Arab Spring countries, you cannot help but pick up on echoes of battles of the past.

Othman was a cool customer. He kept on his aviator shades at almost all times; when not inside, that is. He was a careful listener and a careful man in general: 'You have to be cautious in Libya,' he said, echoing the advice of Sotyn. It was almost the unofficial motto of post-revolutionary Libya. He laid down a few rules. We would not drive anywhere at night – 'too dangerous, you do not know who is police or soldiers, or people pretending to be police or soldiers at fake checkpoints'. We would stick to the main tourist sights – he worked for a travel company, not as a bodyguard for a gung-ho reporter, he pointed out. If I was to take pictures in non-tourist places, I was to do so discreetly and fast, in order not to draw unwanted attention.

All of which seemed more than reasonable to me as we drove eastwards along Mussolini's road in the blustery wind, sand swirling in mini-tornadoes. Burnt-out cars lay by the side of the street. We swerved to avoid a dead cat. We slowed to cross a thick rope at our first checkpoint, where two young men wearing bandanas, Yasser Arafat-style scarves (known as *keffiyehs* in Arabic) and khaki trousers lazily waved us through. I began to count the number of checkpoints we passed, but soon gave up as there were so many. The men – who could well have been teenagers – held rifles and were unshaven and generally slapdash. I found something worryingly casual about them. Was Libya's national security being held together by youngsters with guns? It seemed so.

As we drove, Othman talked. And I quickly sensed that as he spoke he was going through a process of catharsis, letting out thoughts to an outsider that had been bottled up for some time.

'I was in Tripoli when the revolution began,' he said, keeping his eyes fixed on the road ahead. The revolution had started in the east of the country, first in the city of Al Bayda on 16 February 2011 (where protests were sparked by local government corruption and delays in the building of housing units), and then in Benghazi, the main city in the east, where a 'day of rage' was organised on 17 February. This demonstration, which is seen by many as launching the full rebellion, was in part brought about by the arrest of a human rights lawyer named Fathi Terbil, who had been representing relatives of 1,270 political prisoners believed to have been killed by Gaddafi's security forces at Tripoli's notorious Abu Salim prison in 1996. It was an atrocity that had gone largely unreported for years and involved many political prisoners from the east of Libya, who were gunned down after staging a protest in pursuit of basic human rights. Some prisoners had not seen daylight for as long as six years, and they were crammed in cells that were regularly flooded for days on end. Tortures included blindfolding men and making them repeatedly run at full tilt into brick walls. Vicious dogs and electric prods were also used. It is unsure whether Gaddafi gave the order for the mass killing, but close observers believe it was likely. He denied responsibility, declaring: 'Libya is the only country in the world with no political prisoners.' Perhaps he really thought this was true... after he had ordered so many murders.

As we slowed down to negotiate pot-holes on the *strada litoranea*, Othman ran through the horrific story of Abu Salim. He also said that there was a strong copycat factor to the uprising against Gaddafi – with great awareness of the revolutions in Tunisia and Egypt, and a sense of seize-the-moment in the air.

Othman explained that when the protests kicked off he returned to his hometown of Bani Walid, a town in the desert about 160 kilometres southeast of Tripoli, to be close to his family. Bani Walid was a Gaddafi stronghold, one of the last places to fall to the rebels, just three days before Gaddafi's death on 20 October 2011. A couple of weeks before my visit there had been a mini-rebellion in the town against the National Transitional Council, during which eight people died, resulting in the formation of a new 'tribal council' that had been subsequently recognised as the local ruling authority by the NTC. Fighting between Gaddafi loyalists and rebel militias was ongoing. Othman stressed that although he was from Bani Walid, he supported the revolution.

'For eight months, we were just watching the troubles,' he said. 'We saw places fall to the rebels over eight months. Tripoli went in August. But Bani Walid and Sirte were still with Gaddafi. Seif al Islam was in Bani Walid up until it fell.'

He was referring to Seif al Islam Gaddafi, the prominent second son of the ex-leader who escaped from the town on 17 October 2011, but whose convoy was struck by a NATO attack that killed 26 of his supporters. He was captured in November and was in prison in the northwestern town of Zintan at the time of my visit.

'Seif ran a small militia and they fought the rebels until the last moment. Then he withdrew. He had mercenaries with him from all over the country. It was an extraordinary time. No-one knew quite what was happening. We didn't know where Gaddafi was. We thought perhaps that he was hiding in the south. It was a surprise that he was found in Sirte. He was stubborn and he was brave: he could have flown to wherever he wanted,' Othman said, as we passed a burnt-out vehicle that looked like an enormous dead insect, and our first pick-up truck with a machine gun fixed to the back. The truck was dented and painted with the colours of the new national flag: red, green and black, with a white crescent and star in the centre of the band of black. As I had with the checkpoints, I started to count trucks-with-guns, but gave up quickly as they became so frequent.

'In Bani Walid the police knew how to deal with the demonstrations. They weren't violent at all. They didn't kill anyone. They just scattered the crowds. That was where the authorities went wrong in Benghazi: they killed people there,' Othman continued. In Benghazi live ammunition was used against protesters on the 'day of rage'.

'A lot of people in Bani Walid believed that the revolution was a Western conspiracy,' he said. 'They believed the state propaganda. They thought the revolution was not for our own good, that it would be worse for the whole country. They thought that tribes would fight each other if Gaddafi went. They believed that Gaddafi was the only man who could provide unity and keep the peace. In a sense, they were right. Now the children have weapons, actually. Now people sell weapons to anyone. During Gaddafi's time, if you found one bullet outside the security forces, it would be a miracle.'

Othman was on a roll and I listened to him rolling onwards – as we did, too, driving towards Libya's capital through misty, sandy landscape, occasionally passing small concrete developments indistinguishable from one another. His monologue was helping me acclimatise to the country.

'Things are not settled now, actually,' he said; Othman had a habit of adding the word 'actually' to sentences for emphasis. 'It takes time. But it will be for the better, actually. Even some families are divided about whether the revolution was a good thing.' He admitted that his own family was split on the matter. 'We never expected Gaddafi would go. It was something like a dream – something impossible. When the revolution happened in Egypt, we just thought that nothing would change here. But it did, and it was started in the east. A lot of people are still pro-Gaddafi. Their mentality is with Gaddafi for life.'

We clattered over a pot-hole. 'Sometimes I feel disappointed by the revolutionaries. There are horrible stories about what happened during the revolution: on both sides,' he said, eyes still staring straight ahead behind his aviator shades.

We arrived at another checkpoint, where a bearded soldier was smoking a cigarette. The checkpoint was larger than the others we had passed. Each was run by a local brigade (there were more than 150 across the country), maintaining order during the interim government in the run-up to the first democratic elections, after which the plans were for a new police and military structure. We had passed through the town of Zuwarah and were on our way to Sabratha. Another pick-up with a gun on the back was parked on the side of the road. 'Sometimes you see ordinary citizens with these,' commented Othman. Guns seemed to be terribly commonplace in post-revolutionary Libya.

As if reading my mind, Othman agreed. 'Too many people have weapons. The most important thing now is to get the weapons to the army.'

Passing near a mosque, Othman began to tell a chilling story. The manager of his tour company, Arkno Tours, had been involved in the revolution from the very beginning. Jemal Ftais had been a long-time opponent of the regime and he wanted the revolution to 'explode' in Tripoli, Othman said.

'It was very early on, late February or early March. He was killed when he finished Friday prayer,' he said calmly. 'He had been part of a group that had said words against Gaddafi in the mosque.' He had been at a mosque by Algeria Square in the city centre.

'He left prayers with the group and headed towards Green Square [known during the Italian rule as Piazza Italia, now renamed Martyrs' Square] calling for Gaddafi to step down,' Othman continued. 'There were a number of vehicles full of Gaddafi militia. They were expecting the demonstration and they shot them down. Actually my manager died, although we were not sure at first as one man was said to have been captured. We made a search of the hospitals and found him – unnamed – in a fridge. It was a big shock to me – to all of us.'

Jemal Ftais's widow had been running the tour company since; they had together formed the business in the 1990s. Ftais was in his forties when he died, and was a Berber from Zuwarah. 'All the time, he was brave. Even during Gaddafi, he would speak, speak, speak. At his wedding party he was captured by the secret police, for something to do with the company. They could do that – if you forgot one single piece of paper they could get you. They would say to him: why are you bringing in spies to Libya? I think they just wanted to spoil his wedding.'

Othman explained that times were hard for all tour operators. He was employed on a freelance basis: 'There has been no work for me. You are my first tourist for one year, actually. Tourism is not yet actually ready in Libya.'

We continued eastwards. A long queue of cars was waiting at a petrol station outside Sabratha, where we passed an unmanned checkpoint. As we did Othman told me casually that the border at R'as Ajdir had been closed for two days before reopening that very morning (I had been very lucky to get in to the country, bribes or no bribes). I asked him if he thought the trip would be safe. I was worried; a lot of things seemed up in the air.

'*Inshallah*,' he replied, deadpan. God willing. He kept looking straight ahead, eyes as ever on the road. Despite all he had already told me, he was an inscrutable man. '*Inshallah*,' he repeated in the same tone. And I didn't know whether to take this as a positive indication of what lay ahead... or not.

We stopped for lunch in Sabratha at a restaurant with orange walls and a picture of a mosque. It was a Turkish restaurant, and we were soon eating chicken and chips with rice accompanied by pots of hummus and hot sauces, flatbread and 'cheese bread' – like little pizzas without a tomato base, these seemed to be thrown into the feast for good luck. We ate heartily and largely in silence, sitting at a table next to a man wearing mechanics' overalls coated with oil. At one point, to attempt conversation, I asked Othman what he did during the recent conflict. 'I was building a loft extension in Bani Walid – and I married in July,' he replied, between scoops of chicken and rice. He had wanted to tie the knot while there was still peace in his hometown: not long afterwards Bani Walid was surrounded by rebels.

Sabratha was grey, undistinguished and consisted of a passage of tall concrete buildings with commercial premises on the ground level. We would be returning to the city later on to see its Roman ruins, but there was not much else to write home about. Before leaving we popped into a cake shop at the base of a construction with the top floors smashed by shelling during the revolution. We ordered 'almond milk' (extremely sweet) and slices of coconut cake to top up on our small lunch. Then we headed onwards along the *strada litoranea*, crossing checkpoints and beginning to see anti-Gaddafi graffiti: 'LIBYA FREE! GADDAFI OUT', 'WE WILL NEVER GIVE UP, WE WILL WIN OR WE WILL DIE', 'ASK NOT WHAT YOUR COUNTRY CAN DO FOR YOU: FREE LIBYA!' and 'GO TO HELL GADDAFI'. The latter remark – written in English as though it were for international broadcasters to capture on camera, as some of the graffiti had been in Sidi Bouzid – came with a picture of the ex-leader holding a tramp's pack and with a noose around his neck. Near Zawiya's oil refineries (close to where Sotyn, my taxi companion, must have fought), another had a cartoon of him with his face coloured green and a scrawl of Arabic writing. I asked Othman what the writing meant and he translated as: 'Where is the algae now?' He said that it was an insult that made reference to Gaddafi's comment during the insurgence about cleansing the streets of 'drug addicts, jihadis and rats'. Algae was considered 'lower' than rats.

Nearing Tripoli the checkpoints became grander, consisting of cargo containers piled three high and then linked at the top with another container, so it appeared as though you were entering an imposing gate. Fierce-looking men with beards and rifles eyeballed us and nodded us through. Pick-up trucks with guns rolled by. We passed an elaborate compound with sentry points and an ornate entrance. This was where Khamis Gaddafi, the seventh son of the dictator (who had eight children in total, including seven sons, born of two wives), had run an elite and much-feared military brigade. It is believed he died during the uprising. The front of the compound had been painted in the colours of the country's new flag.

On the edge of Tripoli the traffic became frantic. Cars zoomed by, the drivers seeming psychotic (and without a care about traffic police, of which there were none). A vehicle limped along with a smashed-out back window and badly crumpled back end. 'It has been in a crash,' said Othman helpfully. We skirted a bypass and turned into side roads where Gaddafi was painted on a wall, dressed as a clown. Another picture showed him holding a gun to his head with the words 'JUST DO IT'. Yet another depicted him with the body of a rat, hanging from an executioner's noose. I got a glimpse of the Mediterranean Sea, where heavy waves were breaking in a spray of spume. Then we turned down a narrow side street with terrible pot-holes and piles of rubbish. The street was alive to the sound of pop music; most of the shops sold car radios – 'This street is known for it,' said Othman. He parked next to a crater-like pot-hole and a pile of rubbish. Ahead was a doorway. The doorway led to my hotel.

Othman left me in the reception on the first floor. He would return in the morning. I found myself in a darkened space with two brass urns and a new Libyan flag. Behind a desk, a porcelain camel sat on a shelf next to an old-fashioned pigeonhole key rack. A silver-haired, grey-eyed receptionist appeared. He had a hollow expression and an interrogating manner. He looked at my passport and inspected me. 'Mr Thomas,' he said, as I was bending to place something in my bag. I straightened up and turned my gaze to him. He stared at me intently, carefully holding the passport open in his hand. 'Mr Thomas,' he repeated sceptically. 'You are Mr Thomas?' I confirmed that I was indeed. His snake eyes flickered; he looked at me even more sceptically.

'Where are you from, Mr Thomas?'

I told him I lived in London.

'Where is this London?' he replied. 'Is it in Scotland?'

I told him that London was not in Scotland. And I drew a rudimentary map of Britain for him, pointing out the whereabouts of England, Scotland and Wales. This, I was to soon discover, was his favourite conversation. I learned to like the silver-haired receptionist who loved asking about Britain and having me point out the geography of the country.

After being offered an Al-Kindi Hotel annual calendar as a welcome gift – there was a large pile of the calendars – I took a lift next to a plastic Christmas tree to the fifth floor.

My room was small and cramped, with two plastic chairs on a tiny balcony and a door that did not lock. From the balcony, I could see a peach sunset across rusty satellite dishes, past minarets and tower blocks. Pop music emanated upwards and there was an occasional raising of voices as though in argument. I lay on one of the two single beds as sunlight filled the room and a muezzin began a long call to prayer. Wind rattled the windows. I closed my eyes, taking in the sounds of a strange new city. It was then that I first heard the *tap, tap, tap, tap*. The noise sounded like fireworks, but had a more precise, rounded-off tone. As the sunlight faded away, the tapping sound became more frequent. It could only be gunfire, I suddenly realised. Someone was celebrating. I'd heard that it was common for guns to be fired into the sky at night in Tripoli, but had not expected to hear the sound so soon (and so often). I was on holiday in a state with a temporary government, run by local brigades, with bullets flying through the sky at night. I decided not to hang out on the balcony for long, and not to go out after sunset in Libya. What was the point in pushing things, and maybe ending up a news story?

In the restaurant I was the only diner – a sensation with which I had become more than familiar on my journey across North Africa's Arab Spring states. The dining room was on the other side of a lounge in which a large bald man was smoking and idly watching the National Geographic channel. The reptilian-eyed receptionist arrived and began to explain that there was lamb or chicken. 'The lamb is from here,' he said, pointing to his legs. 'The chicken is from here,' he indicated his chest. It was not the most appetising of sales pitches. I opted for the chicken. 'Would you like the chicken breast or would you like the woman's breast?' he asked. He was a comedian as well. He laughed at his own joke and disappeared. My food arrived and I ate an incredibly dry piece of chicken accompanied by pasta and chips and a selection of pots of aubergine, hummus, harissa hot sauce, tomatoes and cucumbers.

Then I returned to my room, after nodding good evening to the bald smoker. Outside, the pop music of earlier had turned to reggae and dance tracks. There was a large bang in the street outside, as though someone had smashed a metal dustbin lid into a wall. The tap-tap of guns was still going strong.

President Obama was on BBC World News talking about Iran, where the Arab Spring had yet failed to take off, thanks to the strength of the military state and the suppression of free speech and movement under the regime of Mahmoud Ahmadinejad. Obama was discussing Iran's 'weapons programme' and saying he was 'very concerned' about a report made by the International Atomic Energy Agency. A militia had recently ransacked the British Embassy in Tehran, forcing the diplomats to pull out, while some Iranian MPs had chanted 'Death to Britain' in parliament in response to British sanctions. It all made Libya sound almost tame by comparison.

Meanwhile, a report on Syria highlighted the result of mortar attacks. A desperate elderly woman was shown scampering across rubble where her home had once stood. Yet again, a reminder of the uncertainty and devastation caused by the dictators of the Middle East.

I turned off the television and closed my eyes: *tap, tap, tap*. It was almost therapeutic. I went to sleep counting gunshots above the rooftops of Tripoli. Libya, I already knew, was going to be quite different to my trip across Tunisia. You had indeed to be cautious in Gaddafi's old hunting ground.

Note: Eight days after I left Libya, two British journalists were arrested and detained by the Misrata Brigade, accused of being 'spies'. Nicholas Davies and Gareth Montgomery-Johnson worked for Iran's English-language Press TV station, and were held after filming late at night in Tripoli. For 24 days they were incarcerated, spending much of the time in a cramped cell that bore the 'hallmarks of torture', including dried blood, shards of glass, pieces of electrical cable, and scorch marks on the wall, according to Montgomery-Johnson, who is from Carmarthen in Wales. The brigade had mistaken Welsh writing on his medical supplies for Hebrew, and they thought the pair were Israeli spies. Every day they were told they were going to be shot. They were not allowed to sleep. They were denied water for two days at a time, and barely fed. On one occasion Davies was dragged away and there was a gunshot. Montgomery-Johnson assumed Davies had been killed and that he was next. The Foreign and Commonwealth Office intervened to arrange their eventual release. Had I heard about such an abduction beforehand, I would not have gone to Libya. In hindsight, deciding not to go out at night was a very good idea.

7

Leptis Magna:

There is a Tourist?

L IBYA CONSISTS of three main regions. Tripolitania in the west, Cyrenaica in the east, and the Fezzan in the south. I was, obviously, in Tripolitania, which got its name from three major coastal cities begun at the time of the Phoenicians: Oea (later Tripoli), Labdah (which became Leptis Magna) and Sabratha. Tripoli is a Greek name that means 'three cities'. I was to see all three of the ancient settlements of the great civilisation established in Carthage in the 9th century BC. But unlike their Tunisian counterparts, there was much more to witness in Libya. The country has some of the finest Phoenician and Roman remains anywhere. After a few days in Tripolitania, Othman and I were going to catch a Buraq Air plane to Benghazi, the capital of Cyrenaica, to see the east of the country, where there are many more ancient ruins along the coast leading to Egypt. We were flying there as the road between Tripoli and Benghazi was deemed too dangerous, particularly as it passed by Sirte, where many pro-Gaddafi supporters lived and conditions were volatile. Othman did not want to risk having his car stolen at a fake checkpoint. And we both didn't want to be left car-less on a roadside in the middle of Libya. That did not sound like a good plan (at all).

So we were to cover Tripolitania and Cyrenaica, leaving out the Fezzan for an adventure another day – we did not have the time to make it to the desert lands of the south.

Outside the Al-Kindi Hotel, gangsta rap music was pumping out of a shop selling Pioneer car stereos. Men lolled in doorways keeping an eye on potential customers. The piles of rubbish had not been cleared away overnight; they seemed a permanent fixture on car-radio street.

We went to look for a bank. Othman had lent me some cash, but was anxious that I got hold of Libyan dinars of my own so I could pay him back. I was under the slight impression he thought I might 'do a runner', though where to I have no idea; as I said, he was a very careful man. We drove along narrow lanes in which vehicles with broken windscreens, many pitted with bullet holes, passed by. Traffic was heavy and at some junctions we had to inch forward against a flow of vehicles and put up with a volley of horns. It was amazing anyone got where they wanted.

A red pick-up truck surged ahead of us, three guys in the front cab wearing bandanas and leather jackets. An anti-aircraft gun was attached to the back. 'They are revolutionaries,' Othman said, noticing my surprised reaction. I had grown quickly accustomed to pick-ups with guns near checkpoints on the *strada litoranea*, but had not expected them in the centre of town. 'They are still offering support as the policemen feel weak.'

Many revolutionaries from Zintan and Misrata – responsible for key rebel victories during the insurgency – had decided to stay on in Tripoli for a while. They were revelling in their triumph and had probably been the source of the sound of guns last night, referred to locally as 'happy shooting'. Bust-ups between the Zintan and Misrata and local Tripoli brigades had also resulted in a fair bit of 'unhappy shooting' among themselves, including the recent stand-off at the beach house of Saadi Gaddafi, the ex-Libyan leader's third son. Many locals wanted them to go home, but the fighters were having fun. The men from Zintan in particular were enjoying playing the role of hero to Tripoli's female population; Zintan is in the Nafusa mountains about 145 kilometres southwest of Libya's capital, with a conservative reputation and few chances for young men to meet women who are not family members. There was quite a bit of showboating, with 'pimped up' pick-ups and blaring music.

Down a cacophonous boulevard we came to Martyrs' Square, where palm trees encircled an ornate fountain decorated with statues of galloping horses. It was a big open space with a concrete surface marked with yellow criss-crossing lines (which seemed to mark out the space to organise people during parades) and surrounded by football stadium-style floodlights. The rose-tinted fortifications of Al-Saraya al-Hamra (Tripoli Castle, dating from the 7th century) stood to one side of the square, while lemon-coloured Italianate buildings with neoclassical façades were on the other. The port of Tripoli and the Mediterranean Sea were at the far end, beyond more palms and a busy street.

I looked up at the fortifications of the castle and imagined Gaddafi standing there. The wall of the castle was a favourite place for delivering his many mad, rambling speeches, though it was not the spot where he'd launched his infamous 'drug addicts, jihadis and rats' address on 22 February 2011 – which, ironically, had helped to galvanise resistance to his regime. By then, he already seemed paranoid about the rebellion and had stayed within his nearby Bab Al-Azizia barracks when he ranted on television about being a 'fighter from the countryside… I will die a martyr at the end'. Wearing a brown woollen *jird*, a Bedouin robe, he said that he would 'cleanse Libya inch by inch, house by house, home by home, alleyway by alleyway, person by person, until the country is cleansed of dirt and scum'. During the broadcast, there were cutaway shots of supporters waving green flags, and of a statue showing a giant golden-coloured fist crushing a US warplane. The latter was a symbol of defiance referring to a 1986 American aircraft attack on Tripoli and Benghazi, in which 60 people were killed and the Bab Al-Azizia barracks were targeted. Gaddafi had escaped injury as he happened to be hidden deep within the underground bunker at the barracks. Ronald Reagan had ordered the attack with the backing of Margaret Thatcher, after a Libyan-backed terrorist explosion at La Belle discotheque in West Berlin, popular with US servicemen, had killed three and injured 230 earlier in that year. Afterwards Gaddafi had called Reagan 'an Israeli dog'.

Stuck in a traffic jam by the castle, I could just imagine his angry quivering voice echoing across the square, as it had so many times in the past. His 22 February speech had been badly misjudged and the phrase 'alleyway by alleyway' (which translates as *zenga zenga* in Arabic) had been adopted by the revolutionaries. The rebels turned the words around and defiantly and mockingly said they would themselves battle to take down the regime '*zenga zenga*'. In a later speech, transmitted over the radio in August 2011 as Tripoli was falling, Gaddafi called on his supporters to defend the city: 'Fight! Oh tribes come from your regions to Tripoli, as you came to Tripoli when the Italians attacked it in 1911... cleanse the great city of Tripoli, the great city of those rats and the cohorts of colonialism.' He went on to accuse NATO of dropping 'sound bombs' rather than real missiles, and telling people they were in no danger from them. He had not just lost his grip on his country, but also on reality.

Along a corridor of trees painted red, green and black, we came to a hotel with a bullet hole in the glass door of the entrance. But the bureau de change inside was closed. Othman shrugged. 'We go some other place, later,' he said, before telling me that every hotel used to have someone working there as the 'government eye' – making me think of all the questions back at the Al-Kindi. Perhaps the strange routine had been a reflex reaction from pre-revolutionary days.

We took the Beach Road along the coast to Leptis Magna, 120 kilometres to the east. Big breakers were crashing on the shore and few cars were about. I commented that the waves looked good for surfing and Othman said that there were no surfers because 'Gaddafi did not encourage sport'.

I asked why.

'Because he was afraid that someone could become more popular than him,' he replied. 'For this reason, football commentators and fans could only refer to numbers, not to players' names. In the *Green Book*, Gaddafi said that it should be a team sport. He said that sport is an activity to be practised, not to be watched.'

The *Green Book* was first published in 1975, six years after Gaddafi took power in a revolution/coup of his own against the post-war, Western-backed government of King Idris. It laid out Gaddafi's political philosophy and included wild sections offering the 'solution to the problem of democracy'. The pages devoted to sport say that sports games are like 'praying and eating... it would be foolish for a crowd to enter a restaurant to watch one or more persons eating... it is unacceptable for a society to permit an individual or a team to monopolise sports to the exclusion of other members of society'.

The exception to this monopolisation was Saadi Gaddafi, said Othman. Saadi fancied himself as a midfielder and he was in the national team, naturally, playing as captain. But he was also disliked by many in the east of the country for schemes to do down the fortunes of the football club Al Ahly Benghazi. He distrusted those living in Benghazi, where there had been rumblings of discontent over Gaddafi's rule. Corrupt referees would regularly intervene to the advantage of opposing teams. The result of all this was great frustration that boiled over into a demonstration at a match in which pictures of Gaddafi were burned and, afterwards, a donkey dressed in a football shirt with Saadi's number was released in the city centre to the cheers of local supporters. This action led to the arrest of around eighty fans, who were imprisoned and tortured. Meanwhile, Saadi Gaddafi went on to play for the Italian club Perugia, but only managed one brief substitute appearance, despite having hired Diego Maradona as his technical consultant and Ben Johnson, the disgraced Canadian sprinter, as his personal trainer. He was not the best of midfielders after all, and it appeared that he had bought his way into the side. He was suspended for testing positive for the steroid nandrolone and went on to gain a reputation as a playboy during his time in Italy. He fled Libya during the revolution and was believed to be living in Niger at the time of my visit.

We passed an army base painted in the colours of the revolution. The new flag, a reversion to the one used under King Idris, was everywhere. Men sat at stalls by the side of the road selling bright mounds of oranges. The city faded away into countryside. Tall, wispy eucalyptus trees lined the road. We slowed to cross a cargo-container checkpoint. The containers were from the Iran Shipping Line. Brigade members lurked in the shade smoking. We stopped at a petrol station with the wrecks of two cars in the forecourt, and filled up. 'Seven dinars for forty-five litres: cheap, eh?' said Othman. Seven dinars is about £3.50.

The new-but-old flag got me thinking about the rise of Colonel Muammar Gaddafi. The Brother Leader and King of Kings – as he variously referred to himself – was the son of illiterate Bedouin parents and born in either 1942 or 1943; no precise records were kept. His hometown was in the desert about fifty kilometres south of Sirte near Abu-Hadi. He went to primary school in Sirte, then secondary school in Sebha, a market town in south-central Libya, from which he was expelled, it is believed, for political activism. He finished secondary school in Misrata and enrolled in the Royal Military Academy in Benghazi in 1963. After graduation he became a communications officer in the signal corps and was sent to Britain in 1966. During the year England won the World Cup, Gaddafi attended an English language course at Beaconsfield in Buckinghamshire, a signal instructors' course in Bovington in Dorset, and an infantry signal instructors' course at Hythe in Kent.

In his engaging book *Libya: From Colony to Revolution*, the historian Ronald Bruce St John quotes the director of the Bovington course as describing Gaddafi as an 'amusing officer, always cheerful, hard-working, and conscientious'; although Gaddafi told an official biographer that he hated his English teacher at Beaconsfield as he considered him a 'colonialist'. There is a photograph from the period of Gaddafi walking near Piccadilly Circus wearing Bedouin robes. He looks quite a sight, proudly striding forwards with The Friar Tuck restaurant in the background – a new snack house run by Charles Forte. A woman behind him is smiling and regarding him quizzically.

'I put on my *al-jird* and went to Piccadilly,' Gaddafi told the biographer. 'I was prompted by a feeling of challenge and a desire to assert myself... I did not explore the cultural life in London. [I] felt alienated by the people shoving past each other and scurrying in and out of endless rows of bars, restaurants and other places of entertainment.' It seems safe to say that he did not partake in the Swinging Sixties. (Though who really knows? He certainly developed a taste for swinging with many women in later years.)

King Idris, chief of the influential Sanussi religious-political order in the east of Libya, had come to power in 1951 after much wrangling in the United Nations about what should happen to the country. As an internationally recognised figure – his family traced its ancestry to the Prophet Muhammad – he was put in charge of a state that unified Tripolitania, Cyrenaica and the Fezzan. He was a shy and distant man, but somehow maintained control until the September 1 coup organised by the Free Unionist Officers' Movement in 1969. Gaddafi, aged 27, was a major player in the uprising. He and the other officers were angered by King Idris's close ties to America and Britain, both of which had military bases in Libya. Further links to the West had come from technical support for the oil industry; oil had been discovered in large quantities in 1959, and within eight years Libya was the fourth-biggest oil producer in the world.

Gaddafi had long been an admirer of Egypt's Gamal Abdel Nasser, whose pan-Arab opinions and defeat of the British during the Suez Crisis in 1956 appealed strongly. Many of his schoolteachers had come from Egypt, and it is believed his early political activism arose from listening to the more radical of them. King Idris seemed the polar opposite of Nasser, with none of the cut and thrust of the Egyptian swashbuckler. And while Idris was in Turkey seeking medical treatment, the revolutionaries struck. There was little resistance. The king never returned.

A revolution had not been unexpected: the Central Intelligence Agency had been aware of the discontent and watching events closely, yet they knew nothing of Gaddafi and the other young officers involved. After the coup, Gaddafi quickly came to the fore through the force of his personality, promoting himself to the rank of colonel. The rest is history. He ruled Libya for 42 terrifying years – paying for his impulsive foreign policy, military excesses, overseas terrorist units, grand projects and secret-police excesses with copious cash from the country's newfound oil.

There was a lot to think about on the long road to Leptis Magna, and a lot of smiling to do too. At each checkpoint both Othman and I grinned at the soldiers. 'It is best this way,' Othman said. He believed doing so disarmed the soldiers, many of whom were very young. The road continued in a sunny haze. The lines of repair-work tarmac on the road's surface twisted onwards, looking like mysterious Arabic script. We talked about the guns at night in Tripoli. 'It is better now,' said Othman. 'In the last few months it has been very bad. It was annoying actually. If a bullet goes up, it must come down. Some people were injured – very critical injuries.' In fact, some had died: another reason not to venture out at night in the capital. As I pondered this, we passed a dusty cement factory, continued a few kilometres and turned into an empty car park next to a deserted café with yellow plastic chairs. We had arrived at Leptis Magna.

🐪 🐪 🐪

When Othman had called ahead to Leptis Magna to speak to a local guide who was to show me round the UNESCO World Heritage Site, he had sounded as though he was trying hard to convince the person at the end of the line about our visit. He had put down his mobile and told me that the guide kept on saying, 'There is a tourist?' He had thought Othman was playing a practical joke.

As we walked towards the unmanned ticket kiosk a large man with a bushy beard, mirror shades and a red Adidas cap appeared from a side room. He was enormous – big enough to play in the front line in American football – and in his mid thirties. He beamed and introduced himself. He was Ahmed Elalem of C-Libya Tours. He must be Libya's toughest, as in physically toughest, tourist guide.

Othman disappeared back to the car, where he went for a sleep. Ahmed and I strode forth to see one of the wonders of Africa, soon arriving at the beautiful honey-hued stone arch of Septimius Severus, who was born locally in AD145 and went on to rule the Roman Empire during AD193–211. The arch was built in honour of a return visit made in AD203 by the 'Grim African', Septimius Severus's nickname brought about by his fierce fighting reputation. While the Phoenicians had first settled in Leptis Magna in the 7th century BC, it was the Romans who made the city special. During the time of its local hero Leptis became the biggest Roman settlement in the whole of the continent. Built of strong limestone, with no modern conurbation ruining the main structures (unlike in Tripoli), many of the remains had remarkably stayed upright over the centuries. I immediately got a strong sense of what life at the time must have been like: the layout of the long avenues, wide marketplaces with stones, public baths, theatres and temples – all quite precisely positioned on a breezy hillside by the sea. The land stretched about half a mile along the coast. We walked past bushes with fish-hook spikes and flint-coloured olive trees that rose between foundation stones and weather-beaten walls. The avenues – little more than paths – led off in narrow straight lines of wobbly flagstones partially covered in mossy weeds. Mounds of rich red earth sprouted beards of silvery shrubs. Wild grass whispered in the wind. As we passed through the Grim African's arch and down a Roman road, the tall pink walls of forums, churches, Hadrianic baths, *nymphaeums* (fountains displayed in elaborate colonnaded recesses), and mighty temples arose. Monuments to Hercules and Augustus had survived the ravages of time, but only just – crumbling, half-collapsing, subsiding, with small, spiky plants growing out of cracks. But they were magnificent. People do not think of North Africa for its Roman remains. But there they were, forming a small city hidden between olive trees and tangled vegetation. The Tunisian and Libyan Roman remains must be equal to anything on the northern Mediterranean shores.

I was the only visitor, and as we strolled around the forgotten city I felt an almost spiritual sensation. I can't say precisely why. Perhaps there is just something about the alignment of ancient stones on an isolated hillside that lifts the spirits and draws out elemental thoughts. It was as though I had come to Africa's version of Stonehenge. The sky was royal blue and the air still. The temperature was not much above zero. The blue above framing the honey stones of the temples and basilicas was somehow perfect. While dictators and revolutionaries continued to take to arms in parts of the Middle East, and Islamists and secularists tussled over the future of the region, history stood still in Leptis Magna. Weeds and wild flowers grew between slabs of rock laid down on foundations created before the birth of Jesus; some of the remains dated from Phoenician times. Sparrows took flight and nestled in fine old olive trees. There was no corruption. There were no UN Security Council resolutions. There was no rush of pick-up trucks mounted with guns or cars with broken windscreens. Hillary Clinton was many miles away. An ancient world hung in the air, minding its own business, amid the silence of the stones.

We talked about the history for a while. The Roman Empire period had ended in AD439 with the arrival of the Vandals, at the same time as rule from Rome finished so dramatically in Carthage. A French consul named Claude Lemaire rediscovered the site at the end of the 17th century and began shipping marble back to Europe to be used as building material. Later, in the 19th century, a British consul by the name of Hanmer Warrington arranged for a shipment of stones to be sent to the Prince Regent (later George IV). These were subsequently used to create a classical fantasy at Virginia Water, on the edge of Windsor Great Park.

But Ahmed was just as keen to tell me about life in post-Gaddafi Libya. No matter the peaceful setting, the real world inevitably crept in – and Ahmed did not mince his words. 'We hated him. We are very happy he is gone,' he said, sounding totally certain of what he wanted to say. Ahmed was less 'careful' than Othman. 'Under Gaddafi you got two dinars per month for each child you have – I have three. And you got four dinars for a wife. So for me, ten dinars a month. If you worked for the government you would be paid 350–400 dinars a month, though during the war Gaddafi increased this to

700 dinars to make people love him. The problem is that to live a normal life in Libya, you need a thousand dinars or more a month. Teachers would end up renting out their cars to make extra money – or people would start other private businesses in their spare time.'

Two dinars per child per month sounded like a complete joke, I commented.

He paused. 'Yes,' he agreed. 'We really hated him,' he repeated.

From the mid 1970s onwards, on paper, the economy of the country under Gaddafi had been socialist, although some limited private enterprise was allowed. During the initial period when Gaddafi decreed that 'socialism' was the way forward, many people emigrated after losing homes and businesses, which were confiscated by the state. By 1979, around a hundred thousand people had left; an especially large number as the population was just three million at the time (now it is about 6.5 million). As many as thirty thousand moved to Britain, with around five thousand alone living in Manchester.

'Socialism' in reality meant dictatorship, although one of Gaddafi's many adopted titles was Supreme Guide of the Great Socialist People's Libyan Arab Jamahiriya (the word *Jamahiriya* was invented by Gaddafi to mean 'state of the masses'). The long-winded name for the country was put on car number plates; since the revolution most people had removed the plates, not wanting to be seen to side with Gaddafi.

As his grip on power strengthened, Gaddafi boasted of having created a 'third way' of running a country, a form of socialism in which local councils consisting largely of tribal leaders were established to decide – in theory at least – the direction of the country. The people could have their say through these local congresses and through Revolutionary Committees. There was no need for a formal government or for political parties (pesky, inconvenient things that were banned). The Brother Leader was not in charge, the people were: or so Gaddafi's twisted logic had his subjects believe.

Another 'benefit' to this passing down of power to local congresses effectively run by tribes – of which there are about 140 in Libya including many sub-clans – was that it acted to divide and conquer, as Tarak had said back in Djerba. Tribes came up against neighbouring tribes, and any disputes were local, not national. The focus of politics was on the minutiae of tribal and town-level squabbles, not on the bigger picture. And that was exactly where Gaddafi preferred it to be.

We walked a colonnaded street in the direction of the sea. 'We suffered a lot here. Towards the end, the military of Gaddafi was looking for us,' said Ahmed. 'They took pictures of us protesting.'

'Was there a picture of you?' I asked.

'Yes, they must have got me,' he replied. 'I went to the countryside for five or six days. Then I came back and went into hiding. They were looking for me. A friend, my neighbour, older than me, he was seen at a demonstration. They caught him. He was just a fisherman. Fifty people came to his house. When he questioned them what he had done, they asked him why he had gone to the demonstration. He said he had gone to try to calm things down. They did not listen to him.'

Ahmed went on to describe the horrific fate of his neighbour, who was locked in one of two cargo containers with another 29 prisoners and held within them for 17 days. Bullet holes in the containers provided the only source of air. The occupants were fed little and received limited water. From time to time they were taken out and tortured. On one day, the temperature rose to a scorching level and the men shouted through the holes that they could not bear the heat. They had hardly had any water for a day. Their guards ignored them. One by one they began to drop off, until 18 were dead. Ahmed's neighbour fell unconscious lying amid the corpses. The guards eventually opened the doors to find the bodies. The dead were buried in Gharyan, a town 80 kilometres to the south of Tripoli that was at the time under the control of Gaddafi's forces. The deaths occurred on 5 June 2011. His neighbour was resuscitated and survived. Ahmed said that after our tour of Leptis Magna he would take me to see him.

We entered the 'Hadrianic Baths', where a large rectangular swimming pool was surrounded by pillars. A few inches of green rainwater had settled in the pool, which had somehow survived in a leakproof state through so many centuries. The smell of herbs rose from banks of grass growing out of the sandy soil at the edge of the pool.

Ahmed told me about the early days of the revolution in his hometown of Homs, next door to Leptis Magna.

'In our street many people wanted Gaddafi to stay,' he said. '"We don't like him, we hate him," they said. "But we don't want to be like Iraq." Sometimes neighbours would tell the police: "Yes, that guy is in his house. You can catch him." Sometimes in the morning we would find papers on our car windscreens. They would say: "We are soldiers of Gaddafi. We don't like you. We will kill you."'

The dreadful spectre of the suicide bombs and chaos of the aftermath of the Iraq War felt like a constant backdrop to my visit.

The regime had caused great disruption and heartache within Ahmed's family. Two of his brothers lived in Canada, one working as a doctor and another studying for a PhD in engineering. 'My brother Mohamed, the engineer, he was held for four years in prison under Gaddafi. For what? For nothing. At the end they said: "Sorry you are not the one we wanted." For four years from 1998 to 2002 we knew nothing about him. There were no judges involved. Nothing. No lawyers. Nothing.' When he was in prison, a guard shot him during one heated interrogation, but luckily the bullet only glanced him.

On being set free, Mohamed understandably wanted out of Libya altogether. He sent a report he had written about antennae on mobile phones to a university in Toronto. It impressed the professors and he was accepted for the PhD. Ahmed told me that it was political prisoners such as his brother, and the memory of the 1996 massacre at Abu Salim, that eventually led to the revolution.

Inside the grand Severan Basilica, there was still no-one else around: we did not even see an attendant during our visit to the greatest Roman site in Africa. It was just us and the grand Ionic columns, the honeysuckle walls and the pervading sense of history. In the centre of the basilica I looked around and marvelled at the simplicity of the beauty of the Roman remains: the colonnades, pilasters, pink granite shafts and limestone pedestals. At one end of the impressive 92-metre by 40-metre basilica, intricate carvings on columns depicted figures playing lutes and riding on horseback. A thick vine bearing grapes wound round them. The stone had a faint pink colour and rose about seven metres. It was next to a matching decorative pillar, but on a second column the figures were missing. 'Four or five years ago this happened. People came and stole them,' Ahmed said. 'They jumped over the fence at night with axes and took whatever they wanted. We believe they were Italians who were here in caravans.'

Not enough was done to protect historical sites under Gaddafi, Ahmed believed: 'He had his oil, so he didn't care about tourism. He wasn't interested about history. He'd say: "Oh, we don't need tourists in Libya."'

🐪 🐪 🐪

Afterwards, we did not go to the gift shop – as there wasn't one. Instead we went to meet Mohamed Ahmed Ettarhoni, the man who was tortured and put in the cargo container with bullet holes. We picked him up in the centre of Homs and, on his insistence, drove to the site of the containers. Mohamed was in his mid fifties and wore a grey robe and a black circular hat. He had a white beard and intelligent deep-set eyes. He was thin and wiry. We arrived at a compound with a green mesh gate and a sign on a concrete wall saying: 'DANGER: WEAK WALL.' A gap-toothed guard eventually let us walk through into a yard surrounded by ugly grey single-storey buildings. We were at the former living quarters of a construction company. A twisted basketball net was on one side and weeds grew amid piles of rubbish.

Beyond were the two cargo containers. One was rusty red, the other white with an Iran Shipping Lines logo. Mohamed pulled open the door of the white container and showed me the spot at the end that could have been his tomb. Dots of sunlight cast through the bullet holes revealed a filthy floor and pieces of cardboard that acted as mattresses. He picked up a plastic bottle with a tube attached and explained that this was their 'toilet'.

Mohamed believed that he was picked upon for being a prominent member of a local mosque. Fearing plots, Gaddafi had arrested many moderate as well as radical Islamists over the years. Ahmed and Othman translated as Mohamed explained what happened in the summer of 2011:

'After my arrest on the first day, they beat me. I was boxed by hand and kicked in the legs and back, and then beaten with a baton. Then I was taken to the container. After a few days they saw me praying in the container and they pulled me out by my beard. They took me to a room in the compound.' He pointed to the far side. 'Then I was beaten on and off for three days – on the face with sticks and wire, with electric shocks. They said I had brought NATO into Libya. I said it was not true: I was trying to say anything that might save my life. Then I was taken back to the container. On the morning of the final day, it was so hot. We said to the guards: "We are all Libyans and Muslims. Be reasonable, let us out." They just listened to us. People about me started beating the floor in desperation. Foam was coming out of their mouths. I became unconscious. Finally they opened the door and the bodies were taken away. Then we were taken to the Agricultural University in Tripoli, where we were held. They were planning to hang a lot of us in Green Square. That is what we believed. It was to be a present to the Leader. On the twenty-first of August, we heard someone trying to open the door of our room. It was the head of the camp. He told us to come out. All the soldiers had guns. We thought we were going to be killed. The soldiers said: "Please forgive us, you are free." We shook hands and were very happy – weeping. There were sixteen of us held there. We split up into groups of four to be less conspicuous and made our way.'

At one point as Mohamed told us all of this, he went to one side and was silent, looking away from us and taking deep breaths. It was obviously extremely painful to remember what happened and to be back at the containers. Following him, we went to the room where he was tortured. Plastic cords used to bind together hands were scattered amid old soldiers' uniforms. A metal rack leant against a wall, and Mohamed showed how he was tied to the rack and beaten. He also pulled up his robe to show red-and-black slug-like welt marks on his back. Some of the men involved in the torture had been caught and there was to be a trial, he said.

🐫 🐫 🐫

After parting, Othman and I drove back to Tripoli. Graffiti on the side of the road said: 'LIBYA IS FREE LIKE A BIRD.' We were silent for most of the way, and remained so when we stopped for a spicy soup and chicken meal at a roadside café. There was plenty to think about. We passed checkpoints manned by brigade members wearing balaclavas. Then we went to a little market where a grocery shop owner changed my dollars into dinars. The market sold anything and everything: CDs, PlayStations, Ronnie O'Sullivan snooker games, pots of olives and dates, barley flour, couscous, socks, T-shirts, sausages, camel heads (the equivalent of £12.50 for a real camel head) and sheep's heads (about £3). A sign by the entrance said: 'NO GUNS.' Above the sign were bullet holes. A poster in the street that appeared to have been put up by the National Transitional Council said: 'TODAY TRIPOLI HAS A NEW HEARTBEAT.' It showed a soldier wearing the colours of the new flag while embracing another man. Another read: 'WITH OUR HANDS WE WILL REBUILD LIBYA.' Beneath the slogan were pictures of grenades, machine guns and soldiers' uniforms, and the poster called for members of the public to hand in these items to the rebels.

Othman and I did not hang around; it was nearly dusk. He had one bit of business to attend to, so we drove beyond the Corinthia Hotel, where many journalists were based during the conflict, coming to tall oil-company offices, a JW Marriott (which was boarded up) and the Bab Al Bahr Hotel. We parked outside the hotel, after passing a security gate. I was left in the car as Othman went into the hotel, and I stepped out to get some air and take pictures of the honeycomb-shaped skyscrapers. I walked up to the hotel entrance, and then on the way back was met by 10 members of a revolutionary brigade. They were carrying guns but seemed extremely cheerful. They wore a mixture of khaki uniforms (none of which quite matched), with fleeces, *keffiyehs*, baseball caps and bomber jackets. Some had beards, but not all. They asked me to take their picture and email it to them. I looked at their rifles: I did not turn down their request. Some of them were from Derna in the east of Libya, close to Al Bayda, where the first protests had begun. The town had fallen to the rebels on 18 February 2011.

I took a snap. Then they crowded round and we tried to communicate the best we could. One of them held forth a shiny AK-47. 'It is Russian,' he said.

Mohanoad, aged 23, said: 'The best thing is freedom. We needed to change the regime. We changed it.'

His friend added: 'We are Libya! We are free!'

Before the war, they had been teachers, students, engineers, lawyers and 'a sales manager for Rolex'. But they had been revolutionary soldiers ever since. They looked proud and confident. We all shook hands and they went into the hotel. It was strange who you could bump into outside the four-star Bab Al Bahr Hotel.

🐫 🐫 🐫

Across the street from the Al-Kindi Hotel (three stars and £32 a night, a quarter of the rate at the Bab Al Bahr), I tried a snack stall for dinner after Othman drove off. I couldn't quite bear another rubber chicken, rice and chips in the hotel's freezing dining room.

There were promising-looking pictures of kebabs. I pointed and asked for one.

'We are fish,' one of three men sitting behind the counter said. At least that's what it sounded like.

'OK, I'll go for the fish,' I replied; suddenly pleased by the prospect of eating something that was not chicken.

They did not move a muscle. 'We are finish,' he said. 'Finish.'

They had sold out of all their food but were hanging around to have an early evening chat. They watched me depart in silence.

Back at the hotel, the Reptilian was in the reception and on his usual form. 'Mr Thomas? You are Mr Thomas?' He did not wait for, or expect, a reply. He asked me again where I was from and added: 'What is the weather like there today?' I said I'd tell him if I could use the internet on the computer in the corner, if the internet was working – it had not been yesterday. 'It works today, Mr Thomas! Will you be dining with us?' I said I would. He seemed very pleased.

I ate my chicken, chips and rice with the Al Jazeera news channel playing in the lounge, showing shots of a latest attack in Syria. The same bald man, smoking once again, was in the lounge and as I passed I said 'good evening'. He spoke a little English and said that he worked in the oil industry. He had just been in Tobruk in the east of the country, but was in town on business. He had worked with BP in recent years, but BP had pulled out of Libya when the revolution began. He seemed sad about this. BP has a long history in Libya and was instrumental in finding major oilfields in 1961. Gaddafi nationalised its assets in 1971, but during the years when Tony Blair was Britain's prime minister relations between the two countries had improved, largely due to Gaddafi's stance against Islamic fundamentalists and the 11 September attacks, and the company relaunched its activities in 2007.

We bade each other good night. There was a certain solidarity among the guests of the Al-Kindi.

Then I returned to my room. The 'happy shooters' of Tripoli were still at it. I dropped off. But I was awoken at 6 a.m. Near the far end of car-radio street, a man was ranting at the top of his lungs over a speaker system. I caught the booming words: 'IRAQ... MUBARAK.' His long speech was punctuated by volleys of gunshots. I had no idea what it all meant, but later in the morning there was a Reuters report of claims that Seif al Islam Gaddafi was to be moved from the place where he was held by rebels in Zintan in the Nafusa mountains to be tried in Tripoli in two months' time.

This was big news, as Gaddafi's heir apparent was much hated for defending his father during the revolution, warning in an important broadcast on 20 February 2012 that 'rivers of blood' would flow if the rebellion continued. Even though he had repeatedly made himself out to be a Libyan reformist, when the chips were down he had sided with his family. Many people would have liked to have seen justice quickly administered: with a bullet to the head, or perhaps a noose on Martyrs' Square. But the Zintan brigade had been holding on to their prize catch. They had found him after a tip-off by a Tuareg guide who had guessed that the 'someone important' in a Land Cruiser who needed directions across the desert could be a Gaddafi on the run. He was spot on. Seif al Islam had been heading to Niger, where his brother Saadi was believed to have been given sanctuary.

As it turned out, the claims about Seif al Islam's imminent move to Tripoli proved false – he was kept in Zintan for much longer. But I guessed that this 'news' must have had something to do with the crack-of-dawn rally and gunshots. Visiting a country with so little regular infrastructure – being held together by bands of brigades and a shaky transitional government – so soon after a revolution, I was finding you had to piece information together. It was unpredictable, exciting, confusing and moving; I will remember the grim interior of those containers and Mohamed's story of what happened forever. It was also raucous, noisy, alien and strange. You just had to go with things, keep smiling, and hope for the best.

8

Sabratha and Tripoli:

In Brother Leader's Old Bunker

THE CARTOON on the wall of a building on Gargaresh Street in a well-to-do neighbourhood of Tripoli fitted the morning's news. It showed Gaddafi wrapped in rope and hanging from a wooden frame, while watching on from beyond a couple of cacti, Seif al Islam Gaddafi peers through rectangular-framed spectacles; his body has been turned into a vulture's, and he is accompanied by another vulture, which lurks behind him. I asked Othman to stop and I got out of the car to capture the striking image. The political street-art in Tripoli really was a cut above any I had seen before.

'Hurry, hurry,' said Othman, invoking one of his 'rules'. I had only been out of the car a matter of moments, but he seemed panicky. 'Very quickly! Get back as there are some people here who are pro-Gaddafi.'

I returned to the car straight away. 'You have to be careful,' Othman said as we rapidly drove off. 'We don't want people to say: "Look at how the Western people are laughing at us."'

He paused. 'There is another thing: if they see a foreigner, they presume you are a journalist or maybe a spy,' he added. It was better that we were considered to be neither of those, he said. Any behaviour that might be regarded as 'political' was out of bounds. I was to remain a tourist, a slightly crazy tourist – and do my best to act like one, too.

This neighbourhood of Tripoli is the setting for much of the novel *In the Country of Men* by Hisham Matar. The incisive book, which was shortlisted for the Man Booker Prize in 2006, describes harrowing times in the late 1970s when Gaddafi's Revolutionary Committees were flexing their muscles. This was the period of turmoil when private homes and businesses were seized by the state, and people were coming to terms with the reality of life post-King Idris, leading to so many emigrations. Revolutionary Committee cars patrolled the streets, keeping a close eye on potential dissidents; making other drivers so terrified they would never dare overtake.

The book's protagonist is a nine-year-old boy named Suleiman whose family lives in Gargaresh. He watches on as his friend's father, who lives across the street, is arrested, and then his own father disappears. His mother turns to her 'medicine' – illegal hooch bought from the baker. Public hangings at basketball courts are shown on the television, creating a frenzied atmosphere. The mother desperately burns potentially incriminating books belonging to her husband. Informers are all about; telling on fellow citizens is 'Libya's national sport'. The mother installs a large picture of the Guide, another of Gaddafi's names, in their living room. The Revolutionary Committee members remain suspicious: does the family know anything about leaflets and meetings near Martyrs' Square? Might Suleiman be able to help?

For his own good, Suleiman is sent to Cairo to stay with a friend of the family; he is too close to the parents' troubles. Not long after he leaves, a decree is issued saying that he has officially become a 'stray dog' for having departed the Guide's domain – which puts him at great risk should he ever return to Libya. In the meantime, his parents cannot visit Suleiman in Cairo as they are parents of a stray dog. It's a dictator's Catch 22: no matter how they might try to be together, 'rules' would be broken. The narrator helplessly laments: 'Why does our country long for us so savagely? What could we possibly give her that hasn't already been taken?' The novel gives a sharp insight into life under the regime.

'It was banned here, actually,' said Othman, when I mentioned the book.

He had, however, read a copy while on a visit to London; a tourist he had
befriended had helped him get a visa and he had visited the United Kingdom
once. 'When I read that book I realised how horrible it was to live in Libya:
the kidnapping, the suppression.' By absorbing a view from outside Gaddafi's
sphere of control, he had been able to see the country in another light. Even
though Othman lived under the harsh realities of the regime, it had been
hard to determine what was 'normal', he said. His comments reminded me
of people living in North Korea, who have been so brainwashed and starved
of outside information by the Great and Supreme leaders of the dynasty of
Communist Kims that they have a warped notion of what to expect from the
modern world.

When Othman was a child his brother used to drive him around
Gargaresh to see Tripoli's answer to Beverly Hills. 'My brother was proud
about Gargaresh. He said: "Look! Look how luxury the shops are!"'

I looked. They did not seem all that 'luxury' now: just a normal run of
stores, perhaps slightly smarter than elsewhere in the Libyan capital. We
turned down a side street and the houses were big and neglected. Most were
detached and many had garages. They reminded me of homes in a once-rich
suburb of an American city, where the glory days were past and troubles were
moving in.

'It was rich here in the 1970s and the early 1980s,' said Othman.
'Then things went into decline. They were owned by generals, judges, rich
lawyers, chairmen of companies. But then their sons took over.' Children like
Suleiman, I could not help thinking. 'Maybe the sons were not as motivated
as their fathers. Maybe the sons were lazy young men.'

Perhaps also, I thought but did not say, they did not see a future worth
exerting themselves for under a regime ruled by a family fiefdom that
arbitrarily took what it wanted from its subjects.

The road led down to the sea. Nobody was about. Rubbish tumbled
across the road in a breeze. We paused by a wall and while we looked out
across the concrete-coloured water, Othman told me that sanctions from the

1990s to the early 2000s had hit the country hard. They had ended only because of Gaddafi's rapprochement with the West as he courted figures such as America's Secretary of State Condoleezza Rice and Britain's Prime Minister Tony Blair post 9/11.

'There is very poor housing. A lot of young people have lived stunted lives. People had to build extensions to family homes.' Just as Othman did during the revolution while living in Bani Walid. 'Only in the last five years had Gaddafi begun building new homes for people. But it was too late and very slow. That is why the revolution started: people were complaining about houses and infrastructure. We are a nation of just six million people. Yet the oil prices were high and we have big oil reserves. How did this happen?'

There is enough oil to last another 75 years at current production levels, and enough gas to last 97 years. Libya is one of the world's top 10 energy-producing countries, responsible for two per cent of oil production.

'Why are we not like rich Arab states in the Gulf?' asked Othman, who was becoming franker by the hour. I could sense his deep underlying frustration. He had visited the West. He had taken Westerners about the tourist sites. He had had a taste of what the modern world could offer. But he had had to bite his tongue and put up with life as it had been dealt to him under Gaddafi. His tongue was beginning to loosen and I realised he was saying things to me that he had perhaps not spoken out loud to many people – if anyone.

'We should be rich like the rich Arabs!' he said exasperatedly. 'We have had to drive to Tunisia or Egypt to get proper treatment in hospitals. The war with Chad in the 1980s cost Libya a lot of money and lives. Why did we have that war? It was a pointless war.'

Gaddafi had gone to war with Libya's southern neighbour over ownership of a stretch of desolate desert known as the Aouzo Strip to which Libya had a flimsy historical claim. The army fought on for almost a decade but in the end conceded the land to Chad; this was recognised by the United Nations. It is likely that a Gaddafi victory in Chad would have led to him taking the whole of the country and potentially moving onwards to Sudan and further afield. But the result was an increasingly dilapidated army that fought in scorching conditions for the best part of a decade, achieving nothing and wasting a lot of money on rockets that exploded in the sand.

'It was Gaddafi's weakest point!' summarised Othman, who had become quite animated.

On the outskirts of Zawiya, on the way to the Roman remains of Sabratha, a partially destroyed apartment block was covered in shell marks. 'FREE LIBYA!' was written repeatedly on walls. It was in Zawiya that the brave, award-winning Sky News reporter Alex Crawford and her crew had reported during the early days of the uprising, risking their lives to describe the horrific scenes as Gaddafi's troops fired into largely unarmed crowds in what was effectively a turkey shoot. On 3 March 2011, Crawford and her team had narrowly survived, metres away from tanks that might easily have destroyed their hideaway had the armoured vehicles turned in their direction. Shells and bullets had whistled by, yet she phoned in stories and her cameraman had taken pictures.

These despatches had been important as they showed the world both how violently the regime was reacting and how vulnerable Gaddafi was: the rebels had regrouped and eventually enjoyed a victory, driving the troops out of the city centre. International opinion was influenced and rebels throughout the country were given hope. Just as in Tunisia, news travelled quickly over the internet and by mobile phones (Gaddafi later switched off internet access, though it unexplainably flickered on several times afterwards). Crawford captured the terrifying moments in Zawiya in her gripping book of reportage entitled *Colonel Gaddafi's Hat*, whose title comes from her later encounter with a rebel who had taken possession of (and wore) Gaddafi's peaked white military hat. 'If we're going to die,' she writes of her lowest moment in Zawiya, 'I'm bloody well going to let everyone know what happened to us, what's happening to these people around us.'

Travelling through Libya when I did was a walk in the park next to the risky work required of a front-line correspondent.

We passed a couple of checkpoints. The soldiers waved us through, looking sleepy. Othman moved on to the subject of who should lead Libya in the future. Elections were due to be held four months after my visit. He was a fan of Mustafa Mohammed Abdul Jalil, the leader of the National Transitional Council who had been the Justice Minister under Gaddafi but had resigned and defected to the rebels on 21 February 2011, after the military shot dead protesters in Benghazi at the beginning of the revolution. He was from Al Bayda, where the revolution had begun on 16 February 2011, and was the first member of Gaddafi's General People's Congress to defect. He once defied Gaddafi and criticised the country's security agencies during a meeting of the congress, gaining many admirers. It is thought that he only managed to hold on to his position because Seif al Islam believed that his presence in the government added credence to the notion that Libya was opening up and reforming.

'He is a moderate Islamist,' said Othman. 'What we want is rule of law. We want to be like Turkey, but in a Libyan style. To be somewhere between Turkey and Saudi Arabia. Abdul Jalil is an honest man. Not corrupt. Moderate. I like him.'

We drove down a road with more 'FREE LIBYA!' graffiti and brightly coloured walls spray-painted with dancing figures holding the new Libyan flag. We turned into a large car park with a couple of vehicles in it. We had arrived at Sabratha and, just as he had at Leptis Magna, Othman passed me over to a local guide (there seemed to be some sort of guides' union) and retreated to his car for a sleep.

🐪 🐪 🐪

'Hello, I am Tarek Ali,' he introduced himself. He wore a tan leather jacket, a striped shirt and beige trousers, and had an open, honest face. He was a far cry from the wheeling-and-dealing Tarak of Djerba. He told me that the only people to have visited Sabratha since the revolution had been schoolchildren, a few diplomats and a group of American teachers ('But I did not think they were teachers,' he said, implying they were spies). We set forth across a plot of land covered in dandelions and purple wildflowers, heading for the caramel-coloured stones of the Roman settlement.

Sabratha is not quite as splendid as Leptis Magna; being built of sandstone, many of its structures have crumbled over the years since the ancient city was founded by settlers from Carthage in the 4th century BC (it was rediscovered by Italian archaeologists at the beginning of the 20th century). Yet a lot remains, including temples, basilicas, forums and a superb theatre – considered superior to its counterpart at Leptis Magna.

Tarek and I ambled along. I'm interested in Roman history... up to a point. It's fascinating to think of the trade in olive oil, animals and ivory in Sabratha, and how the Roman Empire shipped goods across the Mediterranean so many hundreds of years ago. The sheer organisation this required speaks of a determination within the human spirit that acts as a thread that connects us to the past. Coexisting with that desire to thrive came the importance of art in civilisation, as witnessed by the flamboyant curls at the top of the Doric columns, the delicate friezes depicting lines of enrobed soldiers, and the Corinthian columns and elegant balustrades of Sabratha's theatre. The auditorium of the latter is 93 metres in diameter and is the largest of its kind in Africa, faithfully rebuilt by the Italians in the 1920s.

But as much as I find the Romans intriguing, I was finding it was Libya in the Arab Spring, as it came to terms with its new world, that I wanted to know about. I began to ask Tarek a few questions about life then and now. But for a while I was unable to get any sense out of him.

For example, if I asked about what happened in Sabratha during the rebellion, he would switch tack and talk about Benghazi, saying something along the lines of: 'The people of Benghazi burned their police stations on the eighteenth and nineteenth of February.' Or tell me something about the remains at Sabratha: 'The sandstone of the temple was local. The flagstones of the streets were made of limestone that came from afar.'

He would make these statements in a quiet, sensible, balanced voice. I would try and make the connection between what he told me and what I'd asked, and fail. It was a little bit frustrating.

But he could not keep it up, and after 15 minutes or so of these verbal skirmishes Tarek opened up. He told me why he was cautious to talk.

'Even after the revolution, I had to be careful,' he said in his soft, measured voice. 'A group of journalists came to Sabratha and I thought: What if they ask me about politics? There were people who were watching, people who were the secret police.'

The group had come during the period when Benghazi had fallen but Tripoli had yet to topple so he was right to be cautious. This circumspection had become second nature. I could tell that he was finding it hard, or at least extremely unusual, to say what he really wanted to an outsider.

'I tried to be outside the group, away from them so that there was no chance I could be accused of saying anything,' he said. 'I am happy that I always stuck to this policy. I am happy because maybe if I had talked about something, I might not be here right now.'

The tendrils of the dictatorship reached into every corner of society – even to its mild-mannered tourist guides. In this early period of post-Gaddafi Libya I got a sense of prison doors having been opened for people who had been incarcerated for a long time and who were still wondering whether it was true that they could step out into freedom. With 42 years in power, Gaddafi had been the world's longest-serving dictator.

'I would know who the secret police were,' Tarek continued. 'They would sit in the tourist coaches, so it was obvious. Sometimes they would hear tourists talking and perhaps laughing. They would ask me what the tourists were saying. I did not want to get involved. I would just reply: "If you want to know what they are saying, learn the language."'

We reached the sea, near a beautiful headless statue of Venus, the goddess of love and fertility. Clouds had cleared and the sky was a perfect blue. The water was aquamarine and waves were breaking with a fizz on rocks on the shore. Tarek looked at the water and told me that there should be sea defences to protect the antiquities from the water. 'Every year part of the ancient city is taken by the Mediterranean,' he said.

'In the 1980s the Minister of Education said that it is a shame that the Sabratha people keep these Roman ruins. The ruins should be taken by a tractor and thrown in the sea, it was shameful to keep Roman things in our country, he said.' The Minister of Education he was referring to was Ahmad Ibrahim, a cousin of Gaddafi, apparently imprisoned in Misrata during the revolution. One of Ibrahim's claims to fame was that he abolished foreign-language education in the 1980s. Yet he sent his own children to fee-paying schools in Britain – typical of the rank hypocrisy of the regime.

We inspected fine mosaics with symmetrical flower patterns. It seemed slightly incredible that tourists were able to walk over these ancient floors. And yet there was not another soul in sight (as usual). Signs explaining what part of the site you were entering were broken and faded. Columns stood proudly amid weeds. Plastic bottles cluttered the shore, washed up by the waves. We crunched along a path to the archaeologically famous theatre, where we stood in the auditorium. The orange-pink columns of the theatre were in three tiers and reached almost 20 metres high above the stage, which faced the semicircular seating. The front of the stage was decorated with exquisite marble carvings depicting philosophers, muses, soldiers, sacrificial bulls and goddesses. One of the panels showed a scene from a tragedy and was accompanied by comic and tragic masks. The stage would have had a curtain, but as it could not be suspended from above (the theatre was roofless) the curtain would have hung from a pole raised in the middle of the front of the performing area. The people of ancient Sabratha clearly loved performances. The seats could accommodate 5,000 spectators.

The Italians found Sabratha in 1921 and went to some trouble reconstructing the theatre, which was reopened in 1937. Mussolini himself attended a production of Sophocles's *Oedipus Rex* to mark the occasion. The thought of a different dictator to Gaddafi sitting in the best seats for the most important spectators was eerie. Nobody is certain precisely when the theatre was constructed but it is believed to have been in the time of Septimius Severus around AD204. First the Grim African, then Il Duce, and finally the Brother Leader – with the East Germanic Vandals making an appearance (AD439–534) just to add to the mix, defeating the Romans after crossing the Strait of Gibraltar in AD429 and bringing a period of darkness to North Africa.

Libya has seen quite a few characters, unsavoury and otherwise, come and go (though I suppose most countries have, when you think about it).

Most of the fighting during the revolution took place in the 'new' part of Sabratha, along the *strada litoranea*, but there was some action at the Roman ruins. Luckily all there is to show of it is a couple of bullet marks, one on a Corinthian column and another on a tall wall on the right-hand side of the stage. After liberation from Gaddafi, locals had held a music show to celebrate freedom, and the new Libyan flag had hung from the top tier of the theatre.

We strolled back to the entrance and as we did so Tarek bent down and picked up a tiny fragment. Earlier he had done the same and shown me a piece of a painted frieze. I had been amazed: we were literally waking over relics. This time he had found an ancient coin with Arabic writing. Again, I was flabbergasted. 'Sometimes I find Roman coins,' he said nonchalantly. 'Usually on a walk like this I find at least one coin of some sort. There are many treasures in Libya.'

🐪 🐪 🐪

There were many pick-up trucks with guns as well. After another grilled-chicken lunch at the Turkish café with orange walls that we'd visited the other day – seemingly it was Othman's favourite – we drove back to Tripoli. By the checkpoint at Zawiya, a dozen trucks with anti-aircraft guns lined the street on the other side. They looked sinister. Sounding a little like a cowboy in a film, Othman commented: 'Maybe something is happening in the West.'

We continued in silence. Apropos of nothing, on the outskirts of Tripoli, Othman said: 'There are many spinsters in Libya now, as many young men died in the war. The new government has changed the law so that men can marry more than once. Before you had to ask your wife's permission if you wanted another wife.'

'How does it work practically? Surely the wives can't like it too much?'

Othman did not answer the second question. 'Sometimes they live in the same house, sometimes in two houses,' he replied. 'There is a saying. One wife fights against you. Two wives fight for you. It's that kind of policy.'

He smirked a bit, staring ahead through his aviator glasses as we headed towards one of the strangest places I have visited in my life.

The oil-office skyscrapers by the waterfront in Tripoli were sparkling in the late afternoon sunlight. For the second time in the day I was reminded of America, but on this occasion it was of 'downtown USA', somewhere like Dallas or Houston perhaps. The skyscrapers with their big satellite dishes, mirrored glass, circular windows, and rooftop helicopter pads clearly made a statement. While young people were struggling to make a way in life and find housing, Gaddafi had made sure that his ego was satisfied with a mini-Manhattan just round the corner from his underground hideaway at the Bab Al-Azizia barracks.

Thinking of the United States at this spot reminded me of an unusual episode in the history of Libya. It came after US victory in its War of Independence with Britain. Being free meant that the previous protection American naval ships had had from North African corsairs – who had an agreement with the British – was withdrawn. Thus began the Barbary Wars; 'Barbary', or 'Berber', was used at the time to refer collectively to the people living on the northwest coast of Africa. The corsairs, pirates and privateers, ran a highly profitable racket, threatening America's trade with Europe. John Adams and Thomas Jefferson conducted talks with Tripolitanian officials in 1786, but they did not go very well, and US ministers were sent to Morocco and Algiers for more talks, with an agreement eventually being made in 1796 for the corsairs to hold off.

This did not last long. In 1801, Yusuf Pasha, the Bey of Tripoli, asked for increased payments and defiantly chopped down the American flagpole outside its consulate in Tripoli. Thomas Jefferson, by this time president, sent naval ships to blockade the port at Tripoli. Unfortunately one of its ships, the *Philadelphia*, was captured with a crew of 307, who were held prisoner (the ship was sunk in Tripoli harbour in 1804 by another American ship so the vessel could not be used by the Tripolitanians). Marines were sent from Egypt in 1805 to invade Libya, but as they made their way westwards a deal was struck involving the exchange of all prisoners and a US payment. In the end the marines did not attack Tripoli. But the invasion is remembered in the first verse of the official hymn of the United States Marine Corps:

> From the Halls of Montezuma,
> To the shores of Tripoli;
> We fight our country's battles
> In the air, on land, and sea;
> First to fight for right and freedom
> And to keep our honour clean:
> We are proud to claim the title
> Of United States Marine.

The whole episode included a number of 'firsts'. It was the first time the US had a navy – built especially to deal with the corsair problem. It was the first occasion in which America tried to unseat a foreign government. And it involved the first US official dealings with the Muslim world; a prelude to rocky times ahead.

Beyond the skyscrapers we came to the place Ronald Reagan bombed in 1986, and where NATO struck during the revolution. Past a dried-out river filled with rubbish, we turned down a dusty track off the traffic-jammed main coast road. A lopsided sentry box marked the entrance to a compound filled with litter and rubble. It looked like a fly-tip. Great slabs of concrete lay about, as though a motorway flyover had collapsed. Rusty barbed wire was scattered in a wide-open yard beyond, with dented old oil barrels lying on their sides. Pale-green buildings with smashed roofs and flame marks were in the centre of the enormous space surrounded by walls pitted with bullets and artillery. Broken swivel chairs were piled on top of splintered window frames and fragments of destroyed air-conditioning units. Weeds poked out of the crumbling surface of the yard.

We had arrived at the Bab Al-Azizia barracks, Gaddafi's former stronghold that was captured by rebels on 23 August 2011, five months before my visit. At the far end of the yard in which Gaddafi had a luxurious Bedouin tent (which he once tried to pitch in Central Park on a visit to New York), a handful of dented vehicles were parked in the shade of scorched olive trees and palms. And beyond the trees, there was an extraordinary sight: an enormous rectangular hole (about 100 metres long and 50 metres wide) that was all that remained of Colonel Gaddafi's underground bunker at the heart of his former compound in the centre of the Libyan capital.

Othman and I went to the edge of the hole, avoiding an open hatch that led down to a complicated network of tunnels. Below us we saw smashed-up armoured vehicles, rusty wires and rubble. Amid the debris, strange treasure-hunters were at work, huddled in groups amid the general devastation. I asked Othman what they were doing. He went to chat to an elderly man who was standing nearby. He returned.

'They collect the copper from the gun bullets,' he said, matter-of-factly.

We soon found that while some were in search of copper, others were hunting for the remains of rifles that might be of use to the many revolutionary brigades. The former Libyan leader's hideaway had become a scavengers' free-for-all.

It looked like a scene from the futuristic film *Mad Max*, in which the modern world has ended, replaced by a desperate struggle for survival. Guys with hooded tops – it was 3°C and one of the coldest days yet – were hauling heavy white sacks filled with Kalashnikov shells on their backs. They stepped carefully over pieces of twisted metal and mounds of earth from the collapsed roof of the bunker, which was destroyed by NATO in May 2011. Hunched under the weight of the shells, they passed from a distance as biblical figures, shuffling through the dust.

We descended a concrete ramp into the hole. Rusty bullet shells were everywhere, mostly burnt out and ruined in terms of the scrap value. There were so many shells that in places we felt as though we were crunching across a weird gravel path made of metal.

Wire jutted upwards from boulders and the occasional support column that had miraculously survived the blasts, looking like striking pieces of abstract art against the solid blue sky. A middle-aged man wearing camouflage trousers and a cap bearing the red, black and green colours of the new flag emerged from a hole with a teenage boy in Adidas tracksuit bottoms and a leather jacket. They were carrying a rusting sniper's rifle and the barrels of several Kalashnikovs.

'These might work for the revolutionaries,' said Abdalla Miloud al-Badrni, who was aged 46 (he insisted I check his ID to confirm the matter) and had signed up to the Lions of Tripoli, an important local brigade (he also showed me the paperwork concerning his membership). 'There is still a lot underneath there,' he said, pointing towards the Armageddon-like landscape at the bottom of the bunker. I wondered if 'a lot' included bodies as well as bullets; nobody seemed to be sure how many might have died at the bunker.

He and Mohamed Sadij, aged 19, held up their haul for inspection – they appeared particularly pleased with a relatively intact telescopic sight from a sniper's rifle. Mohamed said he was committed to working for the country as 'many of my friends died during the revolution'. They posed proudly for pictures and then Abdalla, who long ago served in the Libyan navy, said that the brigades needed more funding from the interim government. They would not need to be picking about the boulders if resources were better. He went on to complain about 'climbers', who had not been part of the revolutionary action against Gaddafi, yet who were finding themselves in prominent positions. Some of these 'climbers' had sneakily changed their colours to make their way in the new Libya, he believed. You don't find them scrabbling about Gaddafi's old bunker in search of spare parts, he commented acidly.

They clambered to their pick-up, and further on we came to a bullet mine: this was not your average day in the life of a tourist. At the top of a wide pit in the rubble, a man in a khaki jacket was making tea using a tin kettle held over a small charcoal fire, sheltering from a brisk wind behind sacks of shells. Few locals could believe how cold the winter had been. Below, men were scraping with picks and shovels, searching for good-quality bullet shells that might be recycled. Not far way, across the wasteland, an armoured vehicle lay crunched on one side. A Russian-made Grad multiple rocket launcher was half-submerged under a collapsed roof of a section of bunker that hung precariously above a column. There were openings to one side leading to more darkened tunnels.

Amid the crunch and scratch of the excavations, Ahmed Jrab stepped forward. He was aged 30 and was the bullet gang's leader. He explained that the copper they found was taken by road to Tunisia where it was sold to dealers who knew how to process the haul; apparently there were no scrap merchants who could handle the job, or pay well enough, in Libya. Each person in his seven-strong team was making about 60 dinars a day (£30), a decent wage.

It was dangerous work, however. The previous week a bullet-miner had lost 'half his face' when he struck live ammunition. Suddenly being in the Brother Leader's old bunker took on another dimension. We watched as a man at the head of the 'mine' struck downwards with his shovel. We winced. No explosion... that time.

Ahmed, who wore a camouflage hat and a dusty black tracksuit, was talkative. He explained that he began the war as one of Gaddafi's soldiers but changed sides when he was fighting near Masrata, as he no longer believed in the former dictator: 'I found a chance to switch, so I did. But they soon told me I was a traitor.'

'How on earth did they communicate that to you, surely you were on the other side of the battle line?'

'Well, they still had my mobile number: so they just phoned me to say so,' he replied simply. 'Then they went to my father's house in Tripoli and intimidated him.' A cloud passed over his face. He was angry, but held back his emotions.

His team of bullet-diggers worked from 8 a.m. to sunset, and they were free to roam across the bunker as they wished. Tripoli and much of Libya seemed to exist in a semi-parlous state in which order was just about maintained, though usual rules did not apply. The team had discovered a particularly good patch of shells, he said, one that would last a few days.

Then Ahmed showed us his war wounds. He had what looked like a scar across the back of his neck, from when an army bullet whistled past during an incident in which three of his rebel compatriots died. He was very lucky to be alive, he said. Altogether he had eight shrapnel or bullet-related wounds. He pulled up his shirt to show the thick circular scar of a bullet that entered his back.

Othman and I thanked Ahmed, shook hands and gingerly stepped across the bunker: crunch, crunch, crunch over bullets that had exploded out of boxes of Kalashnikov supplies. We soon bumped into Abdalla and Mohamed again, who were keen to show us something. We stumbled across boulders, traversing a crater full of the charred and twisted remains of dozens of useless Kalashnikovs, which looked like peculiar driftwood washed up on a beach. Then we arrived at a concrete overhang with one of the largest tunnels of the bunker beneath it. Abdalla shone a mobile phone's light into the darkened depths of Gaddafi's escape network.

So this was where the dictator had lurked. It was a fearful-looking place, and it was not one to hang about in. Who knew what might happen to the roof above.

'We hate Gaddafi,' said Abdalla. Those three words were a kind of mantra for the new Libya. 'We hate him because he spent so much money on arms. All that oil money wasted.' He said Gaddafi was the rat, as he is depicted in so many of the cartoons in Tripoli, not his subjects.

After passing through a corridor with a jungle of twisted wire and ammunition boxes that said they were loaded in the remote Russian port of Oktyabrsk on the River Volga, Othman and I made our way back up the ramp to the yard at the centre of the Bab Al-Azizia barracks. The clink and scrape of the unusual miners continued down below.

When we reached the top, Othman looked back at the scene and simply said: 'I never in my wildest dreams expected I would ever go here.'

Neither did I. And soon we were driving back across the vast litter-strewn yard, where flea markets were apparently held on Fridays, returning to the traffic-jam horns of Tripoli. 'GAME OVER GADDAFI' said graffiti on the wall of the compound. The words summed up his fate perfectly.

🐪 🐪 🐪

Othman parked by the arch of Marcus Aurelius, not far from the oil-company skyscrapers, and went to pray in a mosque. The arch, its stones looking a bit wobbly and grimy in the centre of a small square, is all of significance that remains of the classical Roman town of Oea. The rest had been built over for centuries, but the arch had survived and was the centre-point of the old town. For an hour or so I roamed about the neighbourhood, having arranged to meet Othman at a café at a certain time. Outside a hotel on one side of the square, I was surprised to find an American talking into a mobile phone by the entrance. He wore cowboy boots, was well over six feet and had a Texas drawl. 'Just callin' to see how y'all doin'' he was saying. He nodded at me as he did so. An oilman, I presumed.

A young guy wearing a camouflage jacket, a T-shirt and a bandana drove past in a shiny BMW. He was driving slowly and had one hand on the wheel and the window down. He wanted to be seen in his cool, expensive motor, which had been polished to perfection. Perhaps he was a member of the Zintan or Misrata brigade, going for a spin to show off his latest acquisition. He was in his teens, or just out of them, and it seemed unlikely that the car had been his before the revolution.

Using my guidebook's map, I walked up a muddy alley, passing the domes of the Gurgi mosque, where Othman was praying. After a short stroll – and being scowled at by a small elderly woman dressed in rags – I came to the old British consulate. The building dates from the 18th century when it was a residence of the dynasty that gave the United States so much trouble in the Barbary Wars. It was home to the British consulate from the mid 18th century until 1940 and was remarkable for the sign erected by Gaddafi's regime that was still on the façade. 'However, the so-called European geographical and explorative scientific expeditions into Africa, which were in essence and as a matter of fact intended to be colonial ones to occupy and colonise vital and strategic parts of Africa, embarked from this same building...' it ranted (though perhaps it had a point).

The doorway was open, and I stepped inside. No-one was around. A faded map of the Great Socialist People's Libyan Arab Jamahiriya hung on the wall next to an old tourist-board poster that said 'LIBYA... IS NEAR' and showed a beach. Short and to the point, I suppose. I left the consulate and ventured further into the alleyways. They smelt of burning rubbish. Another small elderly woman dressed in rags scowled at me. After a while I arrived at the medina, which sold anything and everything and twisted and turned in a labyrinth of lanes. In a section selling flamboyant fabrics and costumes decorated with golden swirls, a bald stallholder in a V-neck jumper introduced himself as Mohamed Bashir and told me: 'We never saw him in here.' He was referring to Gaddafi. 'But we saw his wife many times. She would come with a

lot of bodyguards and buy the traditional fabrics.' Sofia Gaddafi fled to
Algeria during the revolution.

I looked into a café named Caffe Casa in which non-alcoholic Holsten
beer was sold alongside KitKats, Red Bull and 'American doughnuts'. Reggae
music played. The café had free Wi-Fi and a no-smoking sign. It was as
Western as Tripoli got; we might have been in Manchester or Manhattan.
Outside, I walked down a crowded lane with stalls selling jewellery,
headscarves, silk negligees and Manchester United and Chelsea shirts. A
muezzin was repeatedly calling 'Allahu Akbar' ('God is the greatest') and
'La Ilaha Ella Allah' ('No God but one God').

The lane led to Martyrs' Square, where long shadows from the castle
spread out across the yellow criss-crosses of its concrete surface. A gazelle
was tied to a chaise longue near the fountain and you could sit and pay to
have your picture taken with the creature. I continued down Algeria Street in
the direction of the enormous dome of the Jamal Abdel Nasser Mosque. It
was on this street that Othman's boss had been shot dead. Not far from this
spot I found Fergiani's Bookshop.

Fergiani's had been the target of my walk – one of the few bookshops
in Tripoli. I entered the cramped, dusty space, and browsed the bright books
(many in English). I was looking for a copy of Gaddafi's *Green Book*, thinking
it would give me an insight into his crazed mind. I could not find one, so I
asked an assistant.

He wore a crumpled grey suit with a jumper and a loose tie. He looked
at me shiftily and sat still for a moment. Then he touched the side of his nose,
rose and shuffled to a back room, urging me to follow. He disappeared behind
some boxes, and emerged with a brown paper bag, through which I could see
the edge of a small green-coloured book.

'Seven dinar,' he said, which was about £3.50. I handed over some
crumpled notes (the one-dinar note had yet to be replaced and still depicted
Gaddafi). The assistant smiled thinly, explained that the 21,000-word book
was not officially forbidden although it was contentious to display. I took the

brown paper bag and went back to Martyrs' Square, where I discreetly read about parliaments having become 'a legal barrier between people and their right to exercise authority'.

Then I went to find Othman. It was hard not to reflect on how odd it seemed that the words of the former regime were being hidden in the back rooms of bookshops... just as so many other books had been during Gaddafi's day.

9

Benghazi, Cyrene and Qasr al-Haj:

Trouble and Tea

THE ELECTRICITY was off at Benghazi Airport. Our bags were heaved into the gloomy arrivals hall and placed on the stationary baggage carousel. The flight had taken just under an hour, after a wait at Tripoli's chokingly smoky domestic terminal. The Buraq Air plane had been cramped and we had sat behind a man listening to a loud and irritating audio version of an Arabic book (annoying to me but normal, it seemed, to everyone else). I had learnt from the in-flight magazine that Buraq was a mythical horse that flew through the air and transported the Prophet Muhammad between Mecca and Jerusalem on a famous 'Night Journey' that is described in the Koran. Othman had closed his eyes and nodded off (he was a master of the catnap). Applause had rippled when we landed.

The airport was festooned with new Libyan flags, and a large official poster outside the exit showed rebels beaming and making V-signs. Beneath the picture ran a message: 'MERCI LA FRANCE.' The words of thanks referred to the key role played by the French in the revolution, and they gave a first indication of the strong local pride that the rebellion against Gaddafi began in the east of Libya, where the atmosphere immediately seemed quite different.

France's part in the uprising was intriguing. The French, under the rule of then President Nicolas Sarkozy, had been the first country to recognise the legitimacy of the National Transitional Council, formed in Benghazi in March 2011 at a time when Gaddafi's forces were regrouping after the 'day of rage' of 17 February that led to Libya's second city being taken by the rebels. As the fledgling revolutionaries were short of firepower and lacking organisation, it seemed highly likely that Gaddafi's better-equipped troops would overwhelm them should they return.

The French act of recognising the Transitional Council had resulted in Britain and America following suit. There was a domino effect, and soon international awareness of the vulnerability of Libya's citizens brought about the United Nations Security Council resolution of 17 March, approving a no-fly zone over Libya and authorising 'all necessary measures to protect civilians'. The resolution had been introduced by the French foreign minister Alain Juppé, who said that 'the situation on the ground is more alarming than ever, marked by the violent reconquest of cities that have been released'. He described Libya as being part of 'a wave of great revolutions that would change the course of history... we have very little time left – only a matter of hours'. Just 48 hours later, French jets attacked Gaddafi's tanks, turning the fight in the rebels' favour.

The most extraordinary, and quite bizarre, aspect of the French intervention was the involvement of the 63-year-old French philosopher Bernard-Henri Lévy. The suave, wavy-haired Lévy had visited Benghazi on 5 March 2011, and assessed the dire situation in which the rebels found themselves. In rapid succession, he had talked to their leaders, telephoned his friend Sarkozy, arranged a meeting between the rebels and Sarkozy at the Elysée Palace, sorted out flights and set the wheels in motion for the UN resolution. It was a stunning piece of DIY diplomacy. BHL, as he is known in France, has since made a documentary film about what happened. The pictures show him in a crisp white Dior shirt unbuttoned to his chest (a style for which he is famous), cavorting with unshaven, battle-hardened revolutionaries wearing black berets and seeming utterly bemused by the debonair philosopher suddenly in their midst. His role in Gaddafi's downfall was very odd indeed.

So Benghazi's rebels had a right to celebrate. If it had not been for their actions, supported by the French, the 'mad dog' might still be in power.

But the country's second city did not only *feel* different to the west of the country – there was something earnest and down-to-earth in the official poster that expressed a deep civic pride – it physically *looked* so too. Although the airport terminal was neat and tidy, if a touch chaotic with the power cut, once we had passed the airport's roadside checkpoint, we were soon moving along squalid roads lined with rubbish. Stagnant water lay in filthy puddles near heaps of black bin-liners. Some of the waste was smouldering, sending up thin, vicious smoke. There was the occasional burnt-out vehicle. Rubble lay all about. The city seemed totally neglected to a level way beyond anything found in Tripoli (outside the compound at Gaddafi's old bunker).

This destitution was not just caused by the conflict: Gaddafi had for years favoured other parts of the country and regarded Benghazi as a hotbed of potential opposition. This mistrust had an historical basis as the city had shared capital status in Libya under King Idris before Gaddafi's *coup d'état* in 1969, when political power shifted to Tripoli. So there was a sense of separation and of having drawn the short straw under the Colonel. There was also a background of Islamic discontent in the 1980s. The historian Ronald Bruce St John points out that six alleged members of Islamic groups were executed in public in Benghazi in 1987, while the regime raided a Benghazi mosque in 1989 to close a section critical of Gaddafi's religious beliefs. Then there was the trouble in 2000 when fans of the local football team, Al Ahly Benghazi, burnt pictures of the Brother Leader and dressed a donkey in the football shirt of his much-hated son Saadi. Gaddafi wasn't at all happy about that and responded by bulldozing the team's ground.

The outcome was that Benghazi had been deliberately left to moulder. It had never received the public cash given to places such as Tripoli, Sirte (close to where the Brother Leader was brought up), and Bani Walid, another of his favoured conurbations. It was rundown and in a bad way: I could see as much within minutes of arriving.

🐪 🐪 🐪

Othman and I had met Zaki, the local contact for his tour company, who was driving us to his house via a short tour of the city. Once we arrived at his place, we were to borrow his car for a few days and continue further eastwards to Cyrene, the 'Athens of Africa', Libya's most complete ancient Greek city. Othman and Zaki were friends and had not seen each other since the revolution. Zaki was soon filling him in on what happened during the uprising. He spoke in Arabic and Othman kindly translated for me. So what I learnt of the early days of the revolution seemed to come in a series of Chinese whispers – with Zaki both speaking and driving fast, while skipping from event to event, and Othman trying to keep up. In snatches, I got a picture of what happened in the run-up to and during the 'day of rage'.

'On the first demonstration, some people were shot in front of me. I lost sight of my brother. I did not know where he was. I was worried about him, but I found him later,' said Zaki, who wore a burgundy and blue striped top and faded jeans. He held one hand on the wheel and was squeezed in to his seat. He was a large, jovial, jowly man in his late thirties.

He was referring to a demonstration on 16 February 2011 in which bullets had been fired to disperse the crowds. The protest had been sparked by the arrest of the human rights lawyer Fathi Terbil, who had represented the 1,270 people killed at Abu Salim prison in 1996.

The trouble continued. 'On the seventeenth, we gathered at five or six places to confuse the undercover security men. Then we went together outside the barracks of the most powerful army brigade. Elderly people went to the front. They wanted to fix the problem without trouble. But then people started throwing stones and petrol bombs,' he continued.

The army began to shoot live ammunition and the crowd scattered. Demonstrations went on and within three days more than three hundred protesters had died. There was great frustration. But on 20 February a breakthrough came. 'A man filled his car with dynamite. He said: "I am going to die to sacrifice myself." He drove at 130 kilometres per hour into the gate. They were shooting at him and the car exploded,' Zaki explained. The man's name was Mahdi Ziu, a manager at the Arabian Gulf Oil Company. His brave sacrifice worked, creating a hole in the wall and allowing the protesters to take the compound.

After crossing a flyover and a bridge, we drove along more desolate streets. A smoke haze of burning rubbish filled the air. Empty expanses of muddy, litter-strewn land spread out in front of ugly concrete apartment blocks. Along the streets I saw repeated pictures of a grey-haired man; I thought he must have been a local hero in the resistance. He *was* a local hero, explained Othman, but from a much earlier campaign of civil unrest: Umar al-Mukhtar, the talismanic leader of a guerrilla group that fought against Italian occupation. In 1931, after much success, he was eventually captured and hanged in front of around twenty thousand Libyan witnesses.

Further on we arrived at the barracks where the main demonstration had been held in February 2011. We went to where the car had exploded – this was another unusual day's tourism – and then Zaki calmly steered through the gate. Inside, a man wearing a red headscarf, desert-coloured trousers and an ill-fitting camouflage jacket gazed our way. He carried a rifle and stood near a pick-up truck with an anti-aircraft gun that was parked by a pistachio-coloured building with burnt-out windows. He was elderly and wiry; a modern-day al-Mukhtar who had taken on the regime and won. Zaki exchanged a few words and the rebel smiled.

'I didn't even dare to speak to a soldier before the revolution,' he said. 'Now I just laugh with them.'

For some time during the demonstrations, he said, Saadi Gaddafi had been in the compound. He had been ill-advisedly sent to talk to locals to try and calm down the situation. It had unsurprisingly had the opposite effect and Saadi had fled before 20 February, narrowly escaping with his life. After the army was driven out, the city was spared its return by the NATO strikes of 19 March 2011. Zaki said that there had been a time during the revolution when he feared that the country would split into two states: one run by the rebels in the east and the other in the west under Gaddafi's continuing control.

NATO's ongoing intervention combined with the uprising in the west in the key city of Misrata had prevented the country dividing, he believed.

During the revolution, Zaki said that he had helped protect members of his family in his neighbourhood. They had feared a 'fifth line' of Gaddafi infiltrators harming innocent people.

He paused and drummed his fingers on the wheel as though deep in thought. Zaki began to explain local anger at the Gaddafi regime: 'There was much unemployment. Loans for developing cities mainly went to Tripoli. Benghazi was ignored… forgotten!'

We passed a series of large well-to-do houses. Zaki pointed at them. 'You see these: we call them the thieves.' Anyone with that much money, he implied, must have been corrupt. He paused once more and added ruefully: 'But you could never really feel rich under Gaddafi. He could take you down at any time.'

Near Zaki's home, posters depicted young men: martyrs from the revolution. One of the pictures contained the message: 'WE HAVE A DREAM.' The eyes of the martyrs seemed by turns defiant, hollow, scared, lost and hopeful. I thought of the families of the deceased and the grief so many people must be going through. Gaddafi may have gone, but his unhappy legacy remained.

By one of the posters, Zaki left us in a muddy side street, after handing Othman the keys to his car. Othman took the wheel. He put on his aviator glasses and we drove eastwards, feeling a sense of freedom as we left behind the stench, sadness and disarray of Benghazi.

🐫 🐫 🐫

It did not last long. On the outskirts of Benghazi, we came to a checkpoint and were about to roll past as usual, but this time our smiles were met by tight, unfriendly faces. A short man wearing a studded belt stared hard at us, without a flicker of friendliness as we grinned inanely, hoping to appear relaxed. It was clear he did not like the look of us. We were waved over to one side, where we parked facing a pile of old tyres and plastic bottles strewn in an empty lot. The rebel came to Othman's window and leaned in, eyeballing us and saying nothing. I caught the shine of a pair of handcuffs connected to his belt. His jacket had been sliced off at the arms and he had a wispy beard. Another small, expressionless man appeared and peered in wordlessly. The first man said something and Othman calmly handed over some papers. The pair disappeared and Othman watched them nervously in the rear-view mirror.

'This was how the system was before the revolution,' he said. 'They asked me who you were and said that tourism is not happening now.'

The men returned and asked Othman to go with them to talk to a supervisor. He was with them for a few minutes. I stared across towards the old tyres and on one occasion turned round to see what was happening. As I did so, I noticed that one of a group of four men with Othman was staring intently in my direction. It was off-putting, but I assumed that everything would be OK. After all, we were just going to see some old Greek stones on a hill overlooking the sea. Surely there was no harm in that.

I phased out for a while awaiting Othman's return. The car door opened and I turned. But it was not Othman. A man wearing khaki trousers, jackboots, shades and a sky-blue Lacoste shirt with the collar up sat down in the driver's seat. He had a five-day beard and greasy curly hair. He smirked and did not look at me.

It was then that I noticed that the car key had been left in the ignition. The man shut the door and turned on the engine. Sounding terribly British, I said: 'Excuse me… This car belongs to my guide – the man over there.' Or something along those lines.

'No inglese,' he replied.

He turned the car and drove towards the checkpoint rope on the road, close to where Othman was standing. I assumed he was just bringing the car round and perhaps fancied seeing how it handled. But he was not testing the vehicle. He was soon driving past Othman and on to the road in the direction of Benghazi. I won't pretend otherwise – I began to get very worried, very quickly. I pulled out my passport from my jeans pocket (where I had kept it for my entire time in Libya, as it felt like a place where you always needed your ID). I showed him the passport and I said: 'English! NATO! English! We helped you!' Or something like that.

'No inglese,' he answered.

He smirked once again. He pulled away from the checkpoint. Was he just messing around? No. He kept going. He faced straight ahead, refusing to look me in the eyes. He made a show of turning on the radio loudly. We began to move very fast. We switched on to a road heading inland and were soon going at 150 kilometres per hour.

This was when I began to panic and wonder whether the whole trip to Libya had been a dreadful mistake. I was being driven in a car at high speed in the direction of the Libyan desert by a man I did not know wearing a gangland-style outfit. I was in a part of the country known to contain Islamic extremists. This man did not look like an extreme Islamist – he seemed Western-leaning in his appearance – but I was no expert in local extreme-Islamist dress sense. I called Othman on my mobile. His phone rang in his jacket on the back seat. The driver smiled to himself. A tinny pop song was playing at great volume on the radio. For a split second I considered tackling the driver – it was a very strong impulse. But that would have just resulted in an almighty crash.

We were overtaken by a red pick-up truck with an anti-aircraft gun and a sickle and a star painted on the back. It settled in front, as though acting as an escort. We were still travelling at 150 kilometres per hour. I was now extremely worried, wondering what to do. So this is what it's like to be abducted, I thought. I imagined a windowless room in a house in the middle of nowhere. I raced through the implications, what this might mean to those close to me (and to the various authorities).

I felt sick and began to think rapidly about what I could do. We had been going down a long straight road for 15 minutes. As we turned at a roundabout on to another road, I called my London contact, who had put me in touch with Othman's tour company. Remarkably there was a strong phone signal and the driver did not seem to mind my making a call. I got through to Craig and began to explain the 'situation' as plainly as I could. As I did so we arrived at a compound with a series of buildings that might have once been a school. The new Libyan flag covered the walls, along with a cartoon of Gaddafi and Seif al Islam with nooses round their necks. Standing in front of the building I recognised Zaki. I had never been quite so relieved to see a familiar face. He wore a black suit – he looked like an undertaker – but was smiling cheerfully. We parked and Othman got out of the red pick-up in front. I had thought he was back at the checkpoint. Again, I was incredibly relieved. Othman had apparently called Zaki from one of the rebels' mobile phones. I told Craig that all seemed to be alright and that I would phone him back to let him know what happened.

We were taken to a cold room with a desk. I was made to sit on a leather swivel chair with wood exposed on its arms; it was as though nervous interviewees had worn away the leather. Othman and Zaki, both clearly anxious though pretending not to be, were on wooden chairs to one side. My driver had disappeared (there was no doubt in my mind that he had been acting oddly on purpose, playing a game with me). Another man in khaki trousers sat behind the desk, which had a laptop on its surface. He had demanded Othman and Zaki's driving documents. It turned out that Othman did not have the correct paperwork to drive Zaki's car and they thought he had stolen it. Their suspicions were raised when they saw that Othman was from Bani Walid, the former Gaddafi stronghold. Add in a foreigner who claimed to be a 'tourist' and they had decided it was all too suspect.

We were moved to another room to await the arrival of the commander of the brigade. We sat on a grimy sofa and smiled at anyone who came in to see us. I don't think I've ever been quite so polite in my life. One by one, lads from the brigade stopped by the office; we obviously made a curious 'catch'. The small grubby room had a picture of hands held together in unity and 'GAME OVER... FREE LIBYA!' behind a desk. A grey safe sat in a corner with a live round of ammunition propped on top. The commander did not appear for a long time. A friendly rebel entered and I showed him pictures on my camera of Leptis Magna and of the big poster of Mohamed Bouazizi back in Sidi Bouzid. He seemed to like this and brought in another rebel to see the shots. After a while, they left and the brigade got used to our presence. We walked out into the yard, where Zaki smoked a cigarette. Nobody minded. The sound of a sports event on a radio drifted from one of the windows. Guys were playing table tennis in an old garage, letting out yells of joy and cries of despair.

Eventually, after about two hours, a large red pick-up truck with streaks of yellow 'lightning' arrived. The commander jumped out. He was jockey-sized with short dreadlocks and startling amber eyes. He wore a large signet ring with a stone that strangely matched his eyes. Although small in physique, he looked tough – as though he had been through quite a few scrapes and more than knew how to handle himself. We stood on a cracked pavement near the Gaddafi cartoons and Zaki urgently showed him the car documents, smiling all along. The commander asked about me, without glancing in my direction. I handed my passport to Zaki, who showed him the page with my Libyan visa. A couple of rebels joined us: they looked like inner-city gang members, with long curly hair, sports tops and bandanas. An ambulance raced past the front entrance of the compound at high speed. All three turned alertly and watched it go, as if ready to spring into action. But they stayed still. The commander seemed satisfied with our documents. He shook our hands. He quietly said 'sorry' to me – and that was all. We were free to go.

All three of us were dazed. As we drove away, Othman told me that we would be staying overnight in Benghazi now, as it was too dangerous to drive on in darkness to Cyrene. We went to a lawyer's office to have a legal paper printed in Othman's name for the car. Then Othman lost his ID. He looked everywhere in the car and we ended up driving *back* to the brigade compound and searching the ground for his ID, as without it he, and we, could go nowhere. We felt at the point of disaster, but then Othman, looking very sheepish, found his ID in his coat pocket. We were not having the best of days.

Othman and I were drained – I had not eaten since breakfast – but we stopped briefly at the Benghazi War Cemetery on the way to find a hotel. This is where 1,214 Commonwealth servicemen who died during World War II are buried; of whom 1,051 are identified casualties. Among those buried is Geoffrey Keyes, who was the youngest lieutenant colonel in the British Army when he died aged 24 during Operation Flipper. He was posthumously awarded the Victoria Cross for his daring raid in November 1941 on what was believed to have been Rommel's headquarters, 250 miles behind enemy lines.

The cemetery is maintained by the Commonwealth War Graves Commission and is a wonderfully restful, contemplative place, surrounded by eucalyptus trees. I squatted by the grave of J R Kerr, a wireless operator/air gunner from the Royal Air Force, who died on 2 June 1944. No age was given. Then I walked around the cemetery, enjoying the last of the day's sunshine as I stepped over the cracked red earth, thinking over the day's events. It had been madness, but we had got through it, and all was well.

We went to an incredibly cold restaurant by the harbour, where we ate a fish dinner under harsh neon lights. We were both starving, Othman deliberately so as it was a Thursday: he had been fasting during the day in line with Islamic practice (which I'd never heard of before). Then we checked into the Benghazi Hotel.

I will never forget the Benghazi Hotel. It was just about the worst in which I have ever stayed. My room on the fifth floor was freezing and smelt strongly of BO. Wind rattled on a balcony door that did not shut properly. Footsteps echoed in the hall. Doors clanged violently. There was no toilet paper. I went to fetch some from the reception and waited for 20 minutes as phone calls were made by a receptionist with dead eyes. In order to find a toilet roll, another zombie of a man was sent to check in all the empty rooms to find one. I heard him shuffling and clattering on the floors above, doors banging. The hotel had just about run out of toilet rolls, it seemed. I looked at an old black and white picture of Umar al-Mukhtar that hung on the wall in the reception. It showed his shrivelled figure being led through a crowd by Italian officials after his capture in 1931. A toilet roll was located. I went to my miserable room and collapsed on the single bed. I suddenly felt terrible, as though my immune system had collapsed. I began to alternate between sweating and shivering. I was violently ill. I took some paracetamol, but they had little effect. It was as though my body had shut down after the sheer intensity of the day. During that drive from the checkpoint with the smirking 'hijacker', I must have tipped over into a state of shock, with which I was only just coming to terms. It was a fitful, restless night.

🐪 🐪 🐪

The next day being Friday, the Muslim day of prayer, we moved off early before the checkpoint at which we had been stopped yesterday was properly manned. I had been in two minds about calling off the trip to Cyrene and returning to Tripoli but reasoned that with the new car document we should be fine. I also felt absolutely terrible and just wanted a simple day – no calamities, no tension, no tearing up of plans, just calm, calm, calm.

From Benghazi to Cyrene is over 200 kilometres, about a three-hour drive. The road takes you through the Green Mountains, where Umar al-Mukhtar hid out during his guerrilla campaign against the Italians. Stalls sold honey by the side of the road, its golden glow suggestive of a rich, fertile land. Bridges crossed great valleys. We skirted Al Bayda, where the Libyan revolution could be said to have started, having been taken by the rebels so early on 18 February 2011. Al Bayda was the hometown of Sofia Gaddafi, so that day would have struck directly into the heart of the Gaddafi family.

Down a lane lined with yellow gorse, we arrived at Cyrene, where I was again met by a local guide who was to take me around the UNESCO World Heritage Site. Cyrene is on a hill a few kilometres inland from the sea and dates from the early 7th century BC when settlers arrived by boat from Thera, modern-day Santorini, because their island in the Aegean Sea was overcrowded. The result was one of the finest city-states in the Hellenistic world, considered by some to be the pre-eminent Greek city during the 4th century BC. For a period it was under the rule of Alexander the Great. When the Greek empire began to crumble, the Egyptians and then the Romans took over.

I was still in an abysmal state, as ill as I could remember being for a long time. My muscles ached and I felt like neither eating nor drinking. I had had nothing all day. Abdul Rahim, my guide, was short and bursting with energy. It was embarrassing not to be able to match his enthusiasm.

'It really is a long time since I was with a tourist!' he pronounced theatrically. He was given to flamboyant statements. 'I have almost forgotten what it is like to walk around Cyrene with a tourist!'

I smiled wanly and we began a tour of the site under a milk-grey sky. Yet again it was very cold. Within a few paces we arrived at a Hellenistic gymnasium that is said to be better than the one at Olympia. The large rectangular space was surrounded by Ionic columns and you could get a sense of how athletes would have run around the perimeter. Three locals from Benghazi were in the gymnasium. They came over and asked Abdul to take a picture of us together. He did so and they talked about being proud to be from the east of Libya, where the revolution started.

After they left, Abdul turned to me and said: 'That was very strange.'

'What was?' I asked.

'You see when Gaddafi was in charge, the whole of Libya was like a big prison. You could not speak against him. And you would never have your picture taken with another person,' he replied.

'Why?'

'Because if you had a picture taken with someone who was found to be an enemy of the regime, you could be in big trouble. You could be seen as a collaborator,' Abdul said. 'A picture with a Westerner, that could cause you trouble as well. You might have to explain yourself. The stakes were high. If you were ever taken as a political prisoner, nobody would speak to you for three to five years afterwards. It was too dangerous. You had to be very careful.'

We shuffled around the remains, which ramble over a wide and prominent space on the windy hilltop, looking down across a valley to the sea. After leaving the gymnasium, we walked along long tall walls, where I learnt from Abdul that Cyrene was famous during ancient Greek times for its harvest of silphium, a now extinct plant that was said to be a contraceptive. I discovered that Alexander the Great was given a four-horse chariot by the people of Cyrene, the first he had ever ridden on. I was told that the word 'Libya' was used by the Greeks to refer to North Africa, although the name came from an ancient Berber tribe. I found out that a legendary dispute about the whereabouts of the border of influence between Cyrenica and Carthage was settled by two pairs of runners setting off along the North African coast from each capital to decide the matter. Where they met would mark the dividing line – which ended up being close to Sirte – but the Greeks accused the Carthaginian runners, who were brothers, of cheating as they had travelled so far. To prove their honesty the brothers offered to be buried alive at the spot (which seemed quite a harsh way of settling matters). This point, known as the Altars of Phillaeni after the Carthaginian brothers, is still regarded as the unofficial border between the regions of Cyrenaica and Tripolitania. The Romans had once built columns to celebrate the spot and Mussolini had erected a grand archway – which British soldiers during World War II had referred to as 'Marble Arch'. The Roman pillars and the Italian monument have since been destroyed.

We walked round a big marketplace of weather-worn rocks and jagged pillars – the occasional torso poked up looking spectral, and there was one wall with the word 'Libya' inscribed in Greek. It was one of the earliest instances of the country's name in writing. Down a steep rocky road, with gaping catacombs to our right looking like blots of ink on a hillside, we came to the Fountain of Apollo. We were at the bottom of a cliff, with the marketplace above. Water from a spring rushed from the mountain and trickled down clever irrigation channels to another section of the city with foundation stones and walls of houses and baths. I asked Abdul if Gaddafi ever visited Cyrene.

'Never!' he exclaimed. He was still bounding with bonhomie. I was still barely able to take in the wonderful site.

'Did Gaddafi care about Cyrene?' I asked, having a good guess as to the answer.

'Never!' he repeated. 'Mussolini came! He stayed over there!' He pointed at a house with a terracotta roof across a valley. 'Never Gaddafi! Never! Never!'

The sound of a muezzin calling prayers filtered from behind some trees. From the top of Cyrene we looked down to the hazy coast. Abdul pointed in the direction of Apollonia, the former port of Cyrene, way down below on the coast. Next door to the site was Susa, where I was staying the night. From the top of Cyrene, you could understand why the Greeks came here: it felt like a position of total dominance, with sweeping views along the Mediterranean. Up on the hill, the Greeks must have seen their enemies coming from miles away.

🐫 🐫 🐫

After having a cup of tea at a café with the fabulous view – the tea given free by the friendly café owner who was amazed to see a Western tourist – I thanked Abdul and apologised for being in a bad way. I still did not feel up to eating anything solid and could hardly drink the tea. We were soon in Susa, where we checked into the Al-Manara Hotel. I collapsed for a few hours and then went for a walk around the quiet town in search of a pharmacy. Rows of pictures of local martyrs lined the empty streets near a square where men were playing chess by a café. Beside the café was a crumbling pink-and-white building from the Italian era. This was where Umar al-Mukhtar had been held on the first night of his capture.

I found a pharmacy and somehow communicated my need for the right drugs. Outside, I wandered up a hill, passing an empty lot with the scorched remains of a BMW; perhaps a car that had belonged to a Gaddafi sympathiser. I came to a ramshackle grocery shop and went in to buy a drink to wash down the pills. The Diet 7UP tasted so good I bought a couple more cans – it seemed to be all my body could handle. Near a sign saying 'FREEDOM FOR LIBYANS', a man was selling fish from a crate of ice attached to the back of a dented bicycle. A mechanic in blackened overalls peered out of an oily workshop. A group of small curious children followed me for a while; a Westerner stood out in Susa (as everywhere in Libya). Down by the harbour, I walked to the end of the sea wall, near a small wooden fishing boat. From the wall I could see the Greek columns rising from the rocky site of Apollonia, which was laid out along the jagged coast for almost a kilometre along a narrow strip of land. The entrance was just a few metres from the hotel.

Feeling marginally better, I went to investigate. There was nobody on the gate. A couple of empty bullet shells lay on the path. In a bit of a daze from drugs and Diet 7UP, I continued onwards, arriving at the peach-stone remains of a Byzantine church. Sheep were wandering about the Corinthian columns, as though on a family outing, lambs hopping along at the back to keep up.

I kept going, examining a partially excavated acropolis on a hilltop and arriving at a Greek theatre, near cliffs dropping sharply into the sea. I sat down on Byzantine stone and closed my eyes. The sun had come out and it was a peaceful spot. I had no thoughts. I was just pleased to feel a little improved. It was a good place to think about absolutely nothing; I was enjoying the sense of solitude. After a while, though, I thought I heard faint voices. I assumed it was just the wind playing tricks with me. But then I definitely did hear

somebody. A voice somewhere close by was talking about 'the Desert Rats…
oh yes, her father served with the Desert Rats'.

This was how I met Steve Hamilton, a 'battlefield guide' working for
Western Desert Battlefield Tours and originally from Burton-upon-Trent in
Staffordshire, and Matthew Arnold, a photographer from New York (not the
19th-century poet). They were in Libya to photograph World War II battle
sites, but dropped in at Apollonia as they were passing. They were pleased to
have gone to Cyrene one day before me, so they could say they were the first
tourists back after the revolution.

'Burnt meat!' said Steve, on ascertaining my condition. 'Burnt meat!
That's the most likely cause, burnt meat!'

He was a bundle of energy and information, wearing camouflage trousers
and smoking a Marlboro Red cigarette. Matthew Arnold was a laid-back
customer with a quizzical expression and a giant camera worth more than
£10,000 (he told me when I asked). He had taken around five thousand
pictures and said he would probably take as many again; they were in the
country for three weeks.

'Driving through minefields in a sandstorm!' said Steve. 'That's what
we've been doing!'

'Luckily there are tracks. People haven't been blown up yet,' added
Matthew, who spotted the sheep and rushed over to capture them.

Steve specialised in taking groups to battle sites in the desert; he had
been on more than a hundred trips and had written a book about the 50th
Royal Tank Regiment in which his grandfather had served. 'That's what I
do – I often take people with family connections to the Desert Rats,' he said.
'People lay wreaths at El Alamein [in Egypt].'

They had a driver-guide 'with connections', who had been looking after
them, and had had no trouble so far. 'It took us about a minute to get into
Libya,' he said. They had crossed at the Egyptian border without hassle. Steve
looked over towards Matthew. He had begun climbing rocks near the Greek
theatre. Steve headed off in his direction to see where his photographer was

going. 'Burnt meat!' he said as he parted. 'Watch out for burnt meat!' And he was gone.

🐪 🐪 🐪

I took a day off. No movement – I was still feeling queasy. No checkpoints. No smirking militiamen. No history. No guides. I confined myself to the lounge of the Al-Manara Hotel, reading a novel and making nodding acquaintance with a tiny, eccentric octogenarian woman who lived next door to the hotel and occasionally dropped by and beamed at me.

The next day, I was a lot less ill. We took it easy, stopping just a couple of times on our way back to Benghazi. The first time was at a small site known as Qasr Libya, with two Byzantine churches that were discovered in 1957. There was a museum full of beautiful mosaics, but the curator had welded the door shut during the revolution to prevent looting, so we could not enter. We looked inside a dusty cross-shaped church. And then we drove onwards down a bumpy dirt track to the ruined Roman city of Tolmeita, which once boasted the largest cisterns in North Africa (and not a lot of people know that). At Tolmeita goats crossed our path as we were making our way back to the car, and Othman seemed to attempt to convert me to Islam.

'You see those goats?' he asked.

I said I did see the goats.

'They are just creatures. They live and they die, just as we live and die. We are just creatures, too. In the Koran it says we should all pray to God. Yes, there are the goats, the birds, the mountains, the desert, the sea. But man was chosen by God to have a brain so he could pray to him. When you stop and think: who gives us this life? All the blood going around the body: how does it work? Why do we live and die? When you look at how beautiful the world is and think about life, it brings you closer to God.'

We stared at the goats for a while. I don't think Othman expected me to convert there and then.

Back in Benghazi we met Zaki at Tahrir Square; no trouble at checkpoints along the way. It may have been less famous than its Egyptian counterpart, but Benghazi's Tahrir Square was a hive of activity. People were constructing a stage with a poster like the one at the airport that said 'WE HAVE A DREAM' and showed rebels punching the air. It was six days before the anniversary of 17 February 2011, and a celebration was planned. A wall of a building on one side was covered in pictures of martyrs. A giant version of the new Libyan tricolour had been daubed on another wall.

Close to Tahrir Square, an enterprising artist had created a mini-sculpture park in front of an old municipal building using pieces of old guns, soldiers' helmets and tanks. The helmets had strange faces drilled into them and hung on a long rack, while fragments of anti-aircraft guns had been turned into peculiar dinosaurs. An effigy of Gaddafi was locked in a cage on one side of the front yard. Inside the municipal building, bullet shells had been twisted into insects and crocodiles. A carpet with a picture of Gaddafi lay in the middle of the hall, and each visitor was invited to wipe their shoes on the face of the former dictator. The artist's name was Ali Elwakwak. He had long grey hair and ushered me around. 'I have five hundred pieces!' he exclaimed. 'I take these pieces to Italy, Rome, Canada, America!' The rusty old bullets and tank parts were about to go on an unlikely world tour.

🐪 🐪 🐪

We flew back to Tripoli, arriving at night and driving across the city in darkness for the first time. The checkpoints were sinister, with barrels alight and thick black smoke rising. The receptionist at the Al-Kindi Hotel met me with a flourish of 'Welcome back, Mr Thomas! What is the weather like in Britain today, Mr Thomas? You are Mr Thomas?' Guns echoed in the darkness. I felt as though I was returning home, but it was my final night in Libya. I was flying back to Europe the following day and then on to Cairo. I had been unsure about crossing the border from Libya into Egypt and this seemed the best way, despite what Steve had said.

On the final morning, Othman and I drove towards the Nafusa

mountains past burnt-out tanks on the way to Qasr al-Haj, a wonderful Berber castle made from mud and stone that dates from the 12th century and was used by locals to store grain in a series of more than a hundred rooms. The castle was circular, with uneven walls around a central courtyard consisting of a gritty sand floor. Windows in the walls gaped open without glass, each slightly imperfect, elongated into oval shapes that reminded me of the mouth of the screaming character from Edvard Munch's artwork. It was otherworldly. And it was African. Keep going south from Qasr al-Haj and the Sahara and desert ways of life would soon take over. Timbuktu and peculiar tribal cultures in the sand awaited. But I was not about to travel to those parts… maybe some other time.

I sat on a Berber ledge and blinked in wonder at the unusual places I was seeing and the indelible experiences I was living through on my journey across the Arab Spring. This was our last tourist site, close to the town of Zintan that was such an important centre of resistance during the revolution. During the drive earlier, we had passed through a place that once had a temperature of 57.8°C, the Libyan and world record, but it was not much above zero up in the mountains, where there had been snow the previous week. It was cold, isolated, windswept, strange and silent. It felt as though we had stepped into a long-gone age hidden in forgotten folds in the Libyan hills.

A Berber family who had got wind of outsiders in town invited us to share some tea at their house. We soon found ourselves sitting on orange cushions in a room with shuttered windows and an open door in a simple dwelling down a narrow dirt lane. They were Sacin, Khalid and Muammar.

'Usually we do not give names as it is too dangerous,' said Muammar, who was in his seventies. 'During Gaddafi we could not talk to you.'

And then they talked… and talked. Over the next hour they unleashed a barrage of criticism of their ex-leader. The Lockerbie bombing ('Why? And all that compensation.'), the war with Chad ('a waste'), Yvonne Fletcher ('killing the British policewoman was crazy'), the country's oil ('Where has the money gone?'), the thwarted return attack on Benghazi after the revolution began ('a crime'). NATO and President Sarkozy were praised. It was as though they were getting it all off their chests; making up for lost time; letting out a long collective sigh. Sunlight shone through the open door as Gaddafi got a roasting. I sat and listened. They were enjoying letting themselves go.

This was what the revolution was all about, I thought to myself: the end of injustice (or so everyone hoped), with the chance to say what was on your mind. And they certainly had a lot to say.

Afterwards, Othman and I drove to Tripoli Airport, where we shook hands and promised to keep in touch. One way or another we had been through a lot together. I entered the ever-smoky terminal. The clock on the departure board told the wrong time and the shops inside were closed. I headed for my Alitalia plane to Rome, ready for further adventure in my third North African country that had just experienced an uprising. I was slowly but surely making my way to the edge of the Middle East.

Note: About three weeks after I visited the Benghazi War Cemetery, a mob systematically desecrated many of the headstones, damaging the graves of more than 150 British servicemen. Hammers were used to smash the headstones and destroy a cross. The group responsible filmed their actions and said of the servicemen: 'They are dogs, they are dogs.' The Commonwealth War Graves Commission promised to carry out repairs and replace stones where needed. It was terrible to think of such a peaceful place being vandalised. Then in June 2012, three months after my tour, extremist militants attacked a British Embassy convoy in Benghazi, injuring two British bodyguards with a rocket-propelled grenade. The ambassador, Dominic Asquith, was unhurt. At around the same time, a bomb exploded near the city's US Consulate, injuring no-one. Later on, the US ambassador to Libya, Christopher Stevens, and three other Americans were killed in an attack at the consulate in September 2012 that had been sparked by a tacky film made in America entitled *Innocence of*

Muslims, which insulted the Islamic faith. President Obama condemned the attack and said 'Chris was a courageous and exemplary representative of the United States'.

Meanwhile, in June 2012 Tripoli Airport was taken for several hours by a brigade from Tarhuna, 65 kilometres south of the capital, who were protesting about the arrest of their commander. They had simply driven on to the runway in a convoy of vehicles and begun firing in the air in front of planes; an Alitalia plane (possibly the one I'd flown back on) had been damaged by a bullet. The brigade was placated by promises from the leadership of the National Transitional Council. But these five incidents highlighted the continuing volatility of the country. Apart from our nerve-racking 'car document' fiasco, I had no trouble on the journey, though I had taken Othman's 'be careful' manifesto to heart and we were very cautious. Even so, had the attacks happened before my journey – just as with the reporters who were held hostage in Tripoli after my visit – I would not have travelled.

The elections in July 2012 brought a victory for the centrist National Forces Alliance led by the moderate, secularist Mahmoud Jibril, who had been involved before the uprising in a project called Libyan Vision to establish a democratic state in Libya. They gained 39 out of 80 seats reserved for political parties, while the Muslim Brotherhood-affiliated Justice and Construction party mustered just 17. The first fully free parliamentary election in Libya since 1952 went peacefully, though there was much wrangling over control of the parliament and who should stand in the cabinet. After this election, in August 2012, a vote was held in the General National Congress for a new president, and Mohamed Magariaf, a moderate on good terms with the Muslim Brotherhood, was made president. He had been opposed to Gaddafi and had spent most of the previous 30 years in exile in the United States.

10

Cairo:

Salafists on Tahrir Square

ON THE plane into Cairo a Welshman and a Cockney in the row behind me were exchanging gossip. They worked as security guards on cargo ships and were about to join vessels heading from the Suez Canal southwards towards the Gulf of Aden. They had just met and were talking loudly. The Welshman had served in the Royal Navy for 24 years, part of the time as a clearance diver (clearing underwater obstructions with explosives), and the Cockney in the British Army for seven. They were dismissive of Filipino crews, who they regarded as 'not hardened enough' though they were 'a good laugh'. They discussed semi-automatic weapons, ''elicopter jobs', and cabins with showers and Wi-Fi.

'You know it's all kicking off on the other side of Africa now,' said the Welshman. He was referring to piracy.

'Whereabouts?' asked the Cockney.

'Gabon, Togo, Ghana, Sierra Leone,' the Welshman replied. 'The ship people are ****ing themselves.'

They really were making a racket. My neighbour, an American woman named Sabrina from Virginia, nudged me and whispered: 'I'm trying to take a nap but I can't, they just keep on going.'

The pair had turned to the qualities of colleagues they had both worked with, who were invariably either 'good lads' or ''orrible lads'. It was hard being with some people for three months on a boat, the Cockney commented. Sabrina and I could just imagine.

She gave me a piece of tangerine gum. She was going to meet friends in Alexandria, on the Mediterranean coast. She had been amazed by last year's revolution, which had seen the former President Hosni Mubarak ousted from power on 11 February 2011 after an uprising that lasted 18 days. He had been in control of the country with the largest Arab population (82.5 million people) for almost thirty years. Sabrina was keen to find out about what happened by talking to her friends, who lived in the city that might be said to be the birthplace of Egypt's upheaval.

For it was in Alexandria that Khaled Said, a 28-year-old businessman, was beaten to death in police custody in June 2010, setting off a chain of events that ultimately led to the removal of Mubarak.

The scene initially had not raised much of an eyebrow – police heavy-handedness was par for the course under Mubarak. Locals in a café had watched on as the young man was frogmarched away by undercover officers. Eyewitnesses said that he was taken from the café into the doorway of a building on the opposite side of the street. So much so normal, maybe he was receiving a warning for something that he may or may not have done, or was being questioned about something he may or may not know about. Indiscriminate hassle from the authorities was part of everyday life. But this was more than an exchange of words. A violent attack took place inside the doorway; it is believed, though no-one is entirely certain, that the police were angry about a video Khaled is said to have posted on a website showing officers sharing out money confiscated during a drugs bust. Whatever the reason, after a delay of some minutes, people near the café saw his lifeless form being removed. By this time many officers had gathered and one of Khaled's brothers had arrived in the street. The brother followed the ambulance to the morgue where he was refused entry to see Khaled. But he returned in the middle of the night, when the morgue was unguarded, located the corpse and took pictures of his shocking find: the smashed-up, ruined features of his younger brother.

This image was posted on the internet. The picture spread. Protests followed in the days and weeks to come in Alexandria and Cairo. The two main policemen involved were detained and put on trial, but the case was postponed for mysterious bureaucratic reasons. Much of the outcry arose as a result of internet campaigns to bring awareness of Khaled's killing. The most effective of these began soon after his death on 6 June and was created by a 29-year-old Egyptian Google employee named Wael Ghonim, who was living in Dubai and who was deeply moved by Khaled's death. He created a page on Facebook displaying two pictures of Khaled: one of the bright young man before the beating, the other of his terribly mangled face in the morgue. He entitled the page 'We Are All Khaled Said' and began a dialogue with his followers calling for justice for Khaled and for an end to police ill-treatment. His first post said: 'Today they killed Khaled. If I don't act for his sake, tomorrow they will kill me.' Within the first day he had 36,000 followers and the number continued to rise rapidly. From 2004 to 2008 the number of people with internet access in Egypt had risen from 1.5 million to 13.6 million, and Ghonim's message struck a chord.

Ghonim remained anonymous throughout the campaign, though he has subsequently written about the period in his book entitled *Revolution 2.0*, published in January 2012. Through his Facebook page, he arranged for 'Silent Stands' of protesters in Alexandria and Cairo in the months following Khaled's death. The people who took part were extremely brave as the Ministry of the Interior began scouring the Facebook page in search of names. Encouraged by his success in creating a stir, Ghonim soon realised that he might be able to organise larger demonstrations. He returned to Egypt from Dubai to co-ordinate opposition to Mubarak's regime. And when his website announced a rally in Cairo's Tahrir Square on 25 January 2011, more than 50,000 turned up. It was a landmark day.

It was not only the police brutality that angered people, there was also a sense of injustice that Mubarak was letting such crimes go unpunished while at the same time ruling over a country in which half the population (about 40 million people) lived below the poverty line on less than the equivalent of

£1.30 a day. After 25 January, the protests continued, escalating in intensity during Mubarak's last 18 days in charge of the country. During this period Ghonim was captured and interrogated for 11 days, all the while being held blindfolded and handcuffed. He was eventually released, ignorant as to the extent that the revolution had moved on as he had been starved of news while in detention. Shortly afterwards, Mubarak conceded the inevitable and stood down.

By a roundabout route, Khaled Said had become Egypt's version of Mohamed Bouazizi, while Ghonim had become a very 21st-century revolutionary hero. *Time* magazine put him at the top of their 2011 list of most influential people in the world and invited him to New York to an awards ceremony.

Only after the revolution were the two policemen eventually found guilty and sentenced to seven years in prison – a term that some family members considered far too lenient.

Sabrina and I talked – quietly – about the revolution, while the cargo ship security men continued their verbal barrage.

'Oh my God, it's like a fish market. Oh my God!' said Sabrina, messing about and covering her ears. She had an inscrutable, Buddha-like expression and a sharp sense of humour.

We landed and filed out past the business-class section of the plane. 'A pity we weren't here,' I joked. It looked very comfortable, and a long way from gabbing cargo ship security men.

'The more you put sugar in the bowl, the sweeter it will be,' she replied, looking at the big seats. With these words of wisdom, she hurried ahead to fetch her bag and catch the bus to Alexandria.

Cairo International Airport was full of adverts for mobile phone companies and international banks – a far cry from the R'as Ajdir border into Libya. A shiny marble corridor led to a booth where I paid US$15 for an Egyptian visa sticker; Sabrina had bought hers in advance. A taxi man had somehow penetrated this far into the airport, 'airside' beyond immigration control. He seemed very disappointed when I told him that my transport had already been fixed. My hotel, which cost US$50 a night and overlooked Tahrir Square, had remarkably emailed to offer to collect me, although I wasn't convinced anyone would be there.

But I was wrong to doubt the City View Hotel. A driver wearing a blue polo shirt and Ray-Bans was holding a sign bearing my name. He seemed as surprised to see me as I was him.

As we walked briskly to his car, he told me, in a manner that suggested that this was quite normal: 'Tomorrow you will see a revolution.'

I asked him what he meant – surely I'd missed the big event by just over a year.

'Tomorrow they will make it large. Maybe five thousand or six thousand, something like that,' he answered casually. He was referring to a protest at Tahrir Square, outside my hotel. I had had no idea about it. He made the 'revolution' sound as though it were part of the city's tourist trail.

We arrived at Mina's car, which had a badly cracked windscreen and a row of stuffed toys on the dashboard.

'I was in the square on January twenty-fifth, of course,' he said. 'The police came and they shoot and it was very difficult. The bombs that make your eyes water. It was everywhere. But when they finally go, it was wonderful. It was the first time that we make something change. Get rid of bad president. It was great.'

We were soon driving down a long boulevard with well-kept flower beds, palm trees and the occasional pharaonic figure in the verge in the middle, real antiquities carved from stone during ancient Egyptian times. A picture on an advertising hoarding showed a smiling soldier holding a baby. A rifle was slung over the shoulder of his body armour. Gentle flute music with a dance beat played on the taxi's cassette stereo. We continued as the road turned in a swoop towards concrete apartments topped with satellite dishes. Pick-up trucks loaded precariously with cabbages idled along as we raced past. Mina was driving fast with one hand and occasionally taking mobile phone calls.

The road was full of dented Fiats honking and driven as though the owners intended to pick up a few more dents very soon. We came to what looked like a country club. I asked what it was and, in between calls, Mina said distractedly: 'It's an army club. Billiards, ping-pong, swimming – something like that.'

So that was where some of the army's elite hung out. During my visit the Supreme Council of the Armed Forces (known as SCAF) was running the country under 'emergency law' in the run-up to the presidential elections due to be held in June 2012. There was much fevered speculation about who would come out on top in the ballot, and during my visit many people discussed the matter. Egyptians love talking politics, and with Mubarak gone there seemed to be an outpouring of chatter. Many were worried that the victor would be a candidate from the Muslim Brotherhood, a party set up in the 1920s and which believes in the introduction of Islamic, or sharia, law. Its slogan states that 'Islam is the solution'. The party was widely popular, partly due to its leading role in opposition to British colonial rule, which ended in 1952. Before my visit, the Muslim Brotherhood had taken the most votes in parliamentary elections, with an impressive 37.5 per cent of the ballot.

Then there were the hard-line, ultra-conservative Salafists, who favoured a stricter, more puritanical version of sharia law that shuns modernity and harks back to the days of the Prophet Muhammad (at least as they choose to interpret the days of the Prophet). The Al-Nour party, which had their support in the recent election, had taken 27.8 per cent of the seats in parliament. Some of the most controversial Salafists talked of jihad, a religious war to advance Islam. Their beliefs about women deeply concerned liberal-minded Egyptians; for example, the requirement to wear face veils, and a proposed ban on bikinis (outside of hotels quarantined from Egyptians, where bikinis would be allowed to maintain the tourist industry) and high heels (outside of private homes). 'A woman can only wear high heels for her husband but she is not to do so outside her house,' one preacher had declared. Another had said that the mingling of opposite sexes in public places should be prohibited. The

Salafists of Egypt were much influenced by the Wahhabis of Saudi Arabia, who held similar beliefs and had spread their ideas into Egypt, partly through converting Egyptians who went to work in the Gulf in the 1970s to escape poverty at home.

Just as in Tunisia, the Islamists had used the structure of the mosques to get people out to vote. But it was the upcoming presidential election that would hold the key to real power. The president, not the parliament, would determine the direction of the country. Could a popular secularist candidate emerge? There was much disappointment over the failure to stand of the widely admired Mohamed ElBaradei, the Nobel Peace Prize winner and former director of the International Atomic Energy Agency. ElBaradei, who was from Cairo, was seen as strong for standing up to America and doubting President George W Bush about weapons of mass destruction in Iraq. He had described the 2003 invasion of Iraq, in an interview in *Le Monde* newspaper, as 'a glaring example of how, in many cases, the use of force exacerbates the problem rather than [solves] it'.

Or would the army refuse to relinquish power, with neither the Islamists nor the secularists taking control? Would another Mubarak emerge? Would the revolution have been for nothing? One way or another, it seemed possible that the liberal-leaning protesters who began Egypt's Arab Spring, the ones who turned up on 25 January after the Facebook call for action, could lose out. It was into this cauldron of uncertainty in the Egyptian capital that I was entering.

Past the army's ping-pong club, the city lay ahead in a haze. Dozens of minarets shot upwards. The Mohammed Ali mosque stood proudly on a hill in the distance, all domes and towers. Yet despite the packed buildings, dense traffic and sense of relentless busy-ness (Cairo's population is said to be as many as 20 million, though nobody is sure of the precise number), there was a gentle aspect to the capital. The minarets seemed to break up all the concrete and soften the horizon. Within minutes I had realised that Cairo was my favourite Arab Spring city so far.

After plunging into a long, dark tunnel, we emerged into the streets of the old town. Women wore headscarves; apparently more were doing so since the revolution due to the rising influence of Islamists. Some men walked along hand in hand. Sirens shrieked. Horns blasted. There was a faint smell of incense. A street stall offered strawberries laid out on wooden trays. We passed a Barclays Bank and a law-court building with a blindfolded figurine on the façade holding scales of justice. Shops sold shisha pipes and Manchester United shirts. Traffic police in white uniforms and wearing black berets at jaunty angles stood at corners. An orange and emerald ambulance squealed behind us. We moved out of the way and noticed that an opportunist driver had used the parting of traffic to follow the ambulance and speed up his journey. 'Ha ha!' chuckled Mina approvingly, rather than scowling and cursing as a taxi driver back home might have. Something about the moment seemed to capture the abundant energy and offbeat vibe with which Cairo was overflowing.

The City View was also my favourite hotel so far. The entrance was between the offices of Sudan Airways and those of Abercrombie & Kent, an upmarket British tour operator whose front window was shuttered throughout my visit, as though the office were closed. You could easily miss the narrow hotel doorway, which led to steps to a lurid pink archway framed by pink columns and topped with a picture of the Sphinx at Giza. A white plastic chair rested by an unmanned reception desk. Beyond was a tiny, old-fashioned lift that creaked through a cage at the centre of a filthy corkscrew staircase (I never saw anyone use the stairs). I yanked open a metal door and pressed a button marked 'hotel' for the fifth floor. There was nothing upmarket or fancy about the City View, but I could already tell I was going to like it.

On the fifth floor, I was met by a welcoming committee of staff including Mr Mohamed, the supervisor of rooms, and Salam Badr, the guest relations manager, a slick fellow with a suit and a quiff. They were in a second reception, next to a couple of well-worn sofas and a television. At most times of day, and well into the evenings, the staff of the City View Hotel could be found on those sofas, chatting among themselves and readily available for conversation. We renegotiated my room rate even though it had been clearly 'negotiated' when I'd agreed to pay US$50 on the internet. The result was I paid the same amount for a twin rather than a double bedroom (they were an extremely courteous but prodigiously sharp lot). Then Mr Mohamed escorted me to my room via the restaurant and the hotel balconies.

The latter were the highlight of the City View, and gave the hotel its name. From the balconies – one of which could fit a small table and two chairs, while the other could fit four sets of small tables and chairs – you looked across to the distinguished façade of the Egyptian Museum. Beyond the museum I could see the charred remains of the block that was once the headquarters of the National Democratic Party, the group that had controlled Egypt's parliament under a single-party system established in the country after President Gamal Abdel Nasser's Free Officers seized power from the British in 1952. Its torching had been a symbolic moment in the revolution. To the left, across an ugly empty lot in front of a half-complete Ritz-Carlton hotel, there was a roundabout and a set of colourful banners and stalls selling T-shirts and flags, with lots of people milling about. The roundabout was where several roads converged, and it was the focal point of Tahrir Square: the epicentre of the uprising.

This was about a hundred metres away and the sight made the hair stand up on the back of my neck. I could not wait to go down and investigate.

'The Nile River,' said Mr Mohamed, who wore a dark suit and a shirt and tie. He was pointing beyond the half-finished hotel. 'The Nile River, Mr Tom.'

I could not see the water, but took his word for it.

'The liberators,' he added – at least that's what it sounded like – indicating towards the square. 'The liberators, Mr Tom.'

He showed me to my room, a shuttered space facing the front of the hotel rather than the square. The walls were pale pink with electrical sockets in unusual places. An almost continuous sound of horns came from below (in the night I counted the periods of silence and the longest gap I reached was 40). The air-conditioning unit had a mini disco-light effect that indicated it was working. These lights were impossible to switch off. There were two small pictures of figures in *gallabiyas*, the long gown worn by many Egyptian men, in a desert. A cramped bathroom contained a crazy shower that sent water flying in all directions at once.

Mr Mohamed turned on the taps in the sinks. 'Hot and cold, Mr Tom,' he said. Then he prodded the bed. 'Very good mattress,' he observed. I thanked him for the insights and slipped him some Egyptian pounds.

I dropped off my bag and headed out to the square. But on the way I was stopped by Salam, the smooth guest relations manager. He wore a grey pinstripe suit as though he was about to set off for a day's trading on an international stock exchange; he was always extremely dapper. 'If you talk to anyone: you come to them,' he said. He was warning me not to let anyone hustle me in the square.

He seemed pleased to have a guest bearing a notebook. 'During the revolution,' he said, 'the whole hotel was journalist. CNN. Russians. *The New York Times. Newsweek.* All the people come here – because we are in the heart of it. It was like a big family. Yari, the photographer, was here: very famous. They were here eighteen days. Very good for business.'

Down the lift and past the Sudan Airways office, I turned on to the main street leading to Tahrir Square. Stalls sold Egyptian flags and umbrella hats bearing the country's tricolour of red, white and black, with a golden eagle in the centre. The red is said to represent the period of struggle before the British colonialists left; the white the coming of the revolution; and the black the ending of colonialism. Next to the flags were T-shirts bearing slogans such as 'I LOVE EGYPT', 'TAHRIR SQUARE: FREEDOM, FACEBOOK' and 'THE DAY WE CHANGE: JANUARY 25'. Boot polishers and sunglasses salesmen operated alongside the tourist stalls. Fresh orange juice carts and men selling sausages and nuts lined the edge of the roundabout, where a confusion of tents and thrown-together marquees existed. A face-painter asked me if I would like the country's tricolour daubed on my face. I politely declined and she seemed so devastated – there were no other tourists that I could see – that I almost changed my mind.

A huge crowd milled about and voices rose from a speaker by a raised platform. People chattered and bustled. Banners with Arabic script had been hoisted on to the platform, between lamp posts and on the frames of the ramshackle tents. Faces of martyrs gazed down. From one lamp post an off-putting effigy of a human hung with a noose tied around its neck. The atmosphere was a mixture of political intrigue and village fete. I bought some sunflower seeds and salted peanuts and tucked them in the top pocket of my shirt, occasionally having a snack as I wandered round the famous square I had seen so often on television. The revolution seemed to be ongoing and to have turned into a highly bizarre day out. I could feel both the electricity of struggle and celebration of victory, combined with an undercurrent of discontent that sometimes bubbled into anger.

Despite the jamboree, serious matters were under debate, as I could tell from the raised voice and tone of the speakers. The demonstration, I gathered, concerned the official disqualification of a Salafist presidential hopeful Hazem Salah Abu Ismail on the grounds that his mother was American – a claim he denied, saying that she only had a Green Card to live in the United States and had not converted nationality. Images of the moon-faced politician with his bushy grey beard were on posters and placards all over the square. A popcorn stallholder, siding with his customers (one sensed his allegiance would switch depending on the day's debate in Tahrir Square), boasted a picture of the Salafist on his wooden cart.

Ismail was in favour of women wearing veils and being segregated from men in the workplace. He would also have liked the age of marriage to be reduced to puberty, as it was during the time of Prophet Muhammad. Some of his supporters favoured the stoning to death of adulterers and for thieves to have their hands cut off. To the West, he was the potential nightmare outcome of the revolution. A few days before my visit, the *Los Angeles Times* had quoted him as saying 'I will never become a puppet for the US or Israel or any Western power.'

I had stumbled into a meeting of some of the most hard-core Salafists in the whole of Egypt. As I made my way through the throng, where some waved sinister black Salafist flags, a bearded man disconcertingly smiled at me and said: 'Welcome.' He was wearing a slightly shortened version of a gallabiya. His gown was white and was at a length so that you could see his socks and sandals below. This seemed to be the regular style of dress for many of the Salafists, while non-Salafists who wore gallabiyas preferred to let the gowns fall to ankle length and chose colours other than white.

I nodded and smiled back and walked towards the platform at the front. To the right of the mini-stage I was surprised to come across a section of swaying black fabric under a white canopy. For a split second I was reminded of a flock of crows. There was something disconcerting about the strange black space. Then I realised what I was seeing. The area under the canopy was where the Salafist women had gathered. They almost all wore full-length black robes with black veils and slits for their eyes – known as *niqabs*. A few did not wear veils and merely had black headscarves. The latter seemed more elderly than the others, though it was difficult to determine ages given how well covered everyone was. The women were penned into the small area behind a barrier and this was clearly the spot given over to the female Salafists.

I found it extraordinary and also sad. And I was suddenly very conscious of being a Westerner, the type of person to whom Ismail would never lower himself to become a 'puppet'. The speaker was intoning clearly important words, his voice echoing across the square. I wondered if Ismail was somewhere among us; I could not see the leader though many men looked just like him, or very similar. I surveyed the scene and ate some sunflower seeds. Then I crossed to the edge of the roundabout, which faced the stage. Behind the bearded speaker a row of palm trees stood sentinel. Beyond the palms was a tall, solid oatmeal-grey building with box-like windows and high antennae poking out of the roof. This was the Mogamma, a building given over to 18,000 bureaucrats working for the central government. It was a notorious place known for its endless paperwork and confusing stamps, with as many as 50,000 visitors each day attempting to negotiate its Kafkaesque systems. The building, which dates from the early 1950s and was constructed on the site of a former British barracks, was an emblem of the bureaucracy, corruption and frustration of Egyptian life under Mubarak that had led to the revolution.

The liberal activists who started the rebellion may not have been in the ascendancy but I felt the raw energy of Tahrir Square. There was not a policeman in sight. The sense of order appeared to come from the restraint of the people. I bought a glass of orange juice and asked the stallholder what he made of the demonstration, as he could speak a little English. He lowered his voice. 'I think bad Islamic,' he replied, looking in the direction of the stage. He was clearly not 'one of them'. But then I looked towards the women and inquired what he thought of their being limited to that corner of the square. 'Only for her husband,' he said, approving of the arrangement. 'Beautiful woman, fine body...' He indicated the shape of women's breasts. '...only for her husband.'

I asked him about the effigy hanging from the lamp post. 'This man is doing everything against them... so they hang him,' he replied.

A glamorous television reporter swept past wearing a white headscarf, accompanied by a cameraman. She appeared to be American. Her eyes flickered in my direction as she strode forth in search of a story. Nearby, a man was asleep with his head resting on a cardboard box, while another was packing up his stall at the end of the day, miraculously balancing a door-sized tray on his head. The wooden tray was piled high with eggs and bread rolls. He walked away through the crowd and people stepped aside. I watched as he amazingly made progress in the direction of Mohammed Mahmoud Street. Then I briefly met a bearded photographer working for the Associated

Press. But as we were talking, the crowd near us suddenly formed neat lines and knelt down to pray. The photographer disappeared to take some snaps.

I wandered down Mohammed Mahmoud Street for a short while, coming to a McDonald's with boarded-up windows. It was open. I stepped inside to take a look, and was confronted by a sign that said: 'Happy Meal: An Excellent Source of Happiness.' But it was drab and gloomy inside with no natural light, so I kept going.

Opposite the McDonald's, vivid street art lined the walls of a building next to the American University. One picture mocked Mubarak, showing him looking dopey with one half of his head wearing a soldier's beret. Another depicted a rebel carrying an orange rifle, seeming to call on his comrades to join him. A third showed young men wearing street clothes and angels' wings; they were presumably among those who lost their lives during the revolt. An official report had found that 846 civilians and 26 policemen died in the 18 days of the uprising.

As I returned to the square, a shambling man veered across the street into my path.

'Are you a journalist?' he asked.

I nodded non-committally and kept on walking, bearing in mind the sharp-suited guest relations manager's advice on talking to people who pick you out.

'Why are you angry with me?' he asked, sidling up to me, even though I'd given no reason to suggest I was.

'I'm not angry with you,' I replied.

'I'm not from here,' the man said, as though that cleared up a question I had wanted answering. Then he began to follow me.

I kept going back to the square. He slipped away into the crowds.

From a distance, I could see the concrete tower of the Ramses Hilton, which was shaped like a series of giant cardboard boxes placed one on top of another. It was marked on my tourist map and was meant to have a terrific view from the roof. I headed northwards, passing El Bostan Street and the entrance to the City View. It was a mild evening. The streets were jammed with traffic and I'd already taken my life into my own hands several times crossing at junctions near Tahrir Square. The Hilton was about 500 metres away, but to reach it meant traversing a series of impossibly busy roads. I watched Cairenes strolling across in the darkness as though the traffic did not exist – the honking cars appeared to dart instinctively to one side and let them go. On the streets near the Egyptian Museum vehicles looked out of control, with no regular lanes and every driver for themselves. No traffic police were about and I did not blame them: where on earth would they begin?

So I caught a taxi for the short distance. There was heavy security at the door of the hotel, with an X-ray machine and a bag search. Inside, the bar of the Sherlock Holmes pub was empty, and I did not see any Western faces around in the lobby. I took the lift to the 36th floor and stepped into the Windows on the World restaurant. I was not intending to dine, just to take a look. The restaurant was empty apart from one table at which three men who might have been politicians were discussing matters conspiratorially. The view across the Nile was superb through tall ceiling-to-floor glass windows. A softly spoken waiter said: 'You can sit here, you do not have to eat.' And he took me to a table right by the window, where I ordered a Stella beer that came with a yellow label that declared it was 'the first beer of Egypt'. As though it was an extremely important matter, the waiter asked: 'Foam or no foam?' I opted for a foamless beer, and I took in the sweep of the city below.

Multicoloured barge-shaped boats lined each bank of the Nile, brightly lit in pinks and greens and blues, occasionally moving off into the coal-black river. They appeared to be ferries, and they buzzed about here and there like fireflies. Larger boats docked on the far side of the Nile seemed to double up as restaurants. As the river curled onwards, a series of bridges lit with sodium lights spanned its dark expanse; the river must have been about 250 metres wide. Across the water beyond a Chevrolet advert, a giant rocket tower stood, bathed in purple light: the Cairo Tower, once the tallest building in Africa.

According to the Egyptian novelist and reporter Ahdaf Soueif, government snipers positioned themselves on the rooftop of the Ramses Hilton and shot at protestors during the revolution, as they did from the Egyptian Museum and the American University. While reporting on and taking part in the uprising on Friday 28 January 2011, Soueif had found herself stuck on the 6 October Bridge directly below the Hilton, attempting to cross with her two young nieces to make their way to Tahrir Square. That Friday subsequently became known as the 'Day of Wrath' in the revolution as so many people took to the streets, with many fatalities.

With their eyes weeping from tear gas despite holding tissues sprinkled with vinegar over their noses – a trick that is meant to limit the effect of the gas – Soueif and her nieces ran into a cordon of soldiers just below where I was sitting with a beer. In her book *Cairo: My City, Our Revolution* Soueif describes begging the soldiers to let them through. The gas 'made you feel the skin was peeling off your face', she writes. The soldier agreed to let them pass and said: 'What can we do? If we could take off this uniform we'd join you.'

I looked down to the bridge and across towards the charred headquarters of the National Democratic Party. The top of the Ramses Hilton is the perfect spot to orientate yourself on a visit to Cairo, and much of the world's media was in the hotel at the time of the uprising; almost certainly looking through these very windows. For a while, reporters are said to have been barricaded in the hotel by Mubarak's forces, and cameramen were at one point asked by the hotel not to film from the hotel for fear of the structure becoming a military target. When Soueif and her nieces passed by on the 'Day of Wrath', hoping to stop at the hotel to wash their eyes, they found the entrance shuttered. They bravely continued onwards to Tahrir Square, where snipers later picked off protesters with shots to the head.

Returning to the City View, I caught another dented taxi. The fare was 10 Egyptian pounds (£E10 – about £1 in Britain), while the bottle of beer I'd just drunk was £E43. Taxis in Cairo were cheap, plentiful and occasionally very lively.

My driver was a slight man with a lot of opinions and a bombastic style. 'Traffic! Cairo! Big problem!' he was soon booming. 'Very tired! Very old roads! Very old cars! The logic is no good!'

We spun past the Egyptian Museum and turned at the roundabout on Tahrir Square. The Salafists were still chanting slogans. Their big demonstration – the 'revolution' that the City View driver had foretold – was to be held the next day. They seemed to be revving up; getting in the mood.

'Abu Ismail!' said the driver, mentioning the Salafist leader. 'For president! No good! No good!'

He paused and then said: 'This!' He was making a pulling motion at the end of his cleanly shaven chin, as though indicating a beard. 'This! No good! Big problem! No cinema! No cafés! No theatre! No travelling! Women: nine years old! Very very problem! No good for women! No school, no study, no English! No college! Women in a different place! Why? Why? This!'

He indicated a beard again. We had stopped by the hotel and he was in full rant mode.

'This very very problem. No trousers! Just gallabiyas! Christians and Muslims cannot meet!' About 10 per cent of Egypt's population is Coptic Christian and they have been subject to regular attacks and persecution.

He waved his arms in a sweeping motion. 'Cairo will close! No tourists come to pyramids! Very very problem!'

The scenes from the balconies of the City View were surreal. To the left, Salafist voices rose from the square and groups occasionally marched resolutely around the roundabout, while to the right a series of dramatic car crashes unfolded. A collision crunched out at least once an hour. The first involved an olive-coloured vehicle that rammed into the back of a van. Its bonnet had twisted upwards and would not come down despite various attempts to yank the metal. One of the passengers was injured and a dozen or so people gathered round as the traffic continued to swirl by. Nobody seemed too perturbed and the car bonnet was eventually pulled back in place thanks to a team of volunteers. It hobbled onwards.

A waiter arrived. I ordered grilled chicken and rice from the menu of the Ali Baba Restaurant (the veal 'enhanced with wild mushroom sauce' was unavailable) and another beer. I was the sole diner.

Up on the balcony, the cacophony of horns below oddly reminded me of crickets in a field. A screech of tyres rose, followed by a thud and a sound of broken glass. Close to the Egyptian Museum another car had skidded into the side of an oncoming vehicle as the driver had attempted a brave, if completely mad, U-turn. Voices were raised and another group gathered. It seemed as though matters were settled by these impromptu panels of eyewitnesses, who established the truth of events before everyone moved on and cars limped away with new dents and scrapes.

Chants rose from the square. The sky was deep purple. A Salafist preacher began intoning importantly. The cars honked and skidded. The sounds were almost hypnotic.

I was joined by another guest. His name was Mohamed Khan and he was a retired bus driver from Hounslow in west London (he had been a driver on the 111 route, he quickly informed me). His son had booked him a fortnight's holiday starting with a few days in Cairo and including a Nile cruise from Luxor to Abu Simbel. He was in his sixties with cropped grey hair and had come out to the balcony for a smoke. He told me he had five children and he proudly listed their various fields of employment: one was an area manager for McDonald's, another a chiropodist, another a banker, and one son ran an ultrasound business. His offspring, it seemed, had some key areas in life covered. Mohamed would never have to worry about corns, interest rates, body scans or Big Macs.

He regarded my chicken and rice, and pulled a face. 'I don't enjoy the food here. I've been going to McDonald's, KFC and Pizza Hut by the square,' he said – maintaining family loyalty while on his holiday. 'I don't like Egyptian food.'

We looked out across the purple sky. Mohamed didn't miss driving buses, he told me. 'Thank God I've finished now,' he said, sounding very relieved. 'I've got no money – my pension's not very good. But thank God I've finished with the buses.'

We talked about Mubarak. The 84-year-old was about to stand trial for complicity in the killing of protesters during the uprising. His sons Alaa and Gamal, born of his half-Welsh wife Suzanne, were to be tried on the same charges. They were also charged with stock market manipulation. After the uprising, Mubarak had initially fled Cairo to live in his plush seaside villa in Sharm el-Sheikh on the Sinai Peninsula. He was soon put under house arrest at the villa. His health had deteriorated and he had been taken to a local hospital. He had since been transferred to the hospital at Tora Prison on the outskirts of Cairo, so he was available for questioning ahead of the trial. Alaa and Gamal were also held at the prison.

Mohamed seemed to know a lot about Gamal, an investment banker. 'He owns a huge home in Knightsbridge,' he told me. Mohamed even knew the address. 'Number twenty-eight, Wilton Place.' I later looked this up and he was, remarkably, spot on. The Georgian house was valued at £8.75 million.

'And Gaddafi,' he continued. 'He owns about a third of Mayfair.'

That wasn't quite true but Gaddafi did own nine properties and a fleet of expensive cars in London, which embassy officials connected to the regime had desperately attempted to sell off to make some quick cash in the final days before the Brother Leader fell.

Another screech and thud came from below. Mohamed returned to his room and for a while longer I listened to the Salafists chanting in the square. 'UNITED... UNITED!' it seemed as though they were yelling, as though supporting a football team. I finished my meal and got an early night. The most ancient sights yet of my tour across North Africa's Arab Spring awaited in the morning... I fell asleep dreaming of pyramids and revolutions.

11

Cairo, Saqqara and Giza:

Pharaohs, Camels and a Yacoubian Building

O N THE road to Memphis we swerved to avoid a dead dog. Rubbish was scattered on the banks of a filthy irrigation channel. The car bumped forwards across pot-holes, slowing to overtake a mule laden with long, thin grass. A tuk-tuk piled high with egg cartons teetered forwards on three wheels. Bright pyramids of oranges and bananas – my first pyramids in Egypt – were laid out on old sacks next to ramshackle concrete houses that appeared as though they might collapse at any moment. A shepherd led his scraggly flock along the edge of another dirty irrigation channel. We halted as an elderly woman directed scrawny cattle across the narrow road.

After being in the cosmopolitan, if slightly manic, centre of Cairo with its five-star hotels, universities and international-brand shops, we had arrived in what looked like the Third World. Yet we were just 20 kilometres south of Tahrir Square. The transformation was absolute – I was getting a first glimpse of the poverty that Mubarak's regime had happily overseen. It was a poverty that had witnessed many dying in scrums for cheap-bread handouts and driven others to suicide. At one point, 14 people a day were committing suicide and in 2009 there were more than 100,000 attempts. How could a family survive on earnings equivalent to £1.30 a day? The answer based on the evidence of some of the neighbourhoods we had passed through on the way to the 5,000-year-old ruins at Memphis, the ancient former capital of Egypt, was clearly: not very well at all.

I was with Alfie, a 33-year-old tourist guide, who was connected to the City View Hotel. As we drove past a field that seemed to have turned into an unofficial rubbish tip, he told me about life working in tourism in a city boasting one of the Seven Wonders of the World.

'We are suffering from no income,' he said plainly. 'We are independent people, not working for the government. If I had not saved money before the revolution I'd be in trouble. I know people who have sold their cars or their apartments. Some have left the tourism field and moved into telecommunications, or they work as taxi drivers or drive buses.'

He was not a fan of the Muslim Brotherhood. He said they had broken a promise by fielding a candidate in the presidential election, having previously said they would stay out of the race in order not to dominate politics and so that the government would be representative of all Egyptians and all faiths. Alfie was a Coptic Christian. 'I am Coptic,' he said. 'The Islamic people, they make trouble with us. Not all of them. So many of my friends are Muslim. My mechanic. He is Muslim and we are friends. But he is not like the people with the beards. He is different.' Alfie was cleanly shaven and was disarmingly honest, with protuberant brown eyes.

He talked about the Muslim Brotherhood's use of mosques to get people to vote for their candidates in the earlier parliamentary elections. He said that many had been in jail for years during the Mubarak regime – the ex-president had been wary of the power base of the Muslim Brotherhood – but people had been wrong to support them simply for having suffered.

I asked him about the rubbish. Some of the places we were driving through looked almost apocalyptic, even though we had almost arrived at Memphis. Alfie replied that the government had never cared about tourist attractions and that complaints he and other guides had made to officials had fallen on deaf ears.

We pulled into a dusty car park. At Memphis, security was tight: armed policemen in white uniforms manned a metal detector by the gate. This was the first port of call on a whistle-stop tour that was also to take in the Step Pyramid at Saqqara and the Great Pyramid at Giza. It was to be a quick half-day, so I could get back to see the planned 'revolution' on Tahrir Square. I did not want to miss the revolution.

Memphis is believed to have been founded in 3100BC, when it was capital of Upper and Lower Egypt, which were united in this period. These terms are still used to describe the country, with Upper Egypt slightly confusingly in the south, 'up' the Nile, and Lower Egypt in the north. After passing security, we came to a row of shops that sold carpets decorated with camels, miniature pyramids made of coloured stone and figurines of pharaohs. A few coachloads of tourists made their way among the shops and it felt unusual having so many people around after my solitary tour of Libya.

We wandered amid statues of ancient pharaohs dotted about a plot of land the size of a hockey pitch, stopping after a while at the sarcophagus of Amenhotep (1290–1224BC). His resting place was long and rectangular, made of pink granite into which tall slender figures had been carved, wearing what looked like sarongs. The figures did not have human heads; instead there were the heads of jackals and what appeared to be lions and hawks. An image showed a dog resting on one side of the sarcophagus, its ears pricked. Around the carvings, intricate hieroglyphics were chiselled in neat columns, depicting birds, fish and pots. It was quite splendid. Amenhotep was from an influential family from the 19th dynasty, Alfie told me. The more closely you looked at the sarcophagus, the more wonderful you realised it was – with so many incredible carvings that had lasted through the centuries. But it was just one of the many superb remains at Memphis: further on we came to a delightful, crumbling alabaster sphinx – a curious-looking creature with a quizzically smiling face. Next up was a statue of Ramses II, who stood proudly near a fence. He was one of the most powerful kings during the period before the birth of Christ, ruling the country 1279–1213BC (during the lifetime of Amenhotep). I learnt that when you see a statue of a pharaoh with a straight beard, the work was completed during the ruler's lifetime. If the beard was 'cur-ved' – as Alfie pronounced 'curved' – it was completed after the pharaoh's death. I was quickly becoming an expert on ancient Egypt. The Ramses II in front of us had a straight beard, and his left leg was stepping forwards to indicate that he had been involved in a military campaign; he launched many attacks on Syria and Nubia.

I also learnt that he was a womaniser. 'A strong man: muscles!' said Alfie. 'Look at them!' he exclaimed, pointing at the bulging muscles of Ramses II. 'Forty women! He was a very good example for Egyptian men: married forty times! One hundred and twenty children!' Or perhaps not such a good role model, as Egypt now is in the middle of a burgeoning population crisis. During Mubarak's rule the population of the country had almost doubled, from 44 million in 1981.

'His name can be found from Alexandria to Abu Simbel!' said Alfie. 'Forty wives!' Of the 40, the most famous was Queen Nefertiti. Ramses the Great, as he was known, inaugurated a huge monument in honour of himself and Nefertiti at Abu Simbel in 1255bc – now such a big part of tourist trips to Upper Egypt.

The highlight of Memphis was an open-air building near the security checkpoint that housed a massive statue of Ramses II lying prone, although it once stood erect; the figure must have been 10 metres long and four wide. He wore a placid expression and looked pretty pleased with life. A man in a brown tunic and a white scarf stood near the head attempting to engage the French tourists in conversation, not having much luck. The statue was mind-boggling, both for having survived in such perfect shape for so long and for its sheer size. The work was completed during his lifetime and must have seemed awesome to his subjects. Egypt has a long history of strong leaders… and, judging by his legacy, Ramses II must have been among the toughest of the lot.

Alfie and I returned to his car. From Memphis, it was not far to Saqqara and the Step Pyramid, and we were soon turning near a herd of goats and pulling into a big car park with three coaches in it. A pack of yellow dogs lazed in the shade of one of the coaches. It was sunny, the warmest day of my journey across North Africa. Saqqara was the necropolis to Memphis during the period of the Old Kingdom in Egypt (2686–2181BC, although some historians use slightly different dates). It was properly 'discovered' in the mid 19th century by the great French Egyptologist Auguste Mariette from Boulogne-sur-Mer, who was taken to the site by Bedouin tribesmen. He employed a team of workmen who uncovered the *serapeum*, a temple to an ancient Hellenistic-Egyptian god, in which many treasures were located. A marvellous statue of an Apis bull-god was transported to the Louvre in Paris, as were other finds. But Mariette went on to work with the Egyptian authorities, sending relics to one of the first museums of Egyptian antiquities in Cairo; he had moved his family to the capital. Over the years to come he made dozens of finds up and down Egypt and was responsible for removing the sand around the famous Sphinx at Giza. At Saqqara, Mariette unearthed the sarcophagus of Prince Khaemweset, one of the many sons of Ramses II; and, suitably for an Egyptologist, Mariette is himself interred in a sarcophagus in the garden of the Egyptian Museum, within view of the balcony at my hotel.

We walked down a sandy path to the tomb of King Teti, which you might easily pass without realising anything was there. But a hole in the sand revealed steps that led into a long, gloomy passage illuminated with neon strip lights. After being led to the entrance by Alfie, I went down alone, hunching over in the passageway. At least I thought I was alone, but I realised after a while that I was being followed by a man wearing an olive gallabiya. Tight hieroglyphics depicting birds and fish had been marked on the walls of the passageway to the tomb of Teti, who came to the throne in 2345BC. I paused to look at these up close, with the man in the gallabiya looming behind. Then I entered a chamber where I was able to stand up straight, with a large black-stone sarcophagus in a corner. I was the only tourist and could imagine how electrifying it must have been for Mariette and his team, scraping away the sand to find rooms such as this – forgotten for 5,000 years.

On discovering a mummified bull at the *serapeum*, Mariette wrote that he 'found the finger marks of the Egyptian who had inserted the last stone in the wall built to conceal the doorway... there were also the marks of naked feet imprinted on the sand which lay in one corner of the tomb chamber. Everything was in its original condition in the tomb where the embalmed remains of the bull had lain undisturbed for 37 centuries'.

The man in the olive gallabiya piped up. 'Look at the sarcophagus,' he said.

I was looking at the sarcophagus. 'Yes, wonderful,' I said.

'Look!' he replied.

'I am!' I said.

'Look, look!' he said pointing at the black stone.

'I don't need a guide, thank you,' I said, guessing that he was attempting to become my one-word guide in return for more than one Egyptian pound.

'I am not a guide. I am a guard!' he said, sounding huffy.

I walked back out of the tomb of King Teti with the man in the gallabiya shuffling behind me.

Alfie and I strolled around the sandy stone remains of Saqqara, passing along a corridor of ancient columns and heading for the Step Pyramid, said to have been the largest building in the world in the 27th century BC, pre-dating the more famous, taller pyramids at Giza. To reach this earliest skyscraper, we passed 'the first wall in Egypt or in the whole world', according to Alfie. I had no reason to doubt him and we admired the 'first wall', which had an elegant inset design of tall rectangles (its style strangely reminded me of Art Deco). The Step Pyramid was constructed as part of the funerary complex of King Zoser. Its cream stones were partially covered in higgledy-piggledy wooden scaffolding making the structure look a little as though Mariette and his men had only just arrived; a restoration of some kind was taking place. It is known as the Step Pyramid because the shape consists of large stone steps, while the later pyramids had smooth outer surfaces. For a short while I looked on feeling slightly dazed, almost in awe. The pyramid rose from the desert as if by magic, lost for centuries before finally being found by Boulogne-sur-Mer's Mariette. It made me wonder how many other worlds were hidden beneath the sands of Africa.

'All around here: treasures,' said Alfie, as if answering my thoughts. 'Many treasures still not found.'

We entered the House of the South, a stone building to the right of the Step Pyramid, poking out of a hillock of rubble and sand. Inside, graffiti had been inscribed on a wall. This was the 'world's first graffiti', the work of Theban scribes, words in praise of King Zoser dating from around 1400BC, Alfie informed me. Given that I'd seen quite a lot of graffiti on my trip through the Arab Spring, it seemed somehow appropriate to witness their oldest ancestor.

🐫 🐫 🐫

Saqqara was intriguing but we were soon heading north to visit Giza, following a truck carrying metal girders that tailed out behind the vehicle and bounced on to the road, sending sparks flying. It would not perhaps have got past 'health and safety' back home. A heron perched on an old tyre in the filthy irrigation channel: evidence, I supposed, that there were fish below. Acrid smoke wafted from plots stacked with rubbish: yet more Mubarak-land. The visage of Mohamed Morsi, the bearded leader of the Muslim Brotherhood, gazed down from red posters attached to lamp posts. We passed the concrete sprawl of 6th of October City. This is the date that Egypt launched its attack on Israel in 1973, surprising the Israelis in the Sinai Peninsula, where they had been ensconced after taking the land in the Six-Day War of 1967. The conflict had ended in a ceasefire on 25 October and eventually led to the Camp David Accords of 1979 in which the Sinai Peninsula was returned to Egypt.

We crept along, with another irrigation channel to our left and simple breeze-block buildings to our right. Women sat on the steps of doorways scrubbing clothing in buckets of water next to grimy gutters. A muezzin called out. And then, just past the 'Principal Carpet School', the Great Pyramid came into view.

There is something mesmerising about the Great Pyramid. If it is within your field of vision you can't seem to help staring at its magnificent triangles of stone – at least I couldn't. There were no queues at the ticket office and we were soon through to the sandy slope leading to the Great Pyramid of Cheops, which stands almost 140 metres tall, about three times the height of Nelson's Column. As we made our way to the foot of its vast shape, an anxious man approached me.

He was a German tourist travelling alone. 'I think it would be better if we go together,' he said. He was pointing towards a collection of men on camels who were gamely trotting in our direction. He seemed to be concerned he might be ripped off or mugged by the men on the camels.

Perhaps I was uncharitable, but I replied that it would be fine and I would prefer to go on with Alfie. I had, after all, paid for my guide. The German looked forlorn. Perhaps I should have been kinder.

The entrance to the Great Pyramid was closed as its keepers had gone to pray. 'It was not like this before the revolution,' said Alfie. 'This is a bad thing.'

Under a bright blue sky, we took in the Pyramid of Chepren, marginally smaller than its neighbour and less prominently placed. A camel man hassled us to go for a ride on his spare camel. 'He said it was ten [Egyptian] pounds for a ride,' Alfie translated. 'But it would have been a hundred [US] dollars to get off. He didn't say that but this is what they do. They take you a long way away into the desert and if you don't have the money they will take your camera or your watch.' I had guilty visions of the German disappearing over dunes, passing over all his valuables and crawling back across the sands, gasping for water.

As if to prove that the hustlers were a tricky lot, a British couple was engaged in a fearful row. 'NO, I WILL NOT PAY YOU FOUR HUNDRED POUNDS!' the man boomed, his features bright red. 'I NEVER WANT TO

SEE YOUR FACE AGAIN IN MY LIFE, DO YOU HEAR ME!' The camel man, who certainly could hear him, continued to implore them to hand over cash. The couple walked swiftly onwards.

Things appeared to have changed little over the years. Mark Twain wrote of his visit in 1866: 'We suffered torture that no pen can describe from the hungry appeals for *baksheesh* that gleamed from Arab eyes.'

I hope the German survived the camel men.

Alfie and I reached a viewing point from where you could see the pyramids below, with Cairo stretched out beyond. It was one of the world's most startling vistas: the sheer scale of the stone rising from its sandy hill, with the city scattered beyond. For a moment or so, I felt inclined to be receptive to 'inspiring thoughts'... to consider matters of human progress, and admire the ancient endeavour the pyramids seemed to represent. But the travel writer Jonathan Raban, who came to Cairo in the late 1970s and wrote about his experiences in *Arabia Through the Looking Glass*, warned against such traps, pointing out that the Great Pyramid was no more than a 'simple-minded megalomaniac's dream come true', with thousands of labourers suffering to satisfy a crude 'fantasy'. I gazed at the pyramids and the camel hustlers and tended to agree. They were big and brash and in your face – and had remained so for many years. But I still could not take my eyes off them.

As we looked down, Alfie opened up. He pointed out a group of women wearing headscarves. 'When I was at university, in my section there were about four hundred people, but only ten women wore headscarves. Now it seems more like seventy-five per cent of women.' By 'now' he meant 'since the revolution'.

He talked about a famous comic actor in Egypt named Adel Imam, who had recently been sentenced to three months in prison for insulting Islam in his films and plays, some of which included parodies of Muslim men wearing traditional Islamic clothing. 'The educated people, all of them are angry about this,' Alfie said, his brown eyes holding steady. 'They say we are going back to the Middle Ages. If there is an Islamic president, we *will* go back to the Middle Ages. One hundred per cent. I'm sure of it. I think that then the young people would do another revolution against the Islamic people.'

He told me about how on Friday 28 January 2011, the 'Day of Wrath', he had been taking a group of Greek tourists around the pyramids. He had attempted to return them to the City View Hotel, but the city centre had become impassable by vehicle. So he had walked with them for the final four kilometres. They had arrived safely at the hotel at about 9.30 p.m., with the revolution taking place below in the square. He had then gone out and helped other young people guard the Egyptian Museum from looters; many had linked arms in a circle around the building. When it became very dangerous – he had seen tanks coming from the direction of the Ramses Hilton – he had retreated to the hotel and watched the revolution from its balconies. He was, he said, a peaceful man and did not believe in violence.

'People attacked the tanks. They burned a jeep. There were gunshots from the army and people were screaming and shouting. There was tear gas. In the morning it was peaceful. There were no police in the city. They disappeared. I heard that some police got rid of their uniforms and cut up their IDs. The 28th of January was the most important day – the defeat of the police,' Alfie said.

We entered the Great Pyramid and climbed its steep steps, rising to the Great Gallery at the top of them, which somehow felt as though it was the centre-point of ancient Egypt, being at the heart of its most prominent structure, while Tahrir Square was the focal point of the modern country, birthplace of the revolution. Then, after seeing the enigmatically beautiful Sphinx, we stopped at a KFC outside the pyramid complex at Giza. I went in to buy Alfie, our driver and me some sodas, and explored upstairs to see the view back across to the pyramids and the Sphinx: it has to be the best fast-food panorama anywhere. I was surprised to find a British family eating chicken nuggets and chips at a table by the window. The parents worked in the visa section of the British Embassy and they lived in Maadi, a southern suburb of Cairo. 'It's where a lot of expats live,' the mother said, but since the revolution there had been 'bag snatches, kidnaps and muggings'.

Were there really kidnappings, I asked.

'Mostly of Egyptian children,' she replied vaguely. 'I don't carry a handbag or money anymore. A maid we know of had her bag taken. The thief snipped it with scissors. There are guys on motorbikes. There's a lot more road rage too since the revolution. There never used to be. Yes, it was chaotic, but people would never lose the plot.'

We drove back to Tahrir Square – calmly – passing a neighbourhood with wonderfully colourful fruit and vegetable stalls. Pumpkins, artichokes, beetroots, oranges and carrots were heaped in great piles; Egypt seemed a place of both enormous abundance and crippling poverty. Then we arrived in Tahrir Square after crossing the river at Qasr el Nil Bridge. Posters of the moon-faced Ismail smiling an unnatural smile stared down at us. There were a few more Salafists milling about than previously. But no 'revolution' as yet.

🐪 🐪 🐪

That was to begin half an hour later. I was sitting on the balcony of the Ali Baba Restaurant at the hotel. Chants echoed from the square, but then grew louder close by. I was eating chicken and salad (the veal enhanced with mushroom sauce was still unavailable) as a group of perhaps three hundred people walked past in a column below with a couple of vehicles in the middle. The face of Ismail was adhered to the side of a van. This was the Salafist 'revolution', finally, but attendance was terrible. It appeared as though those who had been camping on the square, plus perhaps a few more bearded stragglers who had been rounded up from somewhere, had simply joined together to march back to where they had started in a feeble show of force. A large man, his legs planted widely so he would keep his balance, stood on the flatbed of a trailer pulled by a motorbike. He pointed and yelled into a microphone. The Salafists half-heartedly repeated his phrases. The most impressive aspect of the performance was that the large man did not topple over. A group held a yellow banner that said: 'NO US AID: AMERICAN'. Many Salafists believed that Egypt should maintain a tougher stance against Israel, rather than keep the peace with American backers (both diplomatic and financial).

The procession petered out as the Salafists shuffled towards the roundabout. It was not going to be a momentous day in the history of Tahrir Square. It was no 25 January, and certainly no 'Day of Wrath' – and I had not, of course, expected it to be.

I asked Tarek, the 'captain' of the Ali Baba Restaurant according to his badge, what the rotund speaker had been saying. 'They want justice. No double-cross. Justice. Freedom and peace and no double-cross,' he replied.

He joined me for a while on the main balcony. The smaller one was taken by the satellite dish of an Arabic television station whose reporter was on the square.

'You are a journalist?' Tarek asked slyly and rhetorically, without expecting an answer. 'You work? You make money?'

I replied that I was just a slightly offbeat tourist who was taking an interest in the demonstration.

He ignored this response. 'You make money. How much money? How about you give some money to me, Tarek?'

He appeared to be negotiating a translation fee. The City View's employees were not ones to miss a trick. 'Queen Elizabeth!' he said. 'Queen Elizabeth! She is on your notes. Let me see your Queen Elizabeth!'

He only seemed to be messing about, but I gave him a larger than normal tip at the end of the meal.

I went down to Tahrir Square. By the time I reached the road, Salafists were in the process of laying coils of barbed wire. They appeared to be attempting to seal off a wider area as part of their territory, though to what end it was difficult to ascertain as they had more than ample space for their numbers by the roundabout. Nobody in authority was around to intervene. The scenes were much as they were yesterday. I took a picture of a pretzel stall and its owner whispered: '*Sheesh... sheesh...* baksheesh.' The travel writer Eric Newby in his 1984 *On the Shores of the Mediterranean* had certainly been right to advise taking plenty of baksheesh to Egypt: 'Wonderful how [baksheesh] softens the hardest Muslim or Coptic heart, better than any nutcrackers. And do not begrudge it; most people, even those quite far up the social scale, are poorer than it is possible for most of us to imagine.'

The snack providers and T-shirt salesmen were in full swing, whistling to attract customers and milking the revolutionary moment the best they could. A woman ambled past wearing a full black robe with only a narrow slit in her *niqab* face veil. On top of her headscarf, however, she wore a baseball cap in the Egyptian colours. It was a startling image – the austere, ultra-conservative conformity mixed with a sense of humour. But I did not feel I could ask permission to photograph her. I got the impression the Salafist men might not like that. Black flags were waved and voices were raised on the stage.

Seeing as the 'revolution' appeared not to have taken off, I left the Salafists and went sightseeing. In the late afternoon I caught a taxi to see the Mosque of Mohammed Ali, part of the Citadel. This was on a hill and was where Egypt's rulers lived for 700 years from the 12th to the 19th century. On the way, down narrow twisting streets, the taxi passed a building that had recently collapsed and crushed two cars parked at its base. A cordon had been put round the rubble, which had yet to be cleared away. The driver had told me that it was simply an old building that had had its day. Yes, I thought, and it could have killed whoever happened to be walking by. I wondered how many other old buildings were about to collapse in Cairo. It seemed that Mubarak had literally allowed Egypt to fall apart.

We arrived at the Citadel, where I paid an entrance fee and walked up a street that had once been the scene of a horrific massacre, conducted by the man after whom the mosque was named. In 1811, Mohammed Ali, who had come to power in Egypt after the French left in 1801, invited five hundred Mamluk leaders to a feast at the Citadel. The Mamluks were of Turkish tribal background and were renowned fighters who had ruled Egypt for many years before the Ottomans and then the French took over. Mohammed Ali had manoeuvred to ensure that the Mamluks, who had remained a force throughout the years of overseas control, did not take over when the French left. He had also destroyed much of their architecture at the Citadel. And after the 'conciliatory' feast, a gate was closed as the Mamluks attempted to leave on horseback. His guests were trapped and gunned down from battlements above. Not a single person survived.

The massacre made me think back to the bloodshed in Tripoli at the Abu Salim prison – a similar turkey shoot.

Onwards past a (wisely) closed police museum, I came to the Mosque of El Naser Mohamed Ibn Qalawoun, where I removed my shoes and entered an open courtyard with archways all around. The Mosque of Mohammed Ali was further along, down more narrow lanes. To one side, stalls had been set up with free booklets explaining Islam in several languages. There were copies in Estonian, Ukrainian, Slovakian, French and English. One entitled *A Brief Illustrated Guide to Understanding Islam* contained page after page showing how the Koran held the answers to the physical make-up of human embryos, the structure of the brain, the origin of the universe, the physics of cloud patterns, the formation of mountains and the mechanics of sea waves. I really had no idea the Koran could be interpreted in such detail. Another booklet, *Women in Islam* by Dr Sherif Abdel Azeem, included chapter headings such as 'Shameful Daughters', 'Unclean Impure Women' and 'Adultery?' It commented that 'the Islamic veil is only a sign of modesty with the purpose of protecting women, all women. The Islamic philosophy is that it is always better to be safe than sorry.' There were many other such booklets.

I continued further into the Citadel. Outside the National Military Museum, a short walk along, tanks and planes that had engaged against the Israelis were lined up in a courtyard. Inside the museum, I found Mamluk costumes, statues of pashas and displays explaining the struggle for independence from the British, the Suez Crisis and various recent conflicts.

Much space was given over to Egypt's 20th-century double victory over Britain. The story of the rise of Colonel Gamal Abdel Nasser in 1952 after the Free Officers revolted against British colonial rule was told in detail. So was the 1956 nationalisation of the Suez Canal – the triumph that so embarrassed and humbled its former colonialists on the international stage. Nasser's rise to become the hero of the Arab world in the wake of his triumphs against the British is told, as is his demise during the Six-Day War of 1967 that saw Israel destroy his air force, taking advantage of a series of his tactical blunders. It was under Nasser, who died of a heart attack in 1970, that the single-party system that led to Mubarak was established. But there were no displays discussing the internal military affairs of the regimes of the country's post-independence leaders. And sections referring to Mubarak seemed to have disappeared... though a mural of the ex-leader solemnly raising an Egyptian flag remained on a wall by a staircase.

I finally reached the Mosque of Mohammed Ali, which was beyond the military museum. It was a grand affair and busy with local and foreign visitors. A sea of red carpets covered the floor and lights dangled from an enormous metal hoop hanging from the high-domed ceiling. Women in robes and *niqabs* sat cross-legged in the centre next to men in casual shirts with open collars. Carrying my shoes, I continued across the carpets to a doorway that led outside to a terrace with a brilliant view of Cairo. I stared out across the hazy jumble of minarets, domes, concrete blocks, highways, aerials and telecommunications towers. A murmur of activity rose from below.

Cairo always seemed to be brimming with life – I hadn't expected to, but somehow or other I had fallen for Egypt's capital.

From the Citadel, I hopped on another taxi to a neighbourhood known as Coptic Cairo; being a tourist in the city is terribly easy with so many taxis buzzing around. But the main street leading to its churches and the Coptic Museum was blockaded; guarded by officers in white uniforms brandishing guns. It was a reminder of what Alfie had told me earlier about the tension between Copts and Muslims running high. This had been particularly so after a terrorist attack at the Al-Qiddissin Church in Alexandria minutes into the New Year of 2011 in which a bomb killed 23 Copts and injured 97 more. This came after a massacre at a church in Nag Hammadi, a city in Upper Egypt, on 9 January 2010, when Muslim gunmen killed nine people who were celebrating the orthodox, Coptic Christmas. Two further Copts were killed in violence that followed the attack.

The taxi pulled up by a sign that said 'OLD CAIRO: WELCOME'. I got out and walked down a street lined with little shops selling lanterns and leather seat covers. Tambourines tinkled behind a wall. Flute music floated from an open window. I left my camera at a desk (pictures were not allowed for security reasons) and entered the Coptic Museum. It was a peaceful, fragrant setting; courtyards were filled with cacti, palm trees and beds of lilac flowers. Women in pale blue uniforms swept leaves and gossiped on benches. There is believed to have been a Coptic Christian presence in Egypt since the 3rd century and the ancient paintings and scripts in the rooms at the back of the courtyards are exquisite – so neat and detailed, in vibrant reds, blues and golds. Some of the manuscripts are kept in solid, 500-year-old wooden gospel caskets. An 11th-century painting showed Adam with Eve, before and after the fall from grace (which seemed to have a sense of humour mixed into its centuries-old strokes, judging from the slight smirk on Adam's face). It was a terrific, well laid-out museum, full of colourful medieval paintings of saints and pieces of parchment dating centuries back. A sign near yet more delicate manuscripts said that 'no other country has yielded more ancient written material than Egypt'.

Looking around, I could believe it – but the panel also reminded me of some more recently written Egyptian words. In *Revolution 2.0*, Wael Ghonim makes a point that touches on great Egyptian pride in its heritage and its place in the Middle East, saying that Egyptians have long considered themselves to be the 'cultural and scientific leaders of the Arab world'. When they saw the Tunisians get rid of President Ben Ali they felt a psychological urge to keep up with their neighbours, he believes. This, he says, played an important part in the revolution.

After the perhaps chaotic (but magnificent) pyramids, the intriguing history of the Citadel and the antiquities of Old Cairo – and from conversations with the many people I had met – I was getting a growing sense of that deep cultural awareness and pride.

I stayed for three nights in Cairo; taking it easy after my first busy day of tourism. It was relaxing to wander around – and not worry about guns at night or hijackings or over-eager military brigades. I hopped on taxis and occasionally took the subway to get about. The latter had a stop at Tahrir Square and the fare was equivalent to 10p (British) to go just about anywhere. Carriages had odd shutters on the windows and were almost always completely full of men, many of them in military uniforms. Each train had two women-only carriages, though occasionally a woman would be with her husband in one of the regular carriages. When this happened, the men would often use their bodies as a form of shield to keep onlookers from seeing their woman. It was very strange; like a bird using its wings to protect a chick from predators.

All the while the Salafists were a constant presence by the roundabout at Tahrir Square. The chanting and waving of black flags continued throughout my stay; I soon got used to it.

During one jaunt across the city, not far from the Salafists, I dropped into an excellent bookshop at the American University with incredibly well-stocked shelves of titles covering the Middle East, and then made my way up Talaat Harb Street, where I was on a book-related mission. On Talaat Harb – on a stretch of road where many revolutionaries were killed during the Arab Spring uprising – a theatrical man wearing a white uniform was playing castanets and skipping along with a metal urn from which you could buy a cup of tea. A clutter of fashion shops displayed very short miniskirts. Men who appeared to have nothing to do hung about on corners by a roundabout with a statue of Talaat Harb, a financier who set up the Bank of Egypt in 1920 in an attempt to break with foreign control of Egyptians' money. The statue, which shows him wearing a *tarboosh* (or fez), was erected after independence. Street stalls sold T-shirts laid out on wooden trays. Taxis darted about.

Not far along, I came to the target of my walk: the Yacoubian Building. The local author Alaa Al Aswany's best-selling novel of the same name is based on characters living and working in a tall, Art Deco-inspired apartment block that exists on Talaat Harb Street. The book captures everyday life under Mubarak, with corruption and bribery so engrained that they have become second nature. The hopelessness of fighting the system and the importance of the right connections come across strongly as the characters – including an aging aristocrat with a roving eye for the ladies, a gay newspaper editor, a businessman hoping to move into politics, and the son of the doorman – get on with things the best they can. The fate of the doorkeeper's son, named Taha, is particularly poignant: his attempt to join the police force despite having achieved the necessary grades is thwarted by a prejudiced official, he drifts apart from his childhood sweetheart (who is being sexually molested by the sleazy owner of the clothing shop at which she works), and moves into the murky and dangerous world of Islamic fundamentalism. The story develops into a stinging indictment of Mubarak; Al Aswany is also famous in Egypt for his journalism attacking the former regime. Meanwhile, there is much bed-hopping and debauchery in *The Yacoubian Building* (there are no real saints among the characters, but there's plenty of amusingly unsaintly behaviour). The book teems with colour and life.

The real building, found near Talaat Harb's junction with Adly Street, was no different. Next to a shop selling men's suits – displaying a picture of a man in a dapper white double-breasted outfit and a panama hat, looking as though he would have fitted in very well in the days of British rule – I entered a dingy doorway. This led to a hallway with aquamarine walls and gold Art Deco lettering saying 'N. YACOUBIAN'. The building is named after its owner and was constructed in the 1930s. It was where Al Aswany's father once had an office and is also where the author operated his first dental practice (he trained as a dentist in Chicago).

I was met by a boy wearing a T-shirt saying 'SIMPLY THE BEST'. He was slumped on a plastic chair and appeared to be the son of the doorkeeper/liftman: a real-life version of Taha. We were joined by a man whom I assumed was his father, wearing a beige gallabiya. He invited me in a creaking lift with old wooden panels and scuffed mirrors to the top floor, where I looked up through a skylight towards the roof – many of the characters in the novel live in simple constructions that form a rooftop shanty town. I could not quite see if they existed for real and the doorkeeper did not seem keen on my trying to go any further upwards to investigate. We walked down the dusty staircase, coming across the offices of a cardiologist, an import-export business and, to my surprise, a hotel and a hostel. The Brothers' Hotel had five small rooms, tiger-striped bedcovers and a very chilled-out receptionist who told me, 'Yeah, we get people who stay because of the book… Keep in touch, man, like for sure, man.' The Miami Cairo Hostel, on the ground floor, offered simple rooms from £E120 a night (about £12). Some American backpackers, perhaps attracted by the Floridian name, were just checking in. I said goodbye to Taha and his father – who replied *'shokran, shokran'* ('thank you, thank you') when I tipped him £E5 for my impromptu tour – and I stepped back into the racket of Talaat Harb Street.

Cairo seemed a wonderful city for walking, so long as you kept away from the maddest main roads. Near the Yacoubian Building, I stumbled upon Garden Groppi. This café is a throwback to the heyday of the 1930s; both the authors Penelope Lively, who grew up in Cairo, and Olivia Manning mention Garden Groppi in their works, as does Al Aswany. The café was a popular haunt of British soldiers between World War I and World War II.

It smelt of figs, icing, lemon and chocolate. It was cool and empty, with wooden-panel walls and circular tables. I sat in the back garden one afternoon, amid trees with trunks painted white halfway up. I was on an old wicker chair and felt incredibly calm, hidden away in the middle of the big city. I sipped a strong black coffee and rested my eyes. The garden was full of positive vibes.

Afterwards, on my final evening, I strolled onwards around Cairo, meandering and occasionally catching a taxi to catapult me along. It was just before sunset. Down on El Bostan Street, a man smoking a shisha pipe by a rubber tree smiled and consented when I asked if I could take his picture. Further on, I found myself next to the Nile, where there was soft yellow light and sparrows twittered amid pink frangipani. Feluccas lazed across the water, their sails gently billowing in a sporadic breeze. Near a bridge, I chatted to another orange-juice salesman, who freely admitted that juice made up 'just ten per cent' of what he sold. The rest, he confided, was water; it was the only way to run at a profit. From a couple of bright-eyed kids, I bought postcards mocking Mubarak. One showed him wearing a pair of shorts and holding out empty pockets to demonstrate that he was broke. Another pictured him asleep and dreaming of better days.

That evening, I returned to Tahrir Square and drank another strong coffee in a smoky café before going next door to an unusual Swedish restaurant. The owner was a blonde Swede named Cecilia Goldsmith, a former nursery school teacher from Gothenburg, who ran the place with her grown-up son Martin, and her husband Kent Olsson. They had bought the premises on 24 January 2011, exactly a day before the revolution began.

'We had absolutely no idea there was going to be a revolution, and that we'd be in the middle of it,' said Cecilia, who was philosophical and practical about the timing of their restaurant purchase. But she did not seem to mind too much. 'We've had to adapt our menu a bit to offer grilled chicken and oriental vegetables as well as Swedish dishes.' The Cairenes, apparently, were not the greatest fans of Swedish meatballs.

I tucked into a plate of the latter served with mashed potato, cream sauce and sweet lingonberry jam, accompanied by a glass of sparkling water, while sitting at a plain wooden table in a dining room of Scandinavian simplicity.

It was a delicious meal. The Tahrir Table had eventually opened in November 2011, I learnt from Cecilia. But it was forced to close after just two days when violence again erupted in the square as demonstrators demanded that the military transfer its power to a civilian government. The revolutionaries had believed that the Supreme Council of the Armed Forces was attempting to take control of the country by stealth. They had feared the Tahrir Square martyrs' lives would have been lost in vain. Many more had died in the November clashes.

'There was shooting and it was terrible,' said Cecilia. 'Tear gas came inside and customers' eyes were streaming.' People had fallen on the pavements directly outside, where Swedish and Egyptian flags now hung.

Despite all the trouble, death and disarray, Cecilia and her family had not given up. The restaurant had proved a winner with the employees of the Swedish Embassy, though not as many casual tourists dropped by as Cecilia would have wished.

Outside, I could see the Salafists on the square. It was a highly bizarre scene: a little piece of Sweden in the heart of Arabia. But I had rapidly come to expect the unexpected in Cairo. It was too big a city to pin down: too much going on, too many people; so many stories and so many lives. I ate a lemon meringue pie and returned to the City View Hotel. I was ready, after a night's sleep, to hit the road again.

Note: The presidential election was eventually won by the Muslim Brotherhood candidate Mohamed Morsi, who took 51.73 per cent of the vote after a run-off against Ahmed Shafiq, a candidate who had been Mubarak's last prime minister and who was regarded a *felool* (remnant) of the old regime. Morsi said he would put the slogan 'Islam is the solution' into action but promised that his policies would have a 'moderate Islamic reference' and that he would be a 'President for all Egyptians', Muslims and Copts. It is uncertain precisely how moderate – and many of those involved in the demonstrations of 25 January 2011 said they felt let down by the outcome of the election, which some point out was the country's first for 7,000 years. After taking office, Morsi was successful in revoking the power of the generals, seemingly ending the possibility of a military leader seizing control of the country. Later, however, Morsi himself was involved in a controversial move in which he assumed sweeping powers granting him immunity from the rule of law. This did not seem so 'moderate' and led to renewed protests on Tahrir Square that continue as I write

Meanwhile, the Salafist protests about the disqualification of their presidential candidate Ismail came to nothing. They eventually backed another presidential hopeful who was eliminated in the first round of voting.

Also after my visit, Mubarak was found guilty of complicity in the murder of protesters and was sentenced to life in prison. Not long after the verdict he suffered a mental breakdown at Tora Prison. His sons were adjudged not guilty, though at the time of writing they were still being held for 'market manipulation'.

12

Suez and Sharm el-Sheikh:

To a Dismal but Profitable Ditch... and on

IN THE morning I saw the Rosetta Stone. Not the actual stone, a copy of it, just inside the entrance of the salmon-pink Egyptian Museum, not far from the resting place of Mariette. The real thing famously resides at the British Museum in London, taken during the British defeat of the French in 1799 and transported for display in Bloomsbury in 1802. I looked at the dense snake-like inscriptions of the replica. It has to be the most remarkable rock in history with its triplicate version of the same piece of text in hieroglyphics, demotic and Greek that helped unlock the messages on the walls of Egypt. Tourists had gathered round the copy: the Egyptian Museum was by far the busiest tourist attraction I had visited yet. I was having a quick look before catching a taxi onwards to the city of Suez, organised by the ever-slick, super-efficient guest relations manager at the City View Hotel. The cost of the ride covering 140 kilometres came to £E250 (£26 British). This worked out as 18p a kilometre; probably the best-value taxi ride of my life.

But first I had one of the best-loved museums in the world to explore. I stepped past the Rosetta crowds and turned to the right. There had been a scrum of guides offering their services by the entrance, but I decided to go it alone and found myself staring at sarcophagus after sarcophagus, mini-sphinxes, a quartzite statue of the God Ptah (found in Memphis), towers of stone covered in hieroglyphics, and 2,800-year-old alabaster statues of priests. Light filtered through tall arched windows, sending dusty streaks into hidden corners, where I took in ancient wonder after ancient wonder. The impassive faces of figures from the past stared down, their characters locked in alabaster, crystalline limestone and pink granite. Cabinets were crammed with delicate porcelain figurines that would have certainly disappeared had looters ransacked the museum during the mayhem of the revolution. Thanks to the bravery of people like Alfie, potential thieves were kept at bay.

Yet the Egyptian Museum did not escape the uprising trouble-free – far from it. After the initial gatherings at Tahrir Square, the museum was requisitioned by the armed forces to become a handy location for the torture of protesters using electric shocks, whips, sticks and metal pipes. Horrific 'virginity tests' of females detained in Tahrir Square were also allegedly conducted; Amnesty International reports that such tests were forced on 17 women on 9 March 2011. One protester who was held at the museum told the *Egyptian Independent* newspaper that women were 'tied to fences and trees' at the back of the building. Meanwhile, the group Human Rights Watch interviewed six witnesses who described thugs (known as *baltagiyya*) attacking encampments at Tahrir Square: 'They started insulting us, [saying] things like, "Get out of here, you dogs." Then an army officer told the men in plain clothes "Take them to the museum."' At the museum, a woman told the human rights group: 'They were kicking in my stomach and hitting me with wooden sticks and slapping my face. They called me dirty names.'

I looked around the beautiful ancient statues, considering the depths to which human beings sometimes descend. It was hard to comprehend. Moments of crisis involving dictators clearly brought out the very worst in people (as I had found in three dusty countries in North Africa). Mubarak had been responsible for turning some Egyptians into monsters.

The museum itself had survived remarkably intact, with just a small amount of damage; a far cry from its counterpart in Baghdad, the National Museum of Iraq, which lost so many treasures in 2003. I walked on through slithers of light, seeing statues that would have been nigh on impossible to move without a crane and a forklift truck: great falcon-headed Horuses and jackal-headed Seths. In a chamber at the centre stood a giant Ramses II, who had certainly left his mark in Egypt (not just with his 120 children).

I took in a carving of a happy couple, still smiling after so many centuries. I examined a seductive-looking Nefertiti. I peered into the faces of servants washing clothes in 2500BC. I regarded a 'man preparing a beer jar', discovered in Saqqara. Then I gazed into the eerily lifelike eyes of a scribe sitting cross-legged and holding a papyrus notebook.

As I did so, a doctor of antiquities from Cairo University introduced himself and muttered: 'The eyes, yes, the eyes – the eyes are made of rock of crystals.'

The doctor – I won't give his name as perhaps he was just having a slightly strange day – must have been in his fifties. He wore gold-rimmed glasses and a lemon-yellow shirt tucked into cargo trousers. He turned out to work at the museum and he offered to be my guide, quickly negotiating a price of £E20. I thought 'Why not?', and we shuffled about the displays for a while. The doctor had a manner that suggested that every word he uttered was revealing a secret that had previously remained unspoken for centuries. 'Cheops,' he whispered, pointing at a figure. 'The builder of the Great Pyramid.'

He looked at Cheops with exaggerated admiration, as though that was part of his 'performance'. Then we turned to another carving, showing a dwarf with his wife and children: 'Seneb. The chief of all dwarfs.'

We gazed at the chief of all dwarfs for a while.

We arrived at a sarcophagus. 'Four thousand years ago and the colour is still there! Look!' he urged. I looked. 'Yes!' he exclaimed, quietly.

After examining the sarcophagus, I asked him about the revolution. Was he at the museum on 25 January 2011?

'No, it was a Friday. It was my day off,' he answered sharply, as though wishing to switch subject.

'What was it like on the days after that?' I enquired, hoping that he might shed some light on torture at the museum.

He acted as though he had not heard me and pointed at the floor. 'Do you know that in the basement there are half as many treasures as you can find up here?'

I replied I did not know that and I repeated my question.

The doctor cleared his throat. 'I have to be neutral,' he said, grey eyes glancing through gold-rimmed glasses. 'In this job you have to be.'

He would not be drawn on politics.

We continued around the antiquities for a few minutes more. At one point he stopped and told me earnestly that he was 'doctor number one – you are lucky'. And when it came to paying him – we had been together for half an hour – he looked at the £20 Egyptian note.

'I said twenty dollars, this is twenty pounds,' he commented, not seeming to want to touch the offending object being passed his way.

I replied that we'd agreed on £E20 (I did not mind the occasional request for baksheesh, but did mind a straight-up swindle). He looked closely at me, shrugged and took the note. I walked out through a doorway that led by an empty gift shop, dodged a committee of men selling papyrus painted with pyramids, crossed the mad road, and checked out of the City View Hotel after only a small disagreement over the number of nights I had stayed (a mysterious 'accounting error' meant that the number of days at the hotel, rather than the number of nights, had been counted).

🐪 🐪 🐪

Egyptian pounds and US dollars variously distributed, I left Cairo, on my way to Suez. My taxi pulled away from the City View and almost immediately joined a horrific traffic jam on a flyover. The driver reckoned there must have been an accident. 'Stupid people!' he announced. 'Stupid! This always happens!'

We inched along, the driver mumbling 'Stupid, stupid people!' from time to time. We eventually made it off the flyover and came to a big triangular structure in the shape of a pyramid. The driver told me it was a monument to President Sadat, who was assassinated by Islamic fundamentalists at the spot while attending a military parade on 6 October 1981. The assassins had killed 11 others and injured 28 including Mubarak, who was vice president at the time (some of his hostility towards Islamic groups such as the Muslim Brotherhood must have dated from that day). Sadat, despite his surprise attack on Israel in the Sinai Peninsula during the Yom Kippur War in 1973, was later seen by fundamentalists as being too close to the Israelis and the Americans.

When Sadat died, President Reagan said: 'America has lost a great friend, the world has lost a great statesman, and mankind has lost a champion of peace.' With his assault on Israel in 1973, then his visit to the Knesset in 1977 (the first Arab leader to visit the state of Israel), Sadat was considered unpredictable and was disliked by many in the Arab world. But in the West, despite his crackdown on freedom of expression within Egypt, he had admirers.

The road turned into six lanes, all of them jammed with vehicles. Finally, after much frustration, we began to move at a regular speed. Near the main airport we turned on to the Suez Road. Various military compounds with tanks outside and soldiers in sentry boxes lined this road, which would make a natural route for an invading army from Israel. Past a bleak-looking place called Badr City, we entered a wide desert. A sign said it was 116 kilometres to Suez and 475 kilometres to Sharm el-Sheikh. A group of soldiers dozed beneath a sign advertising an unfinished mall. A red pick-up truck overtook us. 'Stupid!' said the driver, reflexively. His phone went and he embarked on an angry conversation. When he finished the call, he added a few words beneath his breath and said nothing for a while.

We continued into the desert. A billboard showed a picture of the footballer Steven Gerrard with the message 'THE WAY LIVERPOOL PLAY'; we were close to the British International School, so perhaps it was erected by expat supporters. We drove along at the maximum speed, 100 kilometres per hour, for a period, overtaking a pick-up truck with a bunch of guys fast asleep on a precarious stack of wood on the back. The truck was crawling along.

'It is big problem. See slow car. Accident,' said the driver. 'Chaos,' he added.

'Are there many traffic police checking the way people drive?' I asked. There was a worrying mixture of Third World-slow and wannabe racing drivers.

'No. They are sleeping now,' he replied.

We continued in silence again, but not for long.

'Arghhh!' the driver said, pointing at another very slow orange truck and slapping the dashboard. 'Like a *gamoose*!'

'What is a gamoose?' I asked. I gathered that it must be some form of abuse: I wanted to pick up a bit of colloquial lingo.

'A buffalo! Gamoose! Gamoose! Buffalo!' he informed me and fell silent once more. He was wearing large shades and had short, grey cropped hair. He was not the type of person who suffered grievances quietly, I had detected.

The desert swept forth ahead of us. The land looked desolate and hopeless. It was good, honest camel-territory – kilometre upon kilometre of bleak nothingness. We passed a lorry that had skidded to one side with a shredded tyre. 'It is too much for this car,' said the driver, looking at the lorry with disgust. 'Too much!'

We came to some traffic cops dressed in white uniforms. They were pointing a radar gun in our direction. 'Ahhh, radar!' said the driver.

'So the police are not all asleep,' I commented.

'No,' said the driver, eyeing them nervously.

Further on, a truck pulling two long containers was swaying dangerously. 'Dancing!' said the driver, looking at the way it moved from side to side. He almost seemed to be admiring the sheer audacity of the lorry driver for taking such a crazily large load. But this was only a temporary admiration. 'Stupid!' he decided as we carefully wheeled by. 'Stupid!'

Jagged mountains appeared in the misty distance. Sand had swept into dunes against the barrier in the centre of the long, straight road. Vehicles were few and far between. We entered the Suez Governorate, where a military memorial stood at the side of the road, surrounded by old tanks. A turning for Sharm el-Sheikh on the Sinai Peninsula was indicated, but we kept going past a statue in the shape of an anchor, a refinery of some sort, and a graffito: 'FREEDOM'. Suez was one of the most important centres of resistance against Mubarak and the city's citizens were famed for their strong sense of independence.

The first demonstrator to die at the hands of the police on 25 January 2011 was in Suez, according to the television station Al Jazeera. Most of the population – rather as those in Benghazi in Libya had felt under Gaddafi, and those in Sidi Bouzid in Tunisia under Ben Ali – believed they were neglected under Mubarak, who did not once bother to visit Suez during his 30 years in power. They did not like him very much. There was bad unemployment, said to be as high as 35,000 out of a population of just under 500,000; and those with jobs tended to work outside of the city. During the 1973 war against Israel, the people of Suez had formed a militia and bravely fought the Israelis. Their reward for that resistance, which some believe prevented the Israelis from advancing on Cairo, had been steady decline for many years. When Facebook activists said 'take to the streets' on 25 January 2011, the people of Suez did not need a second invitation.

We turned on to a causeway that ran along the Red Sea. Few cars were on the road as we curved by a bay and came to a roundabout. The driver rolled down his window to make a joke to a boy sitting on the back of a moped with his father. 'Your father is very fast!' he said in English. The boy looked totally nonplussed. I think the driver was meaning the opposite: he had strong views on the speeds at which other motorists travelled.

Past a dreary windswept park, we reached the Red Sea Hotel, which I had found on the internet and appeared to be the best place in town despite what you might describe as diffident, and in some cases downright damning, reviews on TripAdvisor: 'A bit rundown but OK', 'Old decor in need of some serious work' and 'Don't go there!'

But I had gone and was indeed there. We pulled into a quiet tree-lined street. I tipped my driver more than I normally would; I never got his name but I liked his gruff take on things. And inside I was soon catching a lift to the fourth floor where I had requested a room overlooking the Suez Canal.

Those reviewers had been harsh. Sure, the Red Sea Hotel was no Ritz, but my room had one of the best and most striking views of any at which I've stayed. Beyond a balcony and the verdant gardens of what looked like plush houses, a giant cargo ship was slowly sliding through the canal. From afar it looked as though the ship was somehow drifting through the land.

I sat on the balcony, transfixed. I was at the southern entry point of a canal through which 7.5 per cent of the world's sea trade is said to travel, including most of Europe's oil. I was looking out towards the source of the argument with Nasser that had brought an end to Britain's illusion of empire. I could see across to the Sinai Peninsula, where Israeli troops had been positioned from 1967 to 1982; much of the population of Suez was evacuated during this period due to regular bombardments. There was a strong sense of being at an important place. After all, the canal linked East to West. When a ship came through from the Orient, avoiding the long route round the Cape of Good Hope, it was taking the world's number one short cut through one of the greatest feats of engineering of all time.

The cargo ship was moving southwards. It was big and blue and piled with grey and rust-red containers with 'MAERSK' written on them. The name on the bow was 'CMA CGM BALZAC'. I had become a cargo ship spotter and I was enjoying every moment. There was something surreal about seeing a vessel so large – each ship was like a mountainous island – making its way so slowly but surely across the desert. For almost an hour, I sat and watched. After the *Balzac* disappeared, accompanied by a pilot boat, another ship loomed in the north. In the water next to the elegant houses, expensive speedboats were moored; the Red Sea Hotel seemed to be in a well-to-do neighbourhood. Noisy Indian house crows, brought to Suez by ships from India in the 19th century, occasionally let out a burst of raucous calls. An egret soared serenely by.

The Suez Canal opened in 1888; construction had begun in 1859 financed by shareholders who were mainly French and also included the ruling pasha of Egypt. The latter, however, went bankrupt halfway through the work and was reluctantly forced to sell his interest. The British stepped in. After striking the deal, Disraeli, the prime minister of the time who had raised cash for the purchase through a loan from the Rothschild family, casually told Queen Victoria: 'You have it, Madam.'

The current canal was not the first attempt at creating a waterway across the landscape. In 500BC Darius I of Persia opened a link between the Red Sea and the Great Bitter Lake, just to the north of Suez. Meanwhile Ramses II (him again) is believed to have dug a canal between the Nile and the Red Sea 2,300 years ago, thus linking the Mediterranean to waters leading to the Far East. It had long ago disappeared under drifting sands.

I had brought with me a copy of Joseph Conrad's second novel, *An Outcast of the Islands*, published in 1896. The main character, Peter Willems, is a dissolute man on the run from a scandal in Macassar in Indonesia. He takes to the high seas to escape his troubles. But somehow the ghosts of his concerns follow him. At one point the narrator ruminates on the nature of the sea and is not in favour of the Suez Canal, which he believes has somehow ruined the 'spell' of the open water. And in this passage Conrad coined a phrase describing the canal that stuck:

[The sea] cast a spell, it gave joy, it lulled gently into boundless faith; then with quick and causeless anger it killed. But its cruelty was redeemed by the charm of its inscrutable mystery, by the immensity of its promise, by the supreme witchery of its possible favour... That was the sea before the time when the French mind set the Egyptian muscle in motion and produced *a dismal but profitable ditch*. Then a great pall of smoke sent out by countless steamboats was spread over

the restless mirror of the Infinite. The hand of the engineer tore down the veil
of the terrible beauty in order that greedy and faithless landlubbers might pocket
dividends. The mystery was destroyed.

The great pall of smoke from the countless steamboats may have gone
but the mystery, to me at least, remained. It was more than a 'dismal but
profitable ditch', although the ditch certainly did bring in cash: about
US$430 million a month in tolls. There was something secretive about the
slow progress across the desert, the ships slipping southwards with their
mountains of sealed containers. What was on board? Where were they
going? Would pirates strike in the Gulf of Aden? How long till the captain
returned with another mountain from the East? There was plenty of mystery
– and another sensation, too. The Red Sea Hotel felt like an *edgeland*; well
away from the mainstream world, yet overlooking somewhere that the main
stream relied upon for so many things. It was hard to put a finger on the
appeal of watching the ships drifting across the horizon. It was an elusive
attraction… perhaps there's an inner cargo ship spotter in us all. Perhaps
one day the cargo ships of Suez would become a tourist attraction, like the
pyramids and the Egyptian Museum. Or then again, maybe it was just me.
Maybe the sandy air and the sun were getting to me.

Suez was a curious, singular place. From the hotel I walked by the few smart
shuttered houses next to the water and continued along an empty road with
drumstick trees towards the heart of Port Tewfik – the part of Suez with
a harbour (technically the Red Sea Hotel was in Port Tewfik). Pilot boats
were moored in a dock. A surprisingly large mosque boasted a pair of tall
minarets. I continued towards a corniche by the canal, crossing a deserted
park with scraggly grass. But I drew to a halt when I realised that the tent
that I saw at the far side was not a stall selling snacks, as I had thought, but
occupied by soldiers with guns, behind a tumble of barbed wire that cut off

the corniche to visitors. The Suez Canal obviously remained a sensitive zone, even if the Israelis were long gone. I ambled along near dull apartment blocks that reminded me of the Soviet Union and rundown parts of eastern Europe, and arrived at the end of the port where a minibus with 'NO GO' written on the side was waiting. Despite its unusual slogan, the bus did in fact 'go' and I went on it, travelling back past the hotel and into the centre of Suez, listening to Arabic music and sitting near a woman who wore sunglasses over her *niqab* so it was impossible to detect any features or emotions whatsoever.

I got off the bus and found myself on a filthy road surrounded by tall, crumbling concrete buildings. I investigated a narrow street with rubbish scattered on the pavements. Tiny fashion shops were squeezed at the base of half-wrecked abodes. At the end of this street, I came to the less famous Ibrahimiya Canal, where cats and crows clambered over piles of rubbish by the water's edge. Just as in Benghazi, the city's neglect was only too easy to see. The canal was a thin channel leading I knew not where. I retraced my steps in search of somewhere to eat, stopping to watch an elderly man who had filled an old bucket with his groceries. Someone from an apartment above dropped a rope and the bucket was attached to the rope. The groceries were then hoisted slowly above to the apartment. There was something touching about the scene.

In another street, stalls were selling *fatir*, a pancake-like pastry served with meat of the sort that is scraped from hunks in kebab shops. As much as I wanted to sample the delights of Suez, I did not feel like sampling that particular delight. So I continued along, shunning a KFC and realising I was very hungry. I ended in an alley at a sticky table in a cramped, furnace-hot pizzeria with three other tables. Dripping with sweat, I waited – and waited. Eventually a small, extremely greasy pepperoni pizza was delivered. I ate the small, extremely greasy pizza and after this fine dining experience walked back towards the hotel, crossing a litter-strewn park overlooking the Bay of Suez. Plastic bags, old fast-food wrappers and rusting cans covered the rough grass beneath gaunt trees. Across the bay, I could see the terminal for the ferries to Saudi Arabia or Sudan. I left the park and caught another minibus back to the hotel, where I had a chat with Adir, the reception manager.

He was a dapper man in a suit with a grey tie, aged 58. I know his age because he told me, without a pause, that on 6 June 1967, when he was aged 13, he was evacuated from Suez after the Israeli invasion of the Sinai Peninsula.

'We moved from here into the valley,' he said. 'Almost everything was destroyed: about eighty per cent of the city. The Israeli army was on the other side of the canal. It was very dangerous. Every person moved to the valley. It was only the army that was left.'

That year was a disaster for Suez, Adir said. 'Before 1967 it was much quieter and nicer and cleaner – much smaller.' He said his family eventually moved back to the city from the valley in 1975, when the situation was calmer.

The ships had vanished on the canal – perhaps there was a gap while the authorities cleared the waters to allow vessels to go northwards. I stayed in my room reading a book of Alaa Al Aswany's journalism and essays entitled *On the State of Egypt* that I'd picked up at the American University bookshop in Cairo. Al Aswany describes how he joined the demonstration on Tahrir Square on 25 January after seeing pictures on his television; he had expected a few hundred people to attend the protest and had been shocked by the huge turnout. He rushed to the square to take part when he saw the images. For the next 18 days he 'lived in the street', except when sleeping, and described the atmosphere as being like that of the Paris Commune. Coptic Christians and Muslims, the young and the old, had risen to take a stand beside one another, and when Mubarak eventually fell there was a 'riotous celebration' that lasted all night.

Al Aswany's many articles on poverty in Egypt and Mubarak's vote-rigging arrogance are gripping. He asks how civil servants could be expected to raise families on £E100 a month (£10.50 British). He describes Mubarak as regarding Egypt as a 'poultry farm', an object that the former president acted as though he owned and intended to pass on to his son Gamal as though it were a mere business, no matter how the chickens (or Egyptians) were treated. He slams the ex-president for spending twice as much on the Ministry of Interior (with its violent secret police) as on the Ministry of Health. He talks about the sexual frustration of poor young men who are not wealthy enough to marry. He attacks Wahhabi ideas about covering up women. And twisting the Muslim Brotherhood slogan of 'Islam is the solution', he ends each of a series of eloquent pieces damning Mubarak's autocratic rule by repeating the phrase 'democracy is the solution'.

In the evening I went upstairs to the top-floor Mermaid Restaurant, stepping along narrow red hallways that smelt of polish. Through high, open windows, sodium lights shone by the canal. A solitary diner wearing a baseball cap sat smoking at a circular table with three different cans of soft drinks before him (he appeared to be pushing the limit with soft drinks as alcohol was not served). I ate a red mullet meal that was the best I had had in North Africa. The TripAdvisor reviewers had been a bit sniffy when they described the food as 'average' and 'OK'.

Two men in wool hats joined the man with the baseball cap. I took them to be members of a cargo ship crew. A musak version of Elton John's 'Nikita' played softly on the stereo. Dogs howled in the streets below. The men on the table ate their food noisily but otherwise in total silence. Suez was indeed a curious, singular place.

🐫 🐫 🐫

After being woken by a very early muezzin who seemed to set off both a car alarm and the family of Indian house crows, I watched from the breakfast room as oil tankers headed north. In the reception I disputed my bill. The price I had been quoted in an email 'made no sense' to the receptionist, and I ended up paying a higher rate. Egyptian hoteliers seem to have mastered the art of confused accountancy (in their favour). The sofas in the reception were taken by a group of Western lads, who had just checked out. Each bore a kitbag. I asked one of them what they were doing in Suez.

'Maritime security – we're about to go on board,' said Chris from York. He had a wary manner.

I asked him where they were heading. They all wore matching, navy blue polo shirts and cargo trousers.

'We don't know where... going south,' he replied.

His pal next to him, who had closely cropped hair and a red face, said: 'Sri Lanka. Protection vessels.'

I asked them if they had any stories about pirates, and said that I would not name them or their company, and that I was just interested. Any information would be off the record. The second lad said: 'I used to be a journalist: nothing is off the record. I did a degree in journalism at Southampton University. Never had a job, mind you.'

A large man, also red-faced, with straw hair and a flat nose came over. He looked as though he wanted to punch me. 'Just talk to our central office,' he said, eyeballing me fiercely. 'Don't talk to any of the lads.'

He delivered this in the manner of an order. I did not talk to any more of the lads, and as I left I overheard the large man with the flat nose say loudly, clearly intended so I could hear: 'At least he wasn't the *Daily Star*, could have been worse.'

I took a taxi to the bus station. The people at the hotel had said the bus to Sharm el-Sheikh would leave in half an hour. The people at the bus station disagreed: the bus would leave at 5 p.m. It looked as though I had most of a day to wait at the Suez bus station. It was a bleak spot. I considered returning to the exciting throng of Suez, with its many high-class pizzeria dining options. Then a fellow who had overheard my questions at the ticket counter approached. His name was Haytham and he was an off-duty ticket inspector. He explained that I could catch one bus through the tunnel under the Suez Canal. Then I could take another down to Sharm el-Sheikh. He was going on the bus under the tunnel and I was to join him.

By some kind of miracle we were almost immediately on the move, sitting in a long orange-gold coach filled with tall, tight seats. The ticket inspector was across the way and I found myself talking to three university students taking petroleum- and engineering-related degrees in Suez. They were returning home to Port Said, at the northern end of the Suez Canal, for a break.

I explained my earlier bus problem. Ahmed said: 'Like so many things in Egypt, this has not got better yet. Sometimes we go to the bus station and the bus does not go: this is one of the things of Egypt.'

They talked about a horrific football match in Port Said earlier in the year in which at least 74 people died when supporters of the local Al-Masry football team stormed the pitch after a rare victory over Cairo's Al-Ahly team, viciously attacking rival fans with knives, clubs, swords and stones. They told me that Mubarak had always encouraged violence between clubs as a way of dividing and ruling in the country.

We discussed the revolution and the various presidential candidates. Hassen said: 'In Egypt we have three main things: Facebook, Yahoo and Twitter. For young people these are the things that matter. Since the revolution, even older people have heard about them. They have heard that these things made the revolution.'

The bus plunged into the Ahmed Hamdi Tunnel, emerging in the Sinai Peninsula a few minutes later. The kindly off-duty ticket inspector showed me where to get off and asked another passenger, a local who I gathered was returning to his workplace in Sharm el-Sheikh, to show me where to wait for the next bus. Together he and I trudged past a roundabout guarded by two sand-coloured tanks manned by soldiers wearing red berets. And we waited with a handful of other travellers on a broken pavement next to a garage. This 'bus station' seemed to be controlled by a man with a medicine-ball belly protruding beneath an enormous gallabiya. He inquired about our desired destination, and importantly rattled off information in Arabic.

The other passenger and I stood wordlessly on the broken pavement for two hours as buses passed – never the right bus. I encountered my first Egyptian Bedouin. He was elderly and wore a white robe with a red headscarf held in place by a black band. When his minibus arrived, he happened to be eating sunflower seeds. The medicine-ball man attempted to hurry him along by helping him with his bag. The Bedouin, who had a long, distinguished face with a bushy moustache, was furious with the medicine-ball man and hurled his packet of sunflower seeds on the pavement in anger. With great show, he slowly took his bag and placed it on the roof rack of the minibus. In his own time, clearly to the irritation of all the other passengers, he took his seat. He was a very stubborn old goat. The other passenger and I had a chuckle as the minibus eventually moved away.

Such excitements helped pass the time before another orange-gold East Delta bus arrived to take us to Sharm el-Sheikh. There was no room to sit. So the other passenger and I stood awkwardly in the aisle, the only two people without berths. After a short distance, the bus stopped and all of us were required to go outside and stand in a line with our possessions before us. Policemen checked our ID and an Alsatian sniffed our bags.

We drove on. From the window I looked out across desolate sands into the Gulf of Suez. A row of tankers appeared to be waiting to enter the canal. We stopped for a toilet break and a shisha smoke near a nowhere town called Ras Sudr. We filed out and some of the passengers went to ignite pipes. There appeared to be no particular hurry to get to Sharm el-Sheikh. I bought a KitKat and a soda and rested on a kerb. The other passenger, whose name I never got as he spoke no English, lurked near by. He seemed to have taken on responsibility for my passage, and was keeping an eye on me.

There were more Bedouins at the café. Their presence reminded me that earlier in the year two American tourists and three South Koreans had been kidnapped by Bedouins in separate incidents in the Sinai Peninsula. This had come shortly after a coach containing 50 German and British tourists was seized for a few hours after the driver failed to stop at a makeshift roadblock set up as a form of protest against the local government. The Bedouin kidnappers had struck on the road to St Catherine's Monastery, the peninsula's main tourist attraction at the foot of Mount Sinai, where the Old Testament says Moses received the stone tablets with the Ten Commandments. Despite these troubles, the Foreign and Commonwealth Office did not advise against visiting the region.

The Bedouins had taken the hostages as a gambit to have relatives released from police custody; they had long complained about police discrimination in the region, which they believed was controlled by cronies of the old Mubarak regime. On each occasion the kidnapping was soon over with the release of the hostages unharmed. The Americans had told the Associated Press that the Bedouins had politely served them tea and dried fruit and 'talked about religion and tribal rights'. They seemed to have had a reasonable time. That said, I did not wish to be kidnapped by a Bedouin.

We continued southwards, seated now, as some people had disembarked at Ras Sudr. The driver turned on a television, which loudly played a film in Arabic starring perhaps the noisiest, worst, drama queen-style comic actor in Arabia (he did not raise a single laugh). The desert rolled ahead with desolate mountains rising in the interior. A Bedouin near me reached into his white robe and answered a call on his mobile. We crept through checkpoints and at around 6 p.m. arrived in semi-darkness at Sharm el-Sheikh bus station.

🐫 🐫 🐫

The other passenger and I shook hands, after he had arranged a taxi and established the fare on my behalf. We had hardly exchanged a word, but yet again I was experiencing the understated charm and good-natured way of life of North Africa, a trait that seemed to run as an invisible thread along the south Mediterranean coast.

The taxi whisked me to my beachfront hotel, the Four Seasons, a golf-buggy land with a giant pool and a Balinese spa. It was by far the most upmarket hotel of my journey. Apparently the former British prime minister Tony Blair had not long ago dined at its Italian restaurant with his wife Cherie and the former French president Nicolas Sarkozy. Blair had regularly gone on holiday in Sharm el-Sheikh during Mubarak's rule, once controversially accepting a six-night stay in two villas in the grounds of another hotel, which he subsequently 'paid' for by making an undisclosed charitable donation to an unnamed charity chosen by Mubarak. Blair seemed to get on very well with Mubarak, whom he on one occasion described as being 'immensely courageous and a force for good'; words that the ex-British prime minister perhaps regretted. The former president's luxury villa, where he spent some of his final days as a free man, was close to the Four Seasons. I was hoping to take a look in the morning.

I sat in a candlelit grill restaurant down by the water's edge and ate another good red mullet dinner. A gentle breeze crossed the water; it was a balmy evening. A waiter asked: 'Sir, would you like any magazines or news summaries?' I said I was fine; I still had the rest of Al Aswany. Out on the Red Sea, muffled music came from a 'party boat'. I could make out a DJ's voice. 'IT'S PARTY TIME!' he yelled. This was the most touristy destination of the trip. Beyond the floating disco, I could see lights on Tiran Island, officially part of Saudi Arabia but administered by the Egyptians and an international peacekeeping force known as the Multinational Force and Observers (MFO). The island has huge strategic importance being at the mouth of the Gulf of Aqaba, leading to Eilat in Israel and Aqaba in Jordan. The MFO was established as part of the 1979 Camp David Accords, signed by President Sadat and Israeli Prime Minister Menachem Begin, and has outposts across the Sinai Peninsula.

I was as far south as I had gone or would go on my journey across the Arab Spring. I drank a glass of Egyptian Shahrazade Chardonnay – named after the Persian storyteller from *Tales from 1,001 Nights* – and looked out to sea. Stars shone in the ink-black sky. Candles flickered. Despite the music from the party boat, it was a very peaceful place to be. I returned to my room on a golf buggy. I was looking forward to the final leg of my trip, northwards to the border with Israel and then deep into the interior to see St Catherine's Monastery.

Vast Bedouin pastures and mighty deserts awaited. Egypt seemed such an enormous country with parts that felt quite divided from one another. The centre of Cairo was so different from its rough-and-tumble outskirts near Memphis. The strangeness of Suez – somehow cut off from the main stream – seemed a million miles from the tourist sights of the capital. The deserts of the Sinai were another world altogether – another country almost. As I had found in Cairo, it was hard to grab hold of Egypt. It was massive and marvellous and seemed to stretch on forever.

13

Sharm el-Sheikh, Taba and St Catherine's Monastery:

Smile: you are in Egypt

THE FOUR Seasons was full of Russians. 'Can you tell me somewhere we can make shop?' asked a tall, ballerina-like woman with a husband with a belly and a gold chain, as though I were a member of staff. I pointed them in the direction of the boutiques by the reception. '*Spasiba*,' she replied. She was wearing a bikini and shoes with heels. They tottered and shuffled away.

I went to the breakfast terrace, where I soon met Yasmina Nouali, the forthright and cheerful 'residences manager' at the hotel. Sipping coffee in the shade of tall date palms, she told me that Russians and Ukrainians were important guests, making up numbers as the 'age of austerity' swept western Europe. She described how to find Mubarak's main villa in Sharm el-Sheikh and said that small groups of protesters had gathered outside the local hospital where Mubarak was treated after he stood down: 'I pass by the hospital each day on the way to work: I saw them.' Apart from that, there had been very little sign of the revolution in the resort.

'Here it was very quiet,' she said. 'We feel like we are a part of Egypt, but not Egypt. When our Egyptian staff here go to Cairo, they say: 'We are going to Egypt.' Almost all the Egyptians here are not from the Sinai Peninsula. The local people, the Bedouins, they don't like to work for other people.'

Yasmina was originally from Algeria but had married an Egyptian. She did not like Mubarak: 'I am very glad and lucky to be here during this moment in the history of the country. He was untouchable. He was the pharaoh...

He spent so much time in Sharm el-Sheikh, in his villas. I think he spent more time in Sharm el-Sheikh than he did in Cairo.'

I asked if he ever visited the Four Seasons.

'Yes, he came here to eat,' Yasmina replied, slightly cagily.

We chatted for a while and Yasmina advised me to see Na'ama Bay at night, where all the 'boom, boom, boom' bars were – I was staying another evening in Sharm el-Sheikh so I could witness the booming bay before heading north into the desert. She recommended the Camel Bar and gave me directions to the Old Market and the Ras Mohammed National Park. She was pleased to offer local knowledge as she said that most guests did not venture out of the hotel grounds. We discussed politics. Yasmina said that, when it came to a future leader of Egypt, she was a fan of Mohamed ElBaradei, the Nobel Peace Prize winner: 'He is the only one with experience.'

🐪 🐪 🐪

It was the start of an unusual day. After collecting my hire car, I followed US highway-style signs along a road lined with hotels and palms, going down a hill to the Old Market. I was hoping to find some evidence of real life away from the golf-buggy lands.

I turned into a street with 'OLD MARKET' written on an archway painted with pharaohs, and parked on an empty stretch of road. I got out next to a series of posters of the politician Amr Moussa, a presidential hopeful who had served as Minister of Foreign Affairs under Mubarak and also for a decade as Secretary-General of the Arab League. His eyes had been scratched out on the posters.

'He will never be president,' said a man wearing multicoloured shorts. He had seen me looking at Moussa and had joined me. He was the owner of a stall selling spices, shisha pipes and flip-flops. We fell into conversation; Egyptians surely must be among the world's most enthusiastic talkers.

Shnouda complained that there were not enough tourists. He said that since the revolution he had also suffered trouble from Bedouins, who had come to the market and attempted to take over his business during a time when the police did not intervene. As he said this, a group of fellow stallholders in multicoloured shorts gathered round and a debate on the future of Egypt ensued. Presidential hopefuls were either damned or praised – and Mubarak took a hammering: 'He was very, very bad... He opened the door to drugs... I hate him, I kill him... For thirty years he was powerful... the first ten years OK, then no good.'

A tall, thin, pale-faced man approached wearing aviator shades. He slipped to the front of the impromptu public forum, and berated the men in multicoloured shorts in rapid Arabic. They had just been getting into the swing of things.

'You,' he drawled, pointing at me slyly with a long index finger. 'You. Are you an Israeli?'

He seemed to think I was an Israeli spy of some sort. I answered that I was not.

'Are you sure?' he replied, his words seeming to slide out of the side of his thin mouth.

I showed him my passport.

'Hmmm,' was all he said. He appeared to be the local 'controller' – or fancied himself as such.

The men in multicoloured shorts dispersed. I continued round the market, the sole tourist. Stallholders half-heartedly attempted to sell me 'nice handbags, nice'. Shops displayed T-shirts bearing the slogan: 'SMILE: YOU ARE IN EGYPT'. There were no mottos referring to the revolution. Despite what the stallholders had said, the emotions of Tahrir Square did not seem to be matched in Sharm el-Sheikh. A man at a café near a large, half-constructed mosque asked: 'You want buy sugarcane?' I said I did, and sat at a little table used by locals where I drank the sweet, fresh, sugary drink, accompanied by a pita bread filled with falafel, tomato and grated carrot. Across the street, a travel agency advertised tours in Russian – I'd had no idea there would be so many Russians. I settled in the café, watching the world go by. I could see the thin 'controller' in the aviator glasses lurking by a wall.

🐫 🐫 🐫

I went for a drive. Through a checkpoint I crossed a stretch of desert into Ras Mohammed National Park. It was an elemental and eerie landscape overlooking a sapphire sea. I spun along kilometres of gritty, empty roads, not really knowing where I was going but enjoying the quiet of the desert. The rocky sands disappeared into the flat horizon. I felt a long way from anywhere, and I liked it. But I soon came to a cove where a solitary minibus was parked. There was life in the desert. Down in the shade of rocks – it was a hot day – yet more Russians were bathing in crystal waters.

From the park, I went in search of Mubarak's favourite villa. This was back on the main road, next to the Jolie Ville hotel. The road to the villa itself was blocked. Instead, to catch a glimpse, you had to go to the hotel next door.

At the Jolie Ville, I was surprised to find a major security checkpoint. A dozen guards with guns were at a barrier and I waited five minutes as a suspicious officer inspected my driver's licence. I later learned that many leaders from countries connected to the Non-Aligned Movement, a group of states unattached to any of the major world power blocs, were staying when I visited.

I entered a large white building through a cavernous green-marble reception and kept on walking past a dining terrace into the gardens at the back; I knew where I needed to go. A lush tropical garden rolled over a hill that led to a café and a wooden snorkelling jetty. Feeling a little as though I was trespassing, and aware that journalists had been thrown out for poking around during Mubarak's time, I progressed towards the jetty in the company of a Danish tourist with whom I had fallen into stride. He was holding flippers and agreed to act as my 'accomplice' as we went down the jetty, where I would pretend to take a picture of him while in fact capturing Mubarak's old villa. I was turning into a spy of sorts (though not an Israeli one).

The villa had a semicircular, whitewashed façade and was up a rocky escarpment partially covered in pink bougainvillea. Hoop-shaped windows opened on to a terrace. A sign warned people not to swim in the water beneath the escarpment.

So that was where Mubarak spent so much of his time as well as his final days under house arrest before being taken to the hospital at Cairo's Tora Prison. It was certainly a long way removed from the slum houses and filthy rubbish dumps I'd seen on the way to Saqqara and Giza. I wondered how many world leaders had been entertained up there. Had the former British prime minister Tony Blair, who was close to Mubarak, been honoured with an invitation? It was a beautiful setting.

I thanked the Dane, who seemed to enjoy the minor subterfuge, and went in search of a location Blair definitely had visited. The New Tower Club (referred to as a 'hotel complex' in articles I had read) was tucked away past Na'ama Bay on a hill with a commanding view of the sea. It seemed to be a gated community of big, white villas hidden behind tall hedges and security gates. Satellite dishes poked from the terracotta roofs like strange mushrooms. The villas were said to be worth £5 million each, and it is believed that Blair and his family visited on holiday three times – including a fortnight's stay over New Year in 2004.

During that visit, the Conservative Party member of parliament, Chris Grayling, had attacked Blair in the British press and called on him to explain exactly who was paying for the trip. In a *Daily Mail* story with the headline 'NEW FREEBIE ROW AS BLAIR TAKES HOLIDAY IN £5M VILLA', Grayling commented: 'Once again there is uncertainty about whether the Blairs are paying for their holidays. People are really fed up with their Prime Minister accepting free holiday after free holiday.' Blair had also been a guest at a villa belonging to the government in Tuscany (when he said he made a donation to charity to cover the cost) as well as that of the pop singer Sir Cliff Richard in Barbados and a Miami Beach mansion belonging to Robin Gibb of the Bee Gees.

In his autobiography, *A Journey*, Blair refers to a 'few happy days in the sun' in Sharm el-Sheikh in 2002 and he admits that he had expected criticism for going ahead with the 2004 New Year trip as his family had left for the villa soon after the tsunami in Asia on Boxing Day, in which many Britons were killed. But he says he had continued as he had needed the break. The autobiography does not explain how such holidays were financed, and Mubarak is not mentioned anywhere in the 718 pages.

I returned to Peace Road, the main street with all the hotels. I was getting to know Sharm el-Sheikh in a slightly unconventional way perhaps, but it was fun driving about. I stopped at a mall with a sign for a bookshop and was soon inside a small air-conditioned room. The Eshta Book Centre was run by Bella, a highly talkative, smiley Australian with a Fijian background, who was in the middle of eating a large tub of ice cream when I met her. She wore orange shorts, a stripy top and had a series of gold chains with crosses hanging round her neck. She had started her business three years ago as there was no bookshop in Sharm el-Sheikh. Her husband was a mining engineer who had worked in the Sudan, Yemen and Egypt. Her son was in a feeder team for the East Grinstead rugby club in Britain. 'What do you do in Sharm other than snorkel?' she said, explaining her decision to set up a business. 'And I'm not about to go sunbathing, I'm from Fiji!'

What do Arab men think of her running a shop?

'They think it's *interesting*,' she said, dragging out the final word. 'They think it's *interesting*... but really, I don't give a ****.'

I asked Bella about Mubarak and the revolution.

'Prior to the uprising Mubarak was a very significant presence in Sharm el-Sheikh,' she said, in between great spoons of ice cream. 'Security was tightened. To some extent, we felt safer because of that. During the revolution there were just a few protests outside the police station and down in the Old Market.'

🐫 🐫 🐫

On Bella and Yasmina's recommendations, I dropped off the car at the hotel and took a taxi into Na'ama Bay in the evening. It was indeed 'boom, boom, boom' – plentifully and excessively 'boom, boom, boom'. It was as Western a holiday spot as I had experienced in North Africa; deserted parts of Libya with ancient Greek remains and bullet shells on the ground seemed a distant memory. An FA Cup match was playing on flat-screen televisions in bars (Chelsea were beating Liverpool 2–1). Belly dancers with Geordie accents wiggled for drinkers. I walked down a promenade, overhearing a snatch of Cockney conversation: 'What you've got to watch out for is the wine…' Beyond a McDonald's, there was a Hard Rock Café. A man crooned Lionel Richie songs by a hotel pool. I stopped at a beach bar with a palm-frond roof and drank a sickly sweet, bright-red cocktail consisting of gin, Cointreau and tonic. Further along the promenade, slippery figures approached every now and then hissing: 'Excuse me, excuse me, my friend. Where you from?' I kept going down Main Street. Souvenir shops sold stuffed camels. Local lads smoked shisha pipes in the occasional café. As far as I could tell, that was as much 'local life' as you got in Na'ama Bay.

I came to the China House restaurant, a Blair haunt during his breaks. I looked inside, finding a mini-pagoda decorated with Christmas tree lights. I had read somewhere that the restaurant once had a big sign outside saying 'OUR GUEST OF THE YEAR: TONY BLAIR', but I could not see the grand advertisement. It was gone (a bit like the reputation of the man himself).

I approached a waiter who wore a black Mao Tse-tung-style outfit and asked him what had happened to the banner.

'We took it down when the revolution happened,' he replied.

'Why?' I asked.

'I don't know,' he answered diffidently.

'Was it because Blair was connected to Mubarak?'

'Yes,' he said with a broad smile.

I went for a nightcap at the Hilton where another crooner was singing 'You Ain't Nothing But a Hound Dog'. It was as though we were in Florida.

Beneath an almost full moon, I listened to more old hits and watched Egyptian men in the midst of heroic attempts to chat up Western (or perhaps Russian) women. As I left, a waiter rushed up and asked gruffly: 'Have you paid?'

I said that I had.

'Really?' he asked.

'Yes,' I replied.

He almost reluctantly let me pass. Sharm el-Sheikh did not feel like Egypt, as Yasmina had said. I could have been anywhere with beaches and sun and bars. It was loud, thoughtless and anonymous: somewhere you could hide away, just as Mubarak had in his villas and Blair on his holidays.

In the morning I headed north. It was 220 kilometres to Taba, next to the border with Israel. Peace Road was clear of traffic and so was the twisting highway through the mountains and desert. I passed a cement factory. I slowed to watch a camel idling on the hard shoulder. An occasional lorry loaded with cars roared by in the opposite direction. I crossed big flat *wadis*, open valleys between the mountains. Desolate sandy landscape disappeared into the distance in a heat haze. Entire *wadis* were devoid of vegetation; a tree was a rarity. The land looked brutal, rocky, empty and uncompromising; nightmarish in its hardness. I may not have been discovering the 'discomforts of desert travel: the biting cold of winter nights, the blazing heat, the blinding glare of summer, the irritation of blown sand, the brackish indescribably foul-tasting water, the hunger, the monotony, the long marches, the lack of sleep' as described by Wilfred Thesiger to the BBC, and in his classic travel book about the Empty Quarter of the Arabian peninsula, *Arabian Sands*. But I could imagine what they might be like.

I stopped at a checkpoint at Dahab, a smaller version of Sharm el-Sheikh, where bored-looking policemen sitting on plastic chairs indicated that I could pass by. And I drove on along the quiet highway. To the west was the Badiet El-Tih, the 'wilderness of the wanderings', where only the

Bedouin really knew what went on. If I went east, across mountains, I would find the Gulf of Aqaba. Across the sea, I would come to Saudi Arabia. It was an exhilarating drive; exciting to be in such an alien and remote setting.

Policemen waved me on at another checkpoint at Nuweiba and the road north moved closer to the sea. It led to cheap hotels and campsites on a pink-sand coast. 'CAMP CLEOPATRA' was followed by the 'FREEDOM!' camp, which was advertised with a picture of the Statue of Liberty. I did not see a soul at any of them; perhaps it was the wrong season for tourists in those parts (though the Russians seemed to have been enjoying themselves in Sharm el-Sheikh). I steered clear of the 'BEER SWEER' bar. Then the road became rougher, with bumps and pot-holes. A mist had settled over the magnesium waters of the Gulf. A *zone de plongée* (diving area) by a bay was deserted. High mountains with a pink-and-orange colouration rose as the highway became narrower. After yet another checkpoint, the road deteriorated even further. I thought I must be going the wrong way, but could not work out where I might have made a mistake. A rusting sign said: 'MINISTRY OF TOURISM PROHIBITED AREA: PHOTOGRAPHY IS PROHIBITED'. How had I got lost, I wondered? It did not seem as though I was coming to a tourist resort.

The sign was next to a military compound with an unmanned sentry box. I kept going, imagining that I'd probably have to turn back, and came to a statue of a woman holding a dove. Near this statue, a woman in a full gown and *niqab* was carrying a heavy bag on her head. I had taken the correct route after all: down an empty street with a few dull concrete buildings, I came to my hotel, the Mövenpick, beyond which I could see the border crossing to Eilat in Israel. Another woman in black sat cross-legged on the pavement, with trinkets spread out before her. A bossy security guard took ages checking my driving licence, passport and letter confirming my room. He handed back the documents, opened the barrier, and swiped an arm to indicate I could enter.

Taba would have fitted in well in the pages of one of J G Ballard's slightly sinister novels describing otherworldly holiday destinations where the 'real' is suspended and consumerism and international branding have taken over. It was not brash in the way of Sharm el-Sheikh. It was not flash or in any manner ostentatious. The resort felt neither in Egypt, nor in the Middle East, nor anywhere. It was a place that seemed to fall between all other places: a true nowhere land.

The Mövenpick was a comfortable hotel with a green garden and a big circular pool. It was next to a Hilton with a casino that had suffered a terrorist attack by Islamic fundamentalists in 2004, killing more than thirty people. The hotels in Taba were popular with Israeli tourists, which had been one of the reasons it was targeted. Egypt had a history of such attacks across the country. In 2005, 88 people were killed in bomb blasts in Sharm el-Sheikh; in 1997, Islamic militants shot dead 58 tourists and four Egyptians at the temple of Queen Hatshepsut, close to the southern city of Luxor. There had been further deaths in smaller incidents. It was no wonder the security guard had taken his time with checks at the front gate. I was glad he had been so thorough.

I went for a swim in the giant pool. A solitary man was drinking a beer in the shallows next to a bar. Near my sunlounger, a Russian couple lay out in the heat, hardly saying a word to one another. An excitable member of staff attempted to enthuse me to join a game of volleyball (he did not succeed). Birdsong rose from hedges and fragrant beds of pink flowers.

After a while, I walked down to the beach. To the north, I could see the hotels of Eilat in Israel. Across the Gulf, the outline of Aqaba rose in Jordan. The black, white, green and red national flag flew from a giant post; clearly designed to impress its neighbours. Meanwhile to the south of Aqaba, Saudi Arabia loomed in the distance. From Taba you could see four countries, if you counted the one you were in.

Being on the edge of the Middle East made me think of Syria, where the Arab Spring was still being bloodily played out. From where I stood by the gentle waters of the Red Sea, Damascus was about 470 kilometres away. It seemed almost impossible to think of the five-star life in Egypt's luxurious hotels so close to the devastation of the continuing uprising-cum-civil-war in Syria, where President Bashar Assad desperately clung to power. The latest estimated death toll, including many massacres of women and children, was more than 20,000 and rising. Human rights groups believed as many as 250,000 refugees had fled Syria into Turkey and Jordan (which alone was hosting 160,000).

Out there, beyond Israel and Jordan, was bloodshed and misery. I could even see a country that was holding refugees of the struggle; presumably in camps in the north. In Taba, beers were being served at the pool bar and Russians were applying suncream to one another's backs. My trip through the Arab Spring states of North Africa had thrown up contrast after contrast, but this was the starkest of the lot. I stood still and imagined the horror over the horizon.

The lawns of the Mövenpick were perfectly mown and bright green, but you were warned not to walk on them as they had been treated with chemicals. Sprinklers fizzed. I crossed a little bridge and came to a post bearing the Egyptian flag. It was in a section of the garden that had been named Flag Plaza. At the base of the flag an inscription said that the flag had first been raised by Mubarak on 19 March 1989, to mark the return of Taba to Egyptian sovereignty. The handover of the territory around Taba had been the last (contested by Israel) return of land on the Sinai Peninsula that sprang from the Camp David Accords.

I returned to my comfortable room and rested, reading *Sugar Street* by the Egyptian novelist Naguib Mahfouz (1911–2006). It was the final volume of his *Cairo Trilogy*, a sweeping masterpiece describing life in Cairo in the early to mid 20th century. *Sugar Street* covered 1935 to 1944, and it was brimming with life as well as concerns about how Egypt should be fairly run. Corruption was as big a worry then as it remained after independence in 1952. Just as Al Aswany's *The Yacoubian Building* captures life under an unjust ruler and the chaotic energy of Cairo, so does *Sugar Street* for an earlier period.

In the evening, I went for a drink with *Sugar Street* at the Hilton. White ducks had appeared on the lawns of the Mövenpick and there was a smell of chemicals in the air; presumably the grass had just been treated. At the gate to the Hilton, I was stopped by a mischievous security guard.

'Where do you want to go?' he asked.

'To the bar,' I said.

'You want to go to the health club?' he replied.

'No, to the bar,' I said.

He grinned and let me by.

At Nelson's Pub I drank a very expensive and small glass of white wine, listening to Janet Jackson hits and sitting at a wooden bar with a nautical rope hanging on the wall as decoration. A few drunk Russians were ordering vodkas. I took my glass to a terrace shaped like a ship's prow and looked across to the lights of Jordan and Saudi Arabia. It was quiet on the water. I could see no ships.

Four countries faced one another, peacefully minding their own business. Yet not far to the north, about the same distance away as London is from Newcastle, terror reigned in Syria.

🐫 🐫 🐫

In the morning I set myself a challenge: to visit three of the four countries in the view. I had one ticked off by default (Egypt), and I intended to cross into Israel and catch a taxi the short distance across Eilat to Israel's border with Jordan, where I hoped to go onwards to take a look at Aqaba, and return through Eilat to Taba in the afternoon. It was as far east as I would go; I would be as close to the centre of the Middle East as I had been yet.

I strolled from the Mövenpick to the border with Israel, about 300 metres away, and soon found myself being taken to a back room for questioning by an Israeli immigration official. The female officer had long pink nails, wore a pink watch and boasted a tattoo on the inside of her right arm that said: 'Free to be whatever.' My visa for Libya had caught the attention of the passport inspector who had dealt with me; I was in a room set aside for extra interrogation.

'What is this?' she asked, looking at the visa.

I explained the stamp.

She quizzed me for 20 minutes, occasionally interrupted by staff requiring her signature.

'You're busy,' I said, trying to win her over.

'Tell me about it,' she replied deadpan.

There was a pause as she signed off another docket. 'Why exactly do you want to come to Israel?' she snapped. It was not the first time she had asked the question. I was not sure my tactics were working. She was an unusual mixture of very casual (pink nails and tattoo) and extremely fierce: difficult to work out.

I re-explained the purpose of the day trip.

She said: 'You write about tourism only – OK?'

I assured her I would stick to tourism; human rights and the Palestinian struggle would be off-limits. She looked at me carefully and sent me to sit in a hallway for the best part of an hour. Eventually, I heard a double thump of stamps: my permission to enter Israel had been granted.

From the Egyptian-Israeli border I caught a 70-shekel (£11 British) taxi to the Yitzhak Rabin Border Crossing to Jordan. Along the way we passed a casino, a series of concrete-monstrosity hotels and Heineken billboards: Eilat was not desperately attractive from its backroads.

At the border, I avoided further interrogation by the Israelis and was soon in another Arab state. I exchanged some US dollars into Jordanian dinars at a tiny exchange bureau where I woke the man in charge; he had been wrapped in a blanket asleep on a sofa. The Yitzhak Rabin Border Crossing, on the Jordanian side at least, was quite literally a sleepy place.

My first sight in Jordan was a sign saying: 'WELCOME TO THE

HASHEMITE KINGDOM OF JORDAN.' My second was a picture of King Abdullah II, who was shown wearing a military uniform. His eyes were half-closed as though he was deep in thought assessing whether someone was telling the truth. After being in three countries where revolutions had ousted dictators, I had arrived in a state where one man still ruled the roost. King Abdullah II, who took over the affairs of state when his father King Hussein died in 1999, was commander-in-chief of the armed forces, in charge of appointing the government and responsible for selecting the members of the senate side of the parliament – which also had a lower chamber of 120 elected representatives. From 2001 to 2003, when matters were not being handled to his satisfaction, the king had suspended the parliament and issued a series of decree-like temporary laws of his own. Press freedom was limited and the country was rated 'not free' by Freedom in the World, a group based in the United States that analyses the state of democracy across the globe.

Jordan was generally regarded favourably in the West, perhaps for better-the-devil-you-know reasons. As well as sheltering Syrian refugees, the country had been briefly touched by its own Arab Spring. During the uprisings in Tunisia and Egypt, protesters took to the streets. But the numbers had been limited and Abdullah had replaced his prime minister in February 2011, promising a 'genuine political reform process'. He went on to dissolve parliament and to call for early elections in the face of calls for genuine democracy from the country's Muslim Brotherhood, which was angry that Abdullah, rather than the people, got to choose who became prime minister. Since then, there had been little change and the group Human Rights Watch had accused Abdullah of doing nothing to protect freedom of expression. The Arab Spring in Jordan continued to bubble beneath the surface.

Along the roads into Aqaba, more portraits of Abdullah stared down. I was in an emerald taxi that I'd hired so that the driver could show me round for a couple of hours. We went first to the giant flagpole in the centre of town and looked at an old crumbling castle nearby. I was not sure which old crumbling castle this was; the driver did not speak any English.

Using hand signals I asked to go somewhere for lunch, which was how I found myself at a table outside a restaurant with a picture of Abdullah saluting and wearing a red beret. I ate a chicken shish kebab with chips, one of the last chicken-and-chips of my trip across the Arab Spring (and I'd had quite a few). As I did so, a flock of women wearing black robes and veils fluttered past, walking – almost floating – along the pavement in the direction of a mosque. They were disconcerting and made me think of ancient times; they did not seem part of the modern world. I squinted my eyes, and they looked like moving shadows – hardly real at all.

After lunch, we drove around again for a while. The driver showed me a street with a McDonald's, a JW Marriott hotel, a 'Spongy Donuts' shop and a KFC. I noticed that he had a wooden baton by the side of his seat. I patted my pocket and checked my dinars, glad I could still feel the notes and would be able to pay the fare.

The road north went in the direction of King Hussein International Airport and onwards to the ancient Nabataean city of Petra. It was from the misty mountains and *wadis* beyond that T E Lawrence had famously attacked and taken Aqaba with Arab irregular troops during the Arab Revolt against Ottoman rulers in 1917, his actions supported by Britain's Foreign Office. He describes arriving in 'whirling dust' to find the city in a 'dirty and contemptible' state in his book *Seven Pillars of Wisdom*. Aqaba had suffered bombardment by French and British warships and much of it was rubble. Lawrence of Arabia's surprise assault led to his promotion to major, and old pictures show him in flowing robes riding a camel in to town. I had a copy of his account with me and a passage from his introduction stood out for being relevant to the Arab Spring and its dictators:

> All men dream: but not equally. Those who dream by night in the dusty recesses of their minds wake in the day to find that it was vanity: but the dreamers of the day are dangerous men, for they may act their dream with open eyes, make it possible.

We travelled along another street named after King Hussein. More pictures of Abdullah gazed from billboards. Was he one of the 'dreamers of the day' that Lawrence described? His recent record regarding freedom of expression and of dissolving parliament did not seem good. His face peered down almost everywhere I looked. It was Big Brother for real. It was also a vivid reminder, if only during a fleeting visit, of what the Arab Spring had been all about in the first place: the subjection of a population to the whims of one ruler. More than five million people lived in Jordan.

On the way back, I stopped for a coffee in Eilat, where youngsters were playing volleyball and Bob Marley was singing 'I'm gonna talk that freedom talk', which seemed appropriate. It was casual and calm with a hippy vibe; a description that would not perhaps hold true for parts of the Gaza Strip or the West Bank. The growing tension between Israel and Iran that had the world worrying was not evident in the faces of the smiling tourists. But I did not stay much longer than it took to drink my coffee. I returned to Egypt and to the strange, chemical-grass world of the Mövenpick hotel.

I had seen three countries in one day, each with its own issues and style. Yet it was the sharp, squinting eyes of King Abdullah II – and the sense of power behind them – that I will remember.

🐫 🐫 🐫

I had one final journey. I was travelling south again and moving into the depths of Bedouin territory, along the same road where Westerners had been kidnapped earlier in the year, to climb Mount Sinai and visit St Catherine's Monastery. What better place to end my trip across North Africa: on a holy mountain in a region where religion was all-important – in a sometimes lawless landscape at the edge of Cairo's control.

I drove back down the coastal road past the empty campsites; it was in fact high season and they ought to have been full, I had been told at the Mövenpick, but tourists were keeping away because of the uncertain political situation. I was staying at the Hilton Coral Resort in Nuweiba, the closest town to the long road through the desert to Mount Sinai. I took a wrong turn and went down a deserted road where I violently struck an unmarked speed bump and screeched to a halt. That minor calamity over, I retraced my steps, stopped at a petrol station to fill up and cool down with a soda (petrol was the equivalent of 21p a litre, compared to £1.35 in Britain), and rolled onwards to the oasis of the Hilton.

The hotel consisted of low villa-like buildings spread around a series of pools and lawns. On the lawns, thin white birds with long, curling beaks stepped carefully like elderly men on thoughtful perambulations. Occasionally, with a rapid snap of the head, beaks would strike the grass to capture an insect. The thin white birds would pause as if silently contemplating the quality of their snack before slowly stepping forth once again. It was somehow restful watching the thin white birds at the Hilton.

In the course of arranging for a Bedouin guide to accompany me to Mount Sinai at the dead of night so I could climb to the top as the sun rose in the morning, I became friends with Aly and Wagdy, two of the hotel managers. We talked for a long time about politics, over coffees and then food at the grill restaurant. There were not many guests due to the world economic downturn, so they had time on their hands and were interested in hearing about Tunisia, Libya and Cairo, as well as discussing Egypt's future. Everywhere you went in Egypt you could find a political forum, or easily create your own.

Aly and Wagdy spoke at speed.

Aly began eagerly: 'From a democracy point of view, I respect the Islamic people in parliament because they were voted in.'

Wagdy jumped in: 'The Salafists will change nothing. They cannot ban alcohol or bikinis. People live on tourists. We are a tourist country. Maybe fewer people rely on tourism in Cairo, but we are a tourist country.'

He paused for a split second, and Aly continued before Wagdy could open his mouth again: 'About six million people live on tourism. Say there are five dependants for each of those six million. That is thirty million people out of a population of eighty-five million.'

Aly hesitated, and Wagdy seized his opportunity: 'Nothing will change in the Sinai or Hurghada. Tourism will continue. I am a Muslim, but when the Islamic people were selected for parliament, what happened? They achieve nothing...'

Wagdy cut him short: 'The wise people realise we need a person with liberal thinking, who understands the political world, has an open mind and believes in God.'

Wagdy cleared his throat, and Aly took over: 'Beards!' he said. 'Do we want to be like Kandahar or Kabul? Do we really want that?'

The Aly and Wagdy show kept going as the sun set on the Red Sea. Like so many people in Tunisia and Libya they admitted that it had sometimes been dangerous to talk to foreigners in the past. Wagdy said that 'before the revolution nobody could talk in groups, definitely not in public'.

The way they both gabbled made me think of plants that had gone unwatered for a long time. Now the water – freedom of expression – had arrived and the plants were blooming. They really did enjoy a natter.

🐪 🐪 🐪

Farag Soliman, my Bedouin guide, arrived at midnight. He wore a white gallabiya and had an initially solemn manner. I drove my hire car and he sat in the passenger seat, giving me driving tips. 'Do not use fifth gear!' he said officiously. 'Never!' He then told me to turn off the air conditioning as it was bad for our health. He opened his window: 'One second of desert air is worth a million pounds!' After a short while he suggested that he drive the car, as I was clearly not up to the task. I declined his kind offer, saying that I was not sure he was covered by my insurance. 'Phfff!' he replied.

We continued in silence and after a while he relaxed. 'Under Mubarak the police could plant hashish on a Bedouin,' he told me. Then he switched subject: 'I am very crazy for the Premier League.'

Down the long, dusty road into the desert we went. It was dark and empty. This was where tourists had been hijacked earlier in the year, but with Farag I was completely safe, he assured me. We were the only car on the road and at 1.30 a.m. we arrived at St Catherine's village, where another Bedouin was to escort me up a moonlit path to the summit at 2,285 metres.

The smell of hashish drifted across the path as a shadowy man walked by, leading a camel. Abdo, who also wore a gallabiya, led me along a thin rocky trail. No-one else was on the path and we did not have torches. At first it was hard to find your footing and a twisted ankle seemed likely, but after a couple of hundred metres we curved round into the moonlit side of the mountain. It was quite magical. Stars glittered in the deep purple sky and a milky gleam covered the slopes.

We kept going in silence, stopping at a wooden hut after about an hour for a coffee. Our path joined a more popular route to the summit and other tourists, many of them holy pilgrims, were about. Donkeys formed a line, ready to take the elderly through a steep section. They brayed and grunted. My guide smoked a shisha pipe with friends at the hut, then we continued to a second ramshackle wooden structure, arriving at 3.45 a.m. I hired a blue and white checked blanket to keep warm and rested inside the hut with a handful of other climbers. A man held his hands together and prayed in a corner. There was no more than a murmur of voices. Out of respect for the holiness of the mountain where Moses received the Commandments, people spoke in a whisper.

About an hour later, Abdo advised I go to the summit for the sunrise. He would not continue with me for this bit; we were just a few hundred metres away. I joined a line of people snaking upwards. There must have been about three hundred tourists, but it was not at all crowded.

It was cool and peaceful on top of Mount Sinai. While others formed groups and prayed, I leaned on a rock in a quiet space near a small mosque and tiny Greek Orthodox church. I breathed the desert-scented air, resting for a while under the still purple sky.

Leaning on my rock, I looked back over my month-long trip across North Africa's Arab Spring.

I did not feel as though I had any grand conclusions to make. By no means did I consider myself an expert on the countries I had visited. Far from it: I had been in them for a short time and anyway, politics changed rapidly in Tunisia, Libya and Egypt… especially so soon after the Arab Spring revolutions.

The journey, a distance of about 2,400 kilometres (1,500 miles) from Tunis to Nuweiba, had had many highs and lows and complications. There had been the delights of the Roman remains in both Tunisia and Libya, the wonderful mosque at Kairouan, the visit to Mohamed Bouazizi's isolated grave, the peaceful seclusion of Djerba, the souks of Tripoli, Berber castles, ancient Greek cities, the magnificent madness of Cairo, pyramids, the strangeness of the Suez Canal, the oddity of Gaddafi's old bunker, the Sinai beaches and desert, racing into Jordan and Israel for a day. I had seen a lot and enjoyed the adventure.

Meanwhile, trouble at borders, over-eager checkpoints, a scary drive with a smirking brigade-man, a close miss in a hire car, hustlers, illness, accusations of espionage, gunshots at night, pick-up trucks mounted with anti-aircraft weapons, Salafists in Tahrir Square, baksheesh for border guards, and many confusing buses and smoky airport terminals had left their mark. It had been at times hairy but I had always tried to be extra-careful – as the cool-headed Othman in Libya had been so wont to remind me. Or at least I was as cautious as my nature would allow.

From Sidi Bouzid, where the Arab Spring had sprung, and onwards I had witnessed the ramifications of the uprisings across Tunisia, Libya and Egypt. The excitement of seeing the ragbag of dictators fall on television screens – Ben Ali first, then Mubarak and eventually Gaddafi – and the seas of protesters on the streets of their capital cities had got me going. And I was glad the images had. The journey may have been a highly bizarre way to spend my annual time off, but it was one I did not regret for a moment. During my month on the road and in the air, staying in wonderfully unpredictable hotels along the way, I had had my eyes opened to a trio of culturally rich societies trying to come to terms with their uncertain futures.

Where would the revolutions lead? Many Middle East experts had many opinions. Some were more optimistic than others about whether 'freedom' would last. One influential writer, John R Bradley, who contributes to the *The Washington Quarterly* and *The Spectator*, believed that radical Islamists would inevitably fill the power vacuum, leaving the liberal voices that began the revolutions unheard. A reporter on the region for many years, Bradley describes in his vivid, polemical book *After the Arab Spring* how the Islamists were hijacking the Middle East revolts.

Rightly or wrongly, from the many encounters and people I talked to during my journey, I was more optimistic, though neither 'taken in' nor 'carried away' by the rhetoric of the Arab Spring. There was just too much uncertainty for that. In Tunisia, the Islamist Ennahda Party ran the show. But in Libya, as I later learnt, the centrist National Forces Alliance led by the apparently moderate, secularist Mahmoud Jibril, was about to do well in elections. Meanwhile, as I also subsequently found out, the Muslim Brotherhood went on to triumph in the presidential vote in Egypt, promising 'moderation', whatever that might eventually mean.

What did all of this amount to? It seemed murky. Who really knew? Who could tell if one of the winners of the revolution would turn out to be, or lead to, the next Ben Ali, Mubarak or Gaddafi? Could a Muslim-run government in North Africa embrace modern pluralism, rather than react in a knee-jerk manner to any form of criticism of Islam (no matter how banal, as in the case of the cheap film *Innocence of Muslims*)? Could a Turkish form of Islamic country succeed on the southern shores of the Mediterranean?

With all of this, freedom of expression seemed crucial to the ultimate success or failure of introducing lasting democracy. And what had struck home and made me positive about the trio of countries was far simpler than politics, though it was connected.

It was the desire to talk.

A few hours earlier, I had drunk coffee after coffee with Aly and Wagdy, chatting about this, that and the other as the sun fell over the Gulf of Aqaba. In Libya, I had discussed Gaddafi at length in a back room in a village in the Berber hills. Near Leptis Magna, a torture victim had told me his story (and shown me his wounds). On Djerba, Hasna had quietly regaled me about her friend's awful experience at the hands of those connected to Ben Ali's family. In Egypt, just about everyone I met had a manifesto for the future of the country... and was ready to tell me all about the ins and outs, often at great length.

Perhaps I was being naive, but all this talk and openness, stimulated by the internet and the likes of Wael Ghonim, had made me optimistic. The democracies were fledgling and delicate, yet all democracies have to start somewhere. The frankness of most of the people I had met seemed to bode well.

Yes, Islamist parties may have won elections but as motormouthed Aly had said in the Hilton in Nuweiba, the outcome of a democratic vote – as opposed to a Ben Ali-style 97.7 per cent vote – was to be respected. The writer Al Aswany agreed with that, and his slogan of 'democracy is the solution' is a strong one.

More than anything, I got the sense from so many conversations that what people wanted was for life to be *fair* for once. They were sick to death of grubby dictators lining their pockets while throwing innocent people in jail for no good reason. Could a change to a more equitable way of life really happen though? Could the cycle of corruption be broken?

Another matter of fairness loomed large. The question of women's place in a society where democratically elected Islamists rule is a minefield. I will never forget the sight of the Salafist women on Tahrir Square: the flock of black crows crammed in a pen to one side of a stage where bearded man after bearded man droned into the night. The wearing of veils was growing in Cairo, the symbolic hub of the Arabic world. Imagine it the other way round: a country in which women forced men to spend their public lives fully covered, peering through slits of fabric. It was impossible to conceive. But it was happening to women, with varying degrees of strictness, across Tunisia, Libya, Egypt and other Islamic states.

Where will democracy take North Africa and the Middle East? Will democracy last? How will it treat its citizens? How will women, in particular, fare? (That outcome will, in my mind, ultimately decide the success or otherwise of the Arab Spring.) The people I talked to seemed uncertain. I was just as unsure. But at least they had been able to talk, to ask questions, to communicate, with no-one listening in or reporting them to the secret police.

🐫 🐫 🐫

The sun rose above the pink slopes of Mount Sinai. The sky turned first cinnamon, then golden yellow, then a deepening blue. The stars of the Milky Way faded in the morning light. Groups of pilgrims whispered prayers. A robin hopped by my rock, twittering happily.

We looked across the mountainous landscape. We might have landed on Mars. Then we filed down a steep path known as the Steps of Repentance to St Catherine's Monastery, with its chapels and courtyards dating back to AD337. People took photos of the 'Burning Bush' where God spoke to Moses: 'Come now therefore, and I will send thee unto Pharaoh, that thou mayest bring forth my people the children of Israel out of Egypt.'

It was an inspiring spot, whether you were religious or not. We returned to our cars and buses, which were to join a security convoy along the recently dangerous road. Tourism, as Aly and Wagdy had so rightly said, was hugely important to Egypt, as it was in Tunisia and could be in Libya. Who knew: maybe one day tourists would also return to Damascus? Though that day felt a very long way off.

My tour of the Arab Spring was over. Out on the road to Nuweiba and down to Sharm el-Sheikh, where I was to catch my flight home, the desert stretched forever.

The dictators had gone. Many kilometres of sand, a multitude of debate and an unknown future lay ahead.

ACKNOWLEDGEMENTS

Many gave their time during my rollercoaster trip across North Africa, for which I am very grateful. During a turbulent period you might expect people to give a traveller with a notebook short shrift, but I found the opposite to be true. I have mentioned a lot of those who assisted me abroad in the text but I would like to add a special thanks to Craig Baguley of Arkno Tours for arranging the tricky section across Libya. And thanks also to Jonny Bealby of Wild Frontiers for his sound advice. Hayley Smith of Citrus PR and DialAFlight provided much-appreciated help with the Egyptian leg; her own experience of motoring in the Sinai Peninsula was useful when preparing for the drive to Taba and St Catherine's Monastery. I am also thankful to Donald Greig, Adrian Phillips and Rachel Fielding at Bradt. I did not have a publishing deal when I set off on the journey and was extremely pleased at their interest and enthusiasm. Jennifer Barclay's editing was terrific, as was the ever sharp-eyed copy-editing of Ray Hamilton. Jane Knight, travel editor of *The Times*, offered her kind support. I also owe a special thanks to The Authors' Foundation, administered by the Society of Authors, for providing financial assistance. My parents Robert Chesshyre and Christine Doyle gave excellent advice and have been incredibly encouraging throughout.

BIBLIOGRAPHY

Alaa Al Aswany, *On the State of Egypt* (American University in Cairo Press, 2011)

Alaa Al Aswany, *The Yacoubian Building* (Fourth Estate, 2007)

Muammar Al Gathafi, *The Green Book* (World Center for the Study and Research of the Green Book, 2009)

Ibrahim al-Koni, *The Bleeding of the Stone* (Arris Books, 2003)

Tony Blair, *A Journey* (Hutchinson, 2010)

John R Bradley, *After the Arab Spring* (Palgrave Macmillan, 2012)

James Canton, *From Cairo to Baghdad* (American University in Cairo Press, 2011)

Christopher Catherwood, *A Brief History of the Middle East* (Constable & Robinson, 2011)

Joseph Conrad, *An Outcast of the Islands* (Oxford University Press, 2002)

Alex Crawford, *Colonel Gaddafi's Hat* (Collins, 2012)

William Dalrymple, *From the Holy Mountain* (HarperCollins, 1997)

Ethel Davies, *North Africa – The Roman Coast* (Bradt Travel Guides, 2009)

Wael Ghonim, *Revolution 2.0* (Fourth Estate, 2012)

Anthony Ham, *Libya* (Lonely Planet, 2007)

Lindsey Hilsum, *Sandstorm* (Faber and Faber, 2012)

Andrew Humphreys, *Cairo* (Lonely Planet, 1998)

Daniel Jacobs, *Tunisia* (Rough Guides, 2009)

Philip Kenrick, *Tripolitania* (Silphium Press, 2009)

T E Lawrence, *Seven Pillars of Wisdom* (first published 1922)

David W Lesch, *Syria: The Fall of the House of Assad* (Yale University Press, 2012)

Malcolm C Lyons and Ursula Lyons (translators), *Tales from 1,001 Nights* (Penguin Classics, 2010)

Amin Maalouf, *Disordered World* (Bloomsbury, 2011)

Naguib Mahfouz, *Sugar Street* (American University in Cairo Press, 1992)

Toby Manhire (editor), *The Arab Spring* (Guardian Books, 2012)

Paul Mason, *Why it's all Kicking Off Everywhere* (Verso, 2012)

Hisham Matar, *In the Country of Men* (Viking, 2006)

Simon Sebag Montefiore, *Jerusalem: The Biography* (Phoenix, 2011)

Eric Newby, *On the Shores of the Mediterranean* (Harvill Press, 1984)

John Oakes, *Libya: the History of Gaddafi's Pariah State* (The History Press, 2011)

Jonathan Raban, *Arabia Through the Looking Glass* (Fontana, 1980)

Dan Richardson, *Egypt* (Rough Guides, 2005)

Barnaby Rogerson, *A Traveller's History of North Africa* (Duckworth Overlook, 2008)

Ahdaf Soueif, *Cairo: My City, Our Revolution* (Bloomsbury, 2012)

Ronald Bruce St John, *Libya: From Colony to Revolution* (Oneworld, 2011)

Wilfred Thesiger, *Arabian Sands* (Longmans, Green, 1959)

Johnny West, *Karama!* (Heron Books, 2011)